I0236002

SONGS OF SEVEN DIALS

Manchester University Press

'An intimate and fascinating account of London's Seven Dials in the period between the two world wars. Matt Houlbrook's vivid portrait provides a multitude of stories that encapsulate the cosmopolitanism, gentrification and everyday racism of one of the city's forgotten "black colonies" on the fringes of the West End's theatreland.'

Hakim Adi, author of *African and Caribbean People in Britain*

'Between Soho and Bloomsbury, between two world wars, between rich and poor lies *Songs of Seven Dials*. A poetic exploration of one of London's most iconic neighbourhoods, this book illuminates histories both intimate and global. Through the story of one interwar libel trial, *Songs of Seven Dials* brilliantly explores the tensions of race, class and social inequality that shaped the modern metropolis – and still resonate in the streets of London today.'

Julia Laite, author of *The Disappearance of Lydia Harvey*

'Absorbing and illuminating, *Songs of Seven Dials* speaks eloquently about a past that is simultaneously distant and familiar, casting a fresh light not just on a cluster of past lives and London streets, but on the evolution of modern cities all across Europe.'

Marek Kohn, author of *Dope Girls* and *The Stories Old Towns Tell*

'Full of brilliant insights, *Songs of Seven Dials* offers an entirely new way of understanding the social dynamics of interwar London.'

Jerry White, author of *The Battle of London 1939–45*

'Thoroughly researched and passionately written, Matt Houlbrook's story of injustice and gentrification in Seven Dials is a powerful contribution to the history of central London.'

Phil Baker, author of *City of the Beast: The London of Aleister Crowley*

'This is an original and compelling read. Matt Houlbrook takes the reader on a fascinating journey of discovery through a little know aspect of London's history.'

Stephen Bourne, author of *Black Poppies* and *Fighting Proud*

SONGS OF SEVEN DIALS

An intimate history of 1920s and 1930s London

Matt Houlbrook

Manchester University Press

Published by Manchester University Press
Oxford Road, Manchester, M13 9PL
www.manchesteruniversitypress.co.uk

British Library Cataloguing-in-Publication Data
A catalogue record for this book is available from the British Library

ISBN 978 1 5261 8195 4 hardback

First published 2025

EU authorised representative for GPSR:
Easy Access System Europe, Mustamäe tee 50, 10621 Tallinn, Estonia
gpsr.requests@easproject.com

Typeset
by Cheshire Typesetting Ltd, Cuddington, Cheshire

Contents

Introduction: Songs of Seven Dials *page* 1

1 From Sierra Leone to Seven Dials 17
Great White Lion Street

2 Monstrous machines 51
Great St Andrew Street

3 The local politics of improvement 77
Shorts Gardens

4 Libel, law, and politics 107
Long Acre and the Strand

5 Slumming in bohemia 139
Great Earl Street

6 The ghosts of modern London 173
Little White Lion Street

7 Names and histories 203
Little St Andrew and Little Earl Streets

Denouement: Full circle 229
Mercer Street

Notes 245

Note on sources 282

Further reading 284
List of illustrations 287
Acknowledgements 290
Index 293

This book quotes things that people said or wrote in the 1920s and 1930s. This material can include words, phrases, or ideas that we recognise as offensive today, and which were often understood that way at the time.

Introduction
Songs of Seven Dials

IT STARTS WITH A LIBEL TRIAL, held over three days in the High Court of Justice in February 1927. Little reported at the time, the trial and its verdict would reverberate from a courtroom on London's Strand across Britain and its empire, prompting questions in Parliament and anxious discussions among civil servants and politicians. In understanding what was at stake in court, we better understand both the making of modern London and Britain in the 1920s and 1930s.

The trial's protagonists were unlikely and remarkable. Jim and Emily Kitten, a Sierra Leonean man and his London-born wife, owned a backstreet cafe in the neighbourhood of Seven Dials. They were an ordinary couple striving for a better life. But, after a series of sensational racist articles destroyed their reputation and business, they sued the newspaper *John Bull*, along with its editor, Edward Roffe Thompson, and publisher, the Odhams Press. This was a desperately unequal struggle, in which a working-class couple stood against the might of the establishment. Odhams were represented by the leading barrister Norman Birkett. The Kittens' solicitor, William Drake, had just been suspended for professional misconduct.

Ranged around the courtroom were an equally disparate group. The hotel proprietor and Conservative politician Bracewell Smith tied the case to the centre of local and national government through his political connections and business interests. The Nigerian-born barrister Ladipo Solanke was beginning the career that would make him a leading anti-racist and anti-colonial activist. Shopkeepers and publicans, waiters and tailors, jazz musicians and tipsters, and merchant seamen from across the world – from Italy, Russia, France, the Caribbean, and West Africa – testified against one other. Beyond the courtroom, arrayed in the trial's background, we might begin to pick out philanthropists, planners, and slumming bohemians, police officers and public health inspectors, journalists and filmmakers, Bright Young People, actors and architects, members of the literary and artistic avant-garde, the heir to the throne, and those who simply made their life in Seven Dials in the decades after the Great War.

It is unlikely that all of those involved realised at the time, although some of them clearly did, but the trial distilled increasingly intense conflicts over the area's character and redevelopment. Shadowing the rancorous exchanges in court were the efforts of powerful and propertied people to remake Seven Dials in their own image and the struggles of a diverse and mainly working-class population to protect their homes and livelihoods. Simmering tensions that exploded in court were formed in the claustrophobic intimacy of a tangled knot of streets and yards at London's heart. A forgotten libel trial was animated by the ferocious struggles through which modern London was brought into being. Its outcome shaped both the lives of its protagonists and the future of Seven Dials. The stakes were high, because beneath the case were pressing questions about race, class, and the boundaries of belonging, the course of what we would now call gentrification, and the kind of city London should become.

* * *

Seven Dials was tiny. You could walk across it in less than five minutes, circle its furthest bounds in not much more than fifteen. Squeezed between the thoroughfares of Shaftesbury Avenue and Charing Cross Road and the sprawling Covent Garden market was a shabby cosmopolitan working-class neighbourhood. Cramped tenements, towering warehouses, thrumming factories, and countless small workshops, shops, and places of refreshment contrasted sharply with the grandeur of the surrounding West End. While the area was changing slowly, it still bore the traces of its nineteenth century past as a notorious slum, a byword for poverty and crime. After the Great War – for a time, at least – it would be known as London's 'Black colony'.

As told by outsiders, Seven Dials' history was defined by failed dreams and precipitous decline. In the 1690s, politician and speculator Thomas Neale laid out what he envisaged as a grand planned development, the unusual radial pattern of its streets intended to maximise frontage and revenue. Ambition soon evaporated. Neale's singular vision fractured into myriad competing landowners and developers. Seven Dials became a mishmash of small businesses, workshops, and markets, with a growing working-class population that included many Irish migrants. The area originally marked the southern limit of the infamous St Giles 'rookery' or slum – the setting for the satirist William Hogarth's scurrilous print *Gin Lane* (1751) and known as a home for Black Londoners from at least the 1780s. As St Giles slowly disappeared, Seven Dials took on its unenviable reputation. From the mid-eighteenth century, it was identified as an underworld of crime and vice, a dangerous hotbed of radical politics and publishing.[1]

It was in this guise that Seven Dials began to draw the attention of some of the best-known observers of nineteenth-century London. Charles Dickens's *Sketches by Boz* (1836) caricatured its 'dirty men, filthy women, squalid children, fluttering shuttlecocks, noisy battledores, reeking pipes, bad fruit, more than doubtful oysters, attenuated cats, depressed dogs, and anatomical fowls'. George Cruikshank's accompanying illustrations depicted the grotesques of urban poverty as drunk women fighting in the Dials. Almost forty years later, French artist Gustav Doré's engraving *Dudley Street, Seven Dials*, printed in Douglas Jerrold's *London: A Pilgrimage* (1872), showed a similar scene – a hansom cab stalled amid a swarm of ragged children scrabbling in the dirt. By then the elegant sundial column that once stood at the centre of the Dials was long gone, replaced with a green cast-iron urinal.[2]

Rakish men-about-town were joined by serious-minded social investigators. Sensation was overlaid by the meticulous surveys, tabulated statistics, and colour-coded maps of poverty and overcrowding of Charles Booth's *Inquiry into the Life and Labour of the People in London*, completed between 1886 and 1903. Seven Dials' reputation remained unchanged. Walking the streets with local police, George Duckworth, Booth's secretary, filled his notebooks with telling vignettes and bourgeois prejudices. Shorts Gardens contained a 'very rough doss house' and tenements 'about as bad as it can be'. Lumber Court was 'poor, rough, noisy' – haunted by 'prostitutes, bullies, thieves'. As he picked his way between 'heaps of peapods, old lettuces & crushed fruit', Duckworth saw the down-at-heel environs reflected in the countenance of the people he met. He singled out the 'hardened look of the women – furtive look of trapped beasts' and children who were 'pale, with an older less healthy appearance than among the East End children'. There was, he surmised, a 'noticeable absence of happiness in these streets'.[3]

By the 1890s, accounts like this had made 'Seven Dials' a shorthand for the problems of the 'slum' – a compelling focus for well-meaning philanthropists and zealous Christian missionaries seeking to improve the physical and moral condition of the poor. Its reputation was enough to inspire the famous line from Gilbert and Sullivan's comic opera *Iolanthe* (1882). In this topsy-turvy satire on the privileges of inherited wealth, Lord Tolloller sings:

Hearts just as pure and fair
May beat in Belgrave Square
As in the lowly air
Of Seven Dials![4]

Jobbing writers would repeat the refrain incessantly in the decades ahead.

Around the start of the twentieth century, seasoned observers began to discern signs of a new-found respectability in Seven Dials. Grand new thoroughfares – New Oxford Street in the 1840s, Shaftesbury Avenue in the 1870s and 1880s, and Kingsway in the 1900s – had displaced the worst slums of St Giles and Holborn. Clearance schemes, sanitary reform, and the efforts of municipal authorities like the London County Council had begun to make a difference. Although the Dials remained poor, it could now occasion not just horror but a nostalgia for a vanishing picturesque old London. Yet as new roads and the expanding West End inexorably tightened the area's bounds, the course of 'improvement' confirmed Seven Dials' position as a strange island at London's heart.

* * *

By the 1920s, Seven Dials was better known than understood. Its notoriety was enough to make a placename a cliché. That name was resonant enough to be borrowed by filmmakers, writers of songs and revues, and one of the best-known British authors of the last century. Agatha Christie's *The Seven Dials Mystery* (1929) was not about Seven Dials at all, though. Christie's Dials was an empty vessel – a container for her formal drama of detection, a caricature devoid of people and recognisable local detail. A vibrant urban world became a cipher for social difference and a tortuous plot device involving alarm clocks and an arcane secret society. 'Not a likely neighbourhood for one of his class', observes a doctor after a fashionable man-about-town dies mysteriously.

But Christie's offhand treatment of Seven Dials was more nuanced than most of her contemporaries', particularly those who traded in tales of the criminal underworld: unusually, *The Seven Dials Mystery* acknowledged the area's growing respectability. The novel's title still depended on the old axiom that this was an infamous slum. And, despite its name's ubiquity, the place itself remained elusive. 'Father, where is Seven Dials?' Lady Eileen 'Bundle' Brent asks Lord Caterham: 'In the East End somewhere, I fancy. I have frequently observed buses going there.' From Agatha Christie onwards, it would be a running joke that no one really knew where Seven Dials was.[5]

Comedies of geographical confusion went along with a propensity to absorb Seven Dials into the bounds of other districts. If the East End was a recurring reference point, the area was most often collapsed into its better-known neighbours, Soho and Covent Garden. Somewhere of distinct character and history slipped from view. The artist Alan Stapleton never drew Seven Dials. That was not unusual in itself: even the most prolific artists and photographers of London in the 1920s and 1930s did not capture its precincts. Stapleton was a jobbing illustrator, known for atmospheric architectural sketches and books like *London Alleys, Byways, and Courts* (1924). Seven Dials' absence from his work was notable because he lived there, making his home among the clerks and pensioners in a boarding house on Castle Street. Stapleton sought out forgotten nooks and crannies across London. He walked the alleys and courts around Castle Street every day. It was Soho and the Adelphi he chose to draw, however, rather than more familiar environs near home.

In print, at least, Stapleton never came closer to Seven Dials than Covent Garden and Drury Lane. One walk in *London Alleys* passed along Long Acre, the neighbourhood's southern boundary and a stone's throw from Castle Street. There Stapleton paused – like many artists and photographers at this time – to capture the picturesque surrounds of Conduit Court. Looking north onto the rear of the Bird-in-Hand tavern and 'quaint old-world' houses, the tiny passageway back on to Long Acre and Seven Dials beyond appeared as a void amid the architectural detail and dense-textured shading – a flash of glaring white light that deflected scrutiny. Perhaps a more revealing trace of the area was concealed in the passing apology that prefaced the book. Publication was 'much delayed', Stapleton observed, 'because, just as the manuscript was finished, it was purloined from me'. Notorious yet invisible, Seven Dials' place in Stapleton's work was entirely symptomatic.[6]

* * *

Songs of Seven Dials tells the entwined stories of a libel trial, the lives of its protagonists, and the making and unmaking of a down-at-heel London neighbourhood in the decades after the Great War. To understand the trial, we must understand Seven Dials. In understanding Seven Dials, we more fully understand forms of modern urban life that we now take for granted. The book thus offers an intimate perspective on how London was reshaped by the competing forces of politics and capital – and how, in turn, ordinary Britons experienced, navigated, resisted, and contributed to that process. A place and its people become a starting point from which to show how local histories and everyday lives distilled wider urban, national, and imperial histories.

We might start with a simple question: what had to happen for such different lives to come together on a run-down backstreet in a place like Seven Dials in the aftermath of war? Jim and Emily Kitten and Bracewell Smith lived and worked less than twenty feet apart. Their names appeared on the same page in directories and electoral registers. They exchanged glances on the street and looked onto each other's premises. They confronted each other in court and, perhaps, in person. If they were of Seven Dials, they nonetheless inhabited completely different worlds. To understand this extraordinary proximity, the book traces their journeys to Seven Dials, and shows how they were shaped by social, economic, cultural, and political conditions that were of their time and place as much as the idiosyncrasies of biography. Taking this approach underscores the privileges and penalties of class, race, and gender, the global circuits of war and empire, and the cruelties of state, law, and politics in modern Britain.[7]

Songs of Seven Dials is thus a new history of London, which explores how the far-reaching upheavals of the 1920s and 1930s looked, felt, and worked from the ground. While the stories it tells are small, the histories are big. Intimate local tensions were inseparable from the global movement of people, goods, capital, and culture that made London an imperial metropolis. Like the neighbourhood they came to call home, the Kittens' libel suit against Odhams Press was braced by explosive debates about the limits of citizenship and national belonging, markets of property and labour, the restlessness of private capital and property developers, the grand schemes of politicians and planners, burgeoning forms of mass consumerism and media, and their insatiable appetite for consumers, workers, and profit, and the self-conscious aspirations of a bohemian avant-garde.

This means that *Songs of Seven Dials* is a book about capital, property, politics, and the making of a modern city. It is about how those marginalised by class or race navigated the challenges of an unequal and often dangerous metropolis. It is about those who were pushed out or left behind by the relentless pace of redevelopment. It is about urban decline and what we might now call gentrification. The libel suit was also underpinned by the desire of ordinary people from Britain, the empire, and Europe – waiters and cooks, labourers and porters, dressmakers and domestic servants, artisans and small shopkeepers – to make a better life. Legal action exemplified recurring struggles within and around Seven Dials to protect homes, livelihoods, and communities against the ambitions of the powerful and the march of 'improvement' across London. The prejudice the

Kittens challenged in court, finally, echoed discussions of the controversial 'colour bar' that increasingly defined the racial limits of Britishness. Playing out at the same time as the trial, the courtroom became an acoustic mirror for debates that reverberated from Seven Dials to Sierra Leone, Cardiff to Calcutta.[8]

* * *

Songs of Seven Dials is also a new history of the 1920s and 1930s, written from London's forgotten margins rather than its centre. It is still the case that metropolitan histories of the period fixate on the city's suburbs and arterial roads, its nightclubs, cinemas, and dog tracks, its underground network, art deco flats and factories, its social housing, and monumental public face. Set against the allure of the new, it is easy for places like Seven Dials to slip from view. Yet places like this – old, poor, and declining – were just as characteristic of the period as the more familiar environs of Soho or Bloomsbury.

Just as Seven Dials slips from view in histories of modern London, so the twenties and thirties are often absent from the area's popular histories. Place and period figure as a kind of caesura – a space between, a time apart. It was in these decades that the area became known as one of London's 'Black colonies', though. It was in the early 1920s that Holborn Borough Council and ambitious developers set out utopian plans to transform Seven Dials. Grand boulevards were to replace a cosmopolitan working-class neighbourhood. Department stores and theatres were to replace tenements, warehouses, and workshops. Leisure and pleasure were to replace work and home. Seven Dials was to be brought into the fashionable West End. Predicated on removing five thousand people and demolishing a swathe of central London, these plans shaped the conflicts around Jim and Emily Kitten's cafe.[9]

The coming together of histories of race and urban change was no coincidence. In taking Seven Dials' volatile postwar histories as a starting point, this book shows how the 1920s and 1930s were defined not by hedonism, opportunity, and progress so much as by conflicts of race and class, the bitter realities of inequality, and the shifting relationship between money, politics, and culture. Exploitation and expropriation made London brighter, as much as the antics of a privileged few and the fantasies of politicians and planners. We see those changes playing out on the streets of Seven Dials, just as we also see how differences of race, class, gender, and sexuality determined how they were experienced. As familiar as the chronological shorthand terms might be, clichés like 'The Long Weekend', 'Roaring Twenties', 'Hungry Thirties', and 'Between the Wars' obscure the far-reaching changes and struggles that made modern London after the Great War. *Songs of Seven Dials* is an intimate history of those vital two decades, in which a place and its people carry the weight of my thinking about 1920s and 1930s London.[10]

Different worlds collided in Seven Dials in the decades after the Great War. The legacies of the past and quickening pace of change determined the course of Smith and the Kittens' lives, drawing them together, animating the conflicts between them, and ultimately driving them apart. The tensions that exploded in court in 1927 betrayed the fissures of a city on the move, the fault-lines of a world coming into being. While the displacement of working-class residents was driven by the growing reach of capital and the power of Covent Garden market traders, the area's 'improvement' remained uneven and incomplete. For Seven Dials, the failed schemes of the 1920s meant planning blight, depopulation, and inexorable decline until the 1970s, when the Greater London Council marked the area for demolition. It would take a new generation of preservationists and planners and a dramatic second wave of capital investment and gentrification to make an earlier period's fantasies reality.

* * *

Finally, *Songs of Seven Dials* is a history of our present, which thinks critically and historically about how a cosmopolitan working-class neighbourhood became what is today a playground for global capital, international tourism, and upmarket consumerism. Once a shorthand for the problems of poverty and the 'slum', 'Seven Dials' has become a lucrative brand for property developers and place-makers. This is now a familiar story in cities like London, Berlin, or New York. This book shows how the foundations of what would be called gentrification were laid in the 1920s and 1930s, when politicians, planners, and entrepreneurs tried and failed to raze Seven Dials and build a new city from the ground up. Forgotten histories of a place and its people afford a critical perspective on why our cities are as they are, on the interplay between capital, culture, and politics, on how power works, and on the modern metropolis's inequalities and exclusions. The area was at the leading edge of the overlapping processes through which the capital was remade after the Great War. Look closely, and we can see modern London coming into being and the contours and conflicts of Britain's twentieth century taking shape in Seven Dials' narrow streets.

Why *there* and why *then*? The intimate relationship between place and time is at the centre of *Songs of Seven Dials*. It is also embedded within the book's structure. The seven chapters that follow pivot around the converging dials that gave the area its name. Anchored upon a single street, building, or flashpoint, each provides a different perspective on how cities change and the competing forces that transformed Seven Dials and London in the 1920s and 1930s. These vantage points include Jim and Emily Kitten's cafe (Great White Lion Street), Bracewell Smith's Shaftesbury Hotel (Great St Andrew Street), St Giles Buildings, the model dwellings opened by the Society for the Improvement of the Condition of the Labouring Classes and Holborn Borough Council (Shorts Gardens), the libel trial at the High Court of Justice, the avant-garde Cave of Harmony club (Great Earl Street), the new Cambridge Theatre (Little White Lion Street), and controversial proposals to rename local streets (Little St Andrew and Little Earl Streets).

These different perspectives allow us to understand what was at stake in court in February 1927. They reveal the tensions between progressive municipal politics, rapacious property developers, and the modern press, between those drawn to Seven Dials in search of profit or pleasure and those – usually working class or recent migrants – trying to make their home or living there. Together, the chapters also show how fashioning usable local histories was central to the contentious politics of urban change. The past weighed heavily on Seven Dials. It determined the sort of place it was thought to be, and those who chose to – or could – live, work, and play there. It shaped how the neighbourhood was described, how it was governed and policed, and the plans powerful people made for its transformation. It braced local markets in commercial and residential property. At times the pace of change in the 1920s and 1930s could seem relentless. Still, the ghosts of the past always lingered in Seven Dials – if you knew where to look.

* * *

IT ENDS WITH A MAP, drawn and carefully annotated in May 1938, as municipal authorities again tried to understand the problems of Seven Dials. Surveying the extent of 'slum' housing, an official from the London County Council colour-coded each property's condition. Blue, yellow, red: sound, borderline, unfit. They added notes to show land use – vacant and occupied plots; theatres, hotels, and shops; 'new dwellings' and 'modern flats'; 'showrooms' and 'industry'. In pencil, they outlined empty spaces where demolished buildings once stood. Here was a vivid snapshot of a neighbourhood on the eve of war.

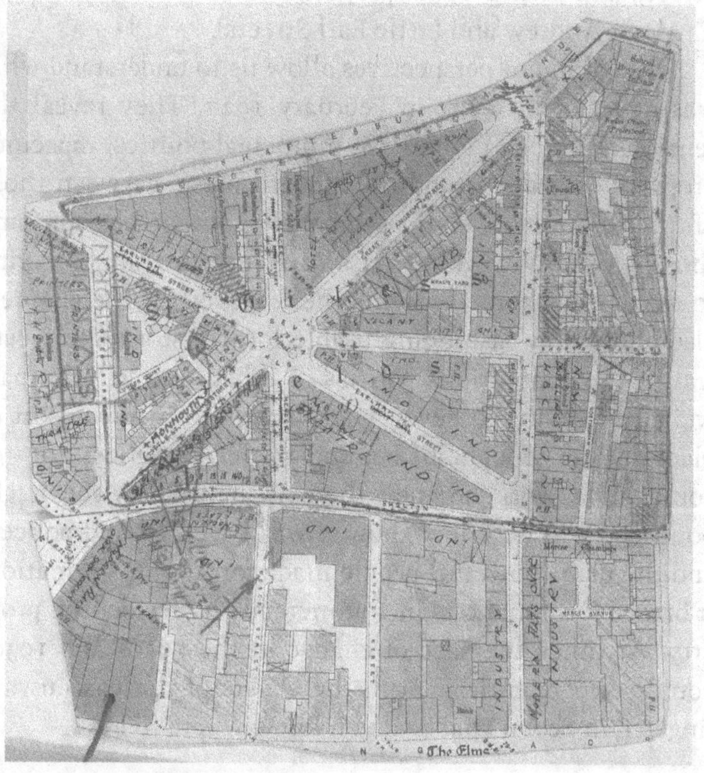

Figure 0.1 Seven Dials, 1938

Yet the pressures of change were uncontainable, and it was impossible to fix Seven Dials. Two-dimensional blocks of colour registered the passage of time as deteriorating ceilings, sagging floors, creeping damp, peeling paint, and the insanitary conditions that made buildings unfit and people leave. Scribbled notes desperately tried to keep step with the incessant rhythms of redevelopment. Printed street names and house numbers were crossed through then written in – showing, in the process, how the past was being reimposed on the identity of the area's streets. Above all, this map was purposeful and forward-looking. Capturing the challenges of decline, depopulation, and dereliction contained the promise of a utopian imagined future – by then receding far into the distance – to be achieved through political will, progressive planning, and private investment.

It is this document's material form which is most striking, though, not how it looks or the detail it contains. The area's boundaries – the curve of Shaftesbury Avenue, the straight lines of Endell Street and Long Acre, the meandering course north from St Martin's Lane – were not just marked in pen or pencil. Instead, this version of Seven Dials was carefully cut out. It survives as an asymmetrical scrap of folded paper tied into a bulging file in the London Archives. Seven Dials was so distinctive – so problematic – that it had to be lifted out of the city of which it was part. This strange fragment embodied the habitual ways of thinking through which the neighbourhood was often isolated from its place and time after the Great War. 'That's not London. That's Seven Dials', a friend told the young Madeleine Gal as they strolled through the West End one Sunday morning a century or so ago. For Gal, better-known now as the prolific autobiographical writer Mrs Robert Henrey, the memory was still vivid over thirty years later.[11]

I have puzzled over this map for a long time now. It contains the prompt and the challenge that animate this book. Against a cartographer's uninhabited abstractions, I have tried to reconstruct a lost urban world and the lives of those who crossed paths there a century or so ago. Underpinning this book is my painstaking effort to reimagine Seven Dials as a place of home, work, and play. Street by street, tenement by tenement, room by room, I interweave archival fragments to put the neighbourhood's people, businesses, and institutions back in their place – to understand those who often left little trace in the historical record. Only by making this effort can we glimpse the world through which Jim and Emily Kitten and Bracewell Smith moved, and appreciate the courtroom conflicts of 1927. Against an idiosyncratic cut-out map, *Songs of Seven Dials* works to stitch Seven Dials back into the city's fabric and, in so doing, provide a new history of London in the 1920s and 1930s.

1

From Sierra Leone to Seven Dials

Great White Lion Street

Jim and Emily Kitten are full of excitement when they open the door to 13 Great White Lion Street. More than the late summer sun has warmed the walk down from their home in Munster Square. Now they step inside and take in the two ground-floor rooms and basement kitchen below. It has taken a while, but they have saved £300, working long hours in poorly paid jobs in kitchens across London – labouring for others, feeding the privileged. It does not matter that the rented premises are small and run-down: this will be a cafe of their own.

The Kittens can still hear the humming traffic of Shaftesbury Avenue. Great White Lion Street joins the main thoroughfare to the open space where the streets that give Seven Dials its name converge. Whatever direction you come from, it appears as a slot in the cityscape – framed by a looming industrial school and the grand Shaftesbury Hotel. In some ways, the central location is deceptive: tucked away on the West End's fringe is almost a world of its own. Once within that world, decorated shop fronts enliven grimy tenements. Colourful signs and window boxes bespeak pride and a cosmopolitan mix of shops, eating places, and workshops.

The Kittens are a striking couple, and as they pass along the footway, they draw curious looks and nodded greetings from playing children and their new neighbours. The place sits alongside Kalman Lieber's tailor's shop and Joseph Pruim's hairdressing salon; Charles Thackeray makes and repairs boots, Etienne Vautro bicycles. Many of those living and working here were born in St Giles, but the street has long welcomed newcomers from across the world.

'The Cafe and Restaurant' opens for business with fresh paint and high hopes. For a while, the Kittens' hard work pays off. Within a few months the cafe has become a popular meeting place: bustling, sometimes overcrowded, and full of life – though, like most places nearby, it can often be rowdy and rough around the edges. A year later, rooms come available above Francesco Russo's wine shop next door, and the couple move to Seven Dials. It is more convenient; and besides, they have grown to like the place. In Great White Lion Street, Jim and Emily Kitten make a new life. In so doing, they build a vibrant social world that will change the neighbourhood's character. For better and worse, this will be their home for the next twenty years.[1]

* * *

There are different ways to tell the story of how Jim and Emily Kitten come to Great White Lion Street late in the summer of 1921. In one sense, this is a deeply personal story. It is about the restless ambition that carries Jim Kitten from Freetown, Sierra Leone to work in the restaurants of Brussels on the eve of the Great War. It is about the shifting fortunes that take him from a German internment camp to wartime London. In turn, it is about how Emily Bridger comes to a rooming house north of Euston Road from one of the poorest streets in London's East End. This account is full of gaps – how might we imagine the couple meeting, falling in love, and marrying in the anxious years of war? We might still say that their journey is defined by hard work and the desire for a better life.

Jim Kitten is born in 1890. His marriage certificate records his father's name as James and his occupation as farmer; there is no space on the form to give the same information for his mother. By the time Kitten is eighteen he is in Europe, working in hotels in Spain and Belgium. In autumn 1914, he is working as a kitchen porter when the German army occupies Brussels. Caught up in the terror and panic of war, Kitten – like other Britons apprehended on the continent – is interned in the civilian detention camp at Ruhleben, a converted racecourse near Berlin.[2] Ruhleben is remembered for the English eccentricities of its theatricals and sports. Its Englishness is equally apparent in brutal hierarchies of class and race.[3] Journalist Israel Cohen recalls

> a little colony of coloured men of different races and shades – Lascars and Jamaicans, West Africans and Zanzibarees – some with princely mutilations on their cheeks, others of a low physiognomical type, but all living happily together in their own barrack, where their love of violin-scraping and banjo-strumming had to be restricted to certain hours of the day in the interests of peace.[4]

Although the *List of Civilian Internees at Ruhleben* (1915) is incomplete, it includes fifteen men from Sierra Leone and dozens more from elsewhere across the empire. Most are merchant seamen, unlucky to be in Hamburg when war begins. There are also waiters, barmen, and performers like Prince Ras Monolulu, born Peter Charles McKay in the Danish Caribbean. A parody of colonial rule places them under command of a white 'barrack captain'.[5] Despite his prejudices, Cohen is struck by their 'remarkable pride of race'.[6]

Ruhleben is a difficult place, particularly for men like Jim Kitten. The Sierra Leonean P. J. E. Thomas, hungry and almost destitute, sends desperate letters through the United States ambassador asking relatives and the British government for support.[7] Disease is rife, particularly in winter. In spring 1916, Johnson Coffeetree dies of tuberculosis in a Berlin sanatorium. He was 'increasingly miserable and sick' for months, writes a German doctor, tortured by 'hallucinations and delusions'.[8] Conditions are bad enough that Kitten tries to escape. He is shot – 'wounded in the left arm' – though the circumstances are unclear.[9]

Kitten is interned for almost twelve months, until he is among 150 men released in a routine prisoner exchange in December 1915. Within days he arrives in London, perhaps for the first time. The following November, Kitten and two other Sierra Leoneans – both merchant seamen – call at the Prisoners of War Department in Downing Street to secure certificates of internment. John Grey had been released with Kitten; Arthur Yorke had followed a month later with others like James Tucker of the SS *Sangara*. The men live in adjacent streets in Earls Court: May Street, Archel Road, Chesson Road.[10]

The addresses are suggestive. At some point in 1916, Kitten is among several Sierra Leoneans – including another internee, Joseph Johnson – who start work at Cadby Hall. Lyons' industrial catering facility in Hammersmith is a 20-minute walk from Archel Road. Lyons' Corner Houses and the iconic 'Nippy' exemplify an increasingly demotic culture of dining out. Cadby Hall supplies the company's restaurants across London. Swiss rolls, bread, and pies roll out in liveried trucks in a 'modern' system of mass production and distribution. Kitten soon moves on, but Johnson works there for decades. Having married and raised his daughter in Shepherd's Bush, he is among 'three well-known personalities at Cadby Hall' caricatured in *Lyons' Mail* in 1950.[11]

Toiling behind the scenes in London's kitchens is exhausting, precarious work, but it brings Kitten close to the symbolic centre of metropolitan life. Lyons' teashops are resolutely middlebrow, but the Savoy Hotel on the Strand – where he becomes a cook – exemplifies high Society. Renowned for its fine dining and dance bands, guidebooks count it among the 'highest class' of West End establishments. The 'cuisine is French and the general arrangements cosmopolitan ... evening dress is almost essential'. So fashionable is the Savoy that it is 'advisable to secure tables in advance by telephone'. Wealthy diners are served by impeccable Italian or Swiss waiters in opulent surroundings. Such exclusive sociability – like Lyons' teashops – is underpinned by the unseen labour of a cosmopolitan workforce: platewomen from Denmark, porters from Britain and Belgium, cooks from Hong Kong and Sierra Leone. While Kitten works in the basement kitchens, upstairs white managers refuse to serve people like him. The famous actor and singer Paul Robeson and his wife Eslanda will be turned away from the Savoy grillroom in 1929.[12]

Kitten finds love as well as work. In December 1917 he marries 19-year-old Emily Bridger at St Pancras Registry Office. Emily's path from Whitechapel leaves little trace – reflecting a peripatetic childhood, her father's early death, a family fracturing through poverty. She grows up in Dorset Street, Spitalfields: it is the 'worst street in London', poor and overcrowded, notorious enough to be photographed for Jack London's *People of the Abyss* (1903). Philanthropic slummers and police alike strive to address the area's problems.

Toynbee Hall settlement and George Yard Charity School are nearby: for a time, Emily attends the school. We do not know how she and Jim meet, but things move quickly. They are already living together in Munster Square, north of Euston Road, when they marry.[13]

* * *

In a roundabout way, it is war that brings Jim Kitten to Seven Dials. The Great War and its aftermath put countless people on the move, throw lives into disarray. It is from a German internment camp and under the aegis of the British state that Kitten travels to London, finds work, meets Emily Bridger. Amid the turmoil of a global conflict new lives take shape.

Just as Kitten carries the memories of Ruhleben in his mind and the aching wound on his elbow, so the traces of war linger when the Kittens move to Great White Lion Street. The conflict's scale and reach make that inevitable. On Long Acre, the ruins of the Odhams Press printworks stand as an awful reminder of that terrifying January night in 1918 when a Gotha aircraft bombs Seven Dials. At the sound of sirens, dozens of people seek shelter in the concrete basement. It takes weeks to clear the rubble and to confirm that thirty-eight people have been killed and eighty-five injured in one of the war's most devastating air raids.[14]

War comes home to the Dials – like so many places – in ways few anticipated. The Royal Army Service Corps sets up a mechanical transport depot in Shorts Gardens.[15] On Endell Street, a new National Kitchen and Restaurant exemplifies the state's commitment to the health and morale of citizens and the mounting crisis of food shortages and high prices. Most remarkable is the Endell Street Military Hospital, established in the old St Giles workhouse by suffragettes, medical pioneers, and partners Dr Flora Murray and Dr Louise Garrett Anderson. Staffed almost entirely by women, the hospital treats around 26,000 casualties between May 1915 and December 1919. For four years, what Madeleine Gal remembers as the 'noise of the traffic ... the roar of the newspaper vans ... [and] the heavy lorries bringing fruit and vegetables to Covent Garden Market' is echoed by convoys of ambulances from the packed hospital trains that arrive at Charing Cross, punctuated by the urgent shouts of staff and cries of pain from the wounded.[16]

War's costs are made visible through the increasingly familiar sight of uniformed medical personnel and damaged men in hospital blues. That those personnel are women underscores the topsy-turveydom of gender roles, exhilarating some and troubling others. As war becomes peace, a terrifying pandemic crashes over Seven Dials. Dozens of local people are admitted to Endell Street with 'Spanish flu'. Just when respite seems near, doctors, nurses, and orderlies who had cared for thousands sicken and die. Cruelly, the hospital's highest monthly death toll – thirty – comes in February 1919. This is an infinitesimal part of a global tragedy: around 228,000 people die of influenza in Britain in 1918–19, over 50 million people worldwide.[17]

It is not just the pandemic that makes the transition to peace difficult. A fragile sense of national purpose dissipates; new conflicts play out as countless small dramas. Moralists worry that the neighbourhood's raucous pubs and cafes betray the brittle hedonism unleashed by the Armistice. Anne Kensit's refreshment house on Little St Andrew Street is loud and lively. When it is raided and Kensit fined for permitting disorderly conduct and allowing 'prostitutes' to gather in July 1919, a solicitor describes the premises as 'in a roughish neighbourhood much frequented by American and Colonial soldiers'.[18] In 1920 local people still cannot use the nearest public baths: that the army is 'clinging to them', protests Labour councillor William Forster Bovill, is 'a perfect scandal ... From the point of view of public health, the situation is a terrible one.'[19] At times, the desire to reconstruct the prewar social order is entwined with a virulent reaction against women's growing personal freedoms and public presence. Politicians summon women 'back' to the home, women are removed from clerical and industrial roles in which they had served the war effort, professions reintroduce marriage bars. The newspaper *John Bull* denounces the 'rich women' still working for 'pin money' in the Shorts Gardens RASC depot when 'our discharged soldiers' are unemployed.[20]

Too much has changed, though: it is impossible to fully move on. In April 1919, the Seven Dials Mission holds a 'grand "Welcome Home"' for 'old boys' who have served during the war. Gathered with loved ones in West Street, Alderman Robert Dibdin thanks 'them all for what they had done for their old country'. I am 'delighted to have [you] back in the Dials', he tells them; I 'hope ... [you will] all have a bright and happy future'. Despite the grand words and local pride, it is a melancholy occasion. Isaac Cutting, retired headmaster of St Giles school, speaks 'feelingly of those old boys who had fallen', sharing 'instances of their bravery and devotion to duty'. As the assembly stands in silence, the well-meaning rituals of remembrance might seem inadequate to the task at hand.[21]

More than a dozen young men never return to Seven Dials. Behind the names inscribed on headstones and memorials are intimate tragedies of loss and grief. Elizabeth McMahon and Mary Ellen Cody live side by side in Neal Street. They are neighbours, but they are also mother and daughter. Caught up in the heady 'rush to the colours', James McMahon – Elizabeth's son, Mary's brother – volunteers in September 1914. He is killed, aged 24, a year later, less than two months after arriving in France. James is buried near Armentières. It costs threepence a letter and Elizabeth is poor – a widow who depends on her adult children's wages – but she requests a special inscription on the headstone: 'Honour, Freedom, Virtue; He Died That You May Live.' There is consolation in believing her son's sacrifice is not in vain.

There is more heartbreak to come. In August 1917, Mary's husband, William Cody, is killed during the Battle of Passchendaele. Their son is five, their daughter just two. Mary raises them with Elizabeth's help while working as a cleaner at the Office of Works. William's body is never identified, and his name appears on the Tyne Cot Memorial in Flanders. It is through the private memorials – framed photographs and mantelpiece shrines – that absence is felt most keenly. A delivery boy hands Elizabeth McMahon her son's personal effects – a handkerchief, postcards and letters, 'RC Emblems' – one wintery day. When she signs for them, her hands shake, and the ink blots and pools on the page. Grief still burns; loss leaves a bureaucratic trail that stretches over years. It is June 1921 when James McMahon's British War Medal and Victory Medal arrive in Neal Street. That same month, his sister Mary completes her census return. In the column next to her and the children's names she writes 'widowed' and 'father dead'.[22]

It is not always obvious, but those who return carry the scars of war. Reverend Wilfred Davies, Rector of St Giles and member of Holborn Borough Council, and his wife Helen grieve for their youngest son, Lieutenant Kenneth Davies, killed in action near Vimy Ridge. Kenneth is interred in

Écoivres Military Cemetery, but his brother Wilfred is invalided home with shell shock – the debilitating condition that provides a ready metaphor for those trying to understand the war's legacies.[23] Horrifically injured in a munitions factory explosion, Mabel Lethbridge's war endures as chronic pain and the artificial leg that prompts her nickname 'Peggy'.[24] From May 1921, the new British Legion works to support discharged servicemen and ease their adjustment from war to peace. The Holborn branch seeks permission to erect a hut – a refuge for the returned – on an empty building site on Shorts Gardens. They are refused, but for two years after the Kittens arrive in Seven Dials the ex-serviceman George Castle is allowed to ply his trade from an all-night coffee stall there, serving Covent Garden porters, down-and-outs, those who cannot sleep.[25]

War changes Seven Dials in other ways. It brings new people. As the German army presses west, stories of atrocities mount, and Jim Kitten is interned, a quarter of a million Belgians flee to Britain – the largest ever number of refugees to arrive in the country. Refugee committees work tirelessly to billet newcomers, but many find cheap housing and work in places like Seven Dials. The Kittens' new business was once a cafe-bar run by Belgian refugees.[26] At least some newcomers settle after the Armistice. The de Clercq family live above their butcher's shop in Little Earl Street.[27] Guillaume and Maria Willscheid manufacture sausages, living and working next door to Elizabeth McMahon and Mary Ellen Cody at 48 Neal Street.[28]

If a row of houses in Neal Street encapsulates how war lingers, so does Frances Bauwens' boarding house, nearby on Great St Andrew Street. Her 1921 census return is a snapshot of a world cast into motion. In her seventies and born in Brussels, Frances has been in London for decades.

Most of her boarders work in West End hotels – a cook and kitchen hand from Belgium, a superintendent from Alsace. Joseph Siegenberg manages a tailor's shop on Shaftesbury Avenue. Until she recently lost her job, Josephine Blatchly was a chamber maid at the Regent Palace Hotel. At twenty-six, she is also a widow. Her husband Charles served in the Australian Imperial Force. Blown up by shelling in Gallipoli, gassed in France, he was in and out of hospital until discharged in February 1919. Then living in Castle Street, the couple marry at St Giles Registry Office. Happiness is fleeting: the explosion has left Charles in agonising pain, and he dies in a military hospital in August 1919.[29]

It means something that Bauwens lists Josephine Blatchly's name below Joseph Siegenberg: a year later the pair share a flat in Old Gloucester Street. It is there a 'well-dressed good looking young woman' bangs on the door, threatens Blatchly – 'I will scar you' – stabs her with scissors, and leaves her for dead. In the ensuing trial, Minnie Siegenberg 'accuse[s] Mrs Blatchly of living with her husband and at the same time drawing a pension as a war widow'. A decade or more later, Blatchly might be found walking the streets of Soho, a regular liaison with the notorious occultist Aleister Crowley. Displaced people, broken relationships and broken lives, jealousy, disputes over the moral boundaries of state support: these are also the Great War's legacies.[30]

* * *

The effects of war are refracted through the networks of empire. Jim and Emily Kitten's journey to Great White Lion Street is also a story about the imperial and maritime connections and rights of nationality and citizenship that allow British subjects to move around the world. It is the ships of the Elder Dempster line that carry people like Jim Kitten between West Africa and Europe, along with the raw materials and manufactured goods of imperial trade. As a subject of empire, Kitten draws on his right to move across the British world, and to live, work, and vote in the metropolis. His path is unusual, but thousands of other Black and Asian men journey to Britain around this time, their movement quickened by the desperate need for wartime labour. Passed in response to the exigencies of war, the British Nationality and Status of Aliens Act (1914) provides that a 'British subject anywhere, is a British subject everywhere'. It allows Sierra Leoneans like merchant seaman Ernest Marke to answer Britain's call to arms and Kitten to build a new life.[31]

The Kittens arrive in Seven Dials at a tense moment in the passage from war to peace. The giddiness of the Armistice has become something more foreboding. When the economy collapses, unemployment rises sharply: by 1921 around two million people are out of work. Attention focuses on the industrial heartlands of northern England, South Wales, and Scotland, but the crisis roils London. In places like the Dials, dozens of waiters, porters, labourers, dressmakers, and tailors are thrown out of work. Perhaps Jim Kitten keeps his job at the Savoy – it is unclear – but many of his friends are less fortunate. Having left the merchant navy to become a waiter, Arthur Yorke is made unemployed. So are his two Sierra Leonean roommates. Here is a cosmopolitan working class: precarious and exploited in the service industry, rather than the heavy industries of coal or steel. The class conflicts of the twenties and thirties look different from Seven Dials.[32]

As industrial conflict escalates and the Miners' Federation strikes against proposed wage cuts in April 1921, powerful and wealthy people fear that Britain will follow Russia and

Germany into revolution. The spectres of Bolshevism and a general strike haunt the aftermath. The downturn also opens the racial fault lines of postwar Britain. Prompted by rising unemployment and competition for jobs in the shipping industry, violence sweeps ports like Liverpool, Cardiff, and Glasgow in 1919. Mass meetings of the British Seafarers Union agitate against 'foreigners'. White crowds attack Black, Arab, and Chinese people and property. Five people die, dozens are injured or hounded from home and work, during what are euphemistically called 'race riots'. Returning to sea after being released from Ruhleben with Jim Kitten, John Grey is often in Liverpool – scene of the most violent disturbances – during this period, staying at the Elder Dempster hostel in Toxteth.[33]

Fears of revolution dissipate, but the racist violence of 1919 casts a long shadow. Neither Seven Dials nor the Kittens are caught up in the riots. It is still impossible to ignore the worsening political climate and panic gripping the popular press. Black Britons, many of whom had served during the war, are identified as an unwelcome presence. While riots were usually started by white men, government and press fixate on the 'alien' threat to public order – those supposedly incapable of integration. The Home and Colonial Offices work to remove Black sailors, deporting 'aliens' and encouraging the 'voluntary' repatriation of British subjects. A battery of legislation, culminating in the Coloured Alien Seamen Order (1925), limits rights to work, welfare, and movement along racial lines. Across Britain and its empire, the 'colour bar' hardens inexorably.[34]

The Kittens' journey to Seven Dials is both commonplace and extraordinary. Their lives are inseparable from the global circuits of empire and the tumult of a world at war. Everyday intimacies are braced by the national and imperial politics of the colour bar. Couples like the Kittens make their home in places like the Dials, but they have little choice. Their marriage threatens the racial hierarchies on which empire depends and raises paranoid fears of 'miscegenation'. Such concerns mean they are prohibited from settling in colonies like Sierra Leone. It is as a British subject that Jim Kitten arrives in London. It is more than love and ambition that keeps him there.[35]

* * *

Perhaps opening a cafe is a response to this turmoil. Kitchen work is ill-paid and uncertain, unemployment is rising. With skills and savings, starting a business makes sense. It is becoming harder for Black or Asian people to find places to meet, eat, or sleep in London. There seems growing need – a market even – for somewhere to gather. Around the cafe are dozens of similar places: shops and eating-houses where Italian, Belgian, Greek, or Jewish entrepreneurs provide for those living and working nearby. Ambition, prejudice, and exploitative labour conditions guide the Kittens onto the well-trodden path of self-employment.[36]

Why does that path lead to Seven Dials? There are prosaic reasons. From Munster Square, Kitten's quickest route to work at the Savoy takes him through the neighbourhood most days. Accommodation is cheap, and close enough to the Strand, that many of his colleagues live there. They include the Italian headwaiter, Egidio Mezzadri, who boards in Neal Street, and American Rudolph Kemphlison, a musician with the Savoy Dance Orchestra. Four of the hotel's Italian waiters live alongside Kemphlison in Estill House, Mercer Street. Guided also by word of mouth, Kitten has chance to explore – to feel the area's character, to cast his dreams into its vacant properties.[37]

The Kittens' journey is about more than the idiosyncrasies of biography. It is a story of a neighbourhood's possibilities and problems – how inequalities of class and race and markets in property and labour determine the choices available to working-class people and recent migrants. Outsiders often dismiss Seven Dials as one of London's 'black spots'. 'Typical of the derelict and worn-out areas often found in the backyards of our town centres', it is – apparently – an 'area to be hurried through, not lingered in'.[38] It is also a place of home and work for thousands. For them, lingering at a market stall, taking a meal in a cafe, chatting on the street, or walking home to a room in an ageing tenement is part of everyday life.

Seven Dials is an anomaly. Once a notorious slum, it is now a jumble of tenements, boarding houses, warehouses, and workshops. Hard-pressed between the West End pleasure districts and Covent Garden's sprawling markets, its narrow streets and courts overflow with noise and activity, people, goods, and vehicles. A backyard, perhaps – but really a behind-the-scenes place servicing the needs of commerce, leisure, and industry in its better-known environs. Box factories and basket stores, warehouses stacked with fruit and vegetables, manufacturers of paints and glues, the stench and commotion of metalworking and chemical treatment encircle the homes where people live. Furnished rooms rise three or four stories high above small restaurants, shops, and workshops where tailors and dressmakers practice their craft. To the south, the thrumming printshops, stores, and offices of Odhams Press mark the line of Long Acre.

The building files of the London County Council that cover Seven Dials contain architects' plans for modernist theatres and model working-class dwellings. They also contain technical drawings for new cranes and stores for

Figure 1.1 Shops in Great White Lion Street, 1913

flammable chemicals like benzine in yards behind the main streets. Chaos can be overwhelming. It is also dangerous. It takes nineteen fire engines and one hundred firemen to deal with the raging fire and thick smoke from an upholsterer's factory in Neal's Yard in August 1929. Seven Dials is a tangle, when the modern city demands straight lines; disorderly and disorienting, when politicians and planners seek order and legibility; unruly and cacophonous, when the age demands harmony.[39]

Cartographers struggle to capture this confusion. In the colour-coded maps of Sir Hubert Llewellyn Smith's *New Survey of London Life and Labour* (1933) commercial, industrial, and warehouse property appears as large unshaded gaps. By then, those empty spaces also betray more and more unoccupied or derelict tenements. It is easier to map Seven Dials' poverty and inequalities. Red lines set against pink shading along the fronts of Little Earl and Little St Andrew Streets suggest more affluent tradespeople and business owners in an area dominated by 'skilled workers and others of similar rates of income'. Blue shading identifies those 'living below Charles Booth's poverty line' around Tower Street and Great Earl Street. Great White Lion Street is first shaded blue, though a cartographer later adds pink lines. Blunt black lines delineate the 'lowest class of degraded or semi-criminal population' around Great St Andrew Street, Neal Street, and Shorts Gardens.[40]

Maps conceal as much as they reveal. It is not obvious that Seven Dials' population – like the wider borough – is collapsing. From a peak of 66,000 in 1891, Holborn's population falls to 43,000 in 1921 and 38,000 in 1931. The drop of 10.1 per cent in the postwar decade is the largest in London. By 1951, only 25,000 people live there.[41] Officials present depopulation as a 'natural corollary of increasing congestion ... created by industry and commerce', but it is accelerated by deteriorating housing, rising rents, and the deliberate decisions made by politicians and planners.[42] Challenged to present evidence of 'exorbitant rents' during a bad-tempered council meeting, Reverend Wilfred Davies cites Great St Andrew Street as an example. 'If you come with me, I will show you cellars ... let at 10s a week ... The people who live in them have to choose between anything and the street.'[43] Such pressures, finds the economist Helen Bosanquet, cause 'steady migration from the district, especially among the sons of old residents, who very rarely remain'.[44]

Seven Dials is also desperately overcrowded – its population density twice London's average. As tenements are demolished and houses further subdivided, overcrowding and insanitary conditions worsen. By the mid-1920s, it is already clear many 'houses were not built for the purpose to which they are now put'.[45] Overwhelmed officials identify further challenges. The area 'stands rather apart ... owing to the general unsuitability of the dwellings for private family occupation' and raising children. Seven Dials residents are older and more male than elsewhere in the capital, particularly as it becomes a transient rooming district for recent arrivals.[46] Then there is the 'difficult problem' of older women living alone 'gradually becoming feebler until they are eventually unable to look after themselves or their homes properly'. The LCC is forced to introduce new powers to intervene since many are 'most unwilling to enter the Poor Law Institutions'.[47]

For a working-class couple with ambitions, Seven Dials is one of few options. For sure, it is run-down and poor. It is also near the restaurants, markets, shops, and factories where locals find work. It is exactly the kind of place where those arriving in central London might find cheap commercial property and somewhere to live. Known affectionately as Jarni, Nellie Rigiani runs a boarding house in Lumber Court. Her husband Victor – a newcomer from Aquila, in the mountains of Italian-speaking Switzerland – is a cook. Their life together is braced by poverty and precarity: living hand to mouth, anxiously peering out from the basement kitchen in case it is the rent collector knocking at the door. Jarni's household also encapsulates a new London emerging in the 1920s. Most of her boarders – the laundress Dobbie Michael, embroideress Christina Russell, and milliner Margaret Hasler – are young single women. Coming from London's burgeoning suburbs, provincial England, Ireland, and beyond, they arrive in search of a cheap room, greater opportunities for work, and the personal freedoms and pleasures of the modern metropolis.

In these surrounds, Connie Aytoun stands out. Worldly and mysterious, she sleeps late and drifts home in the early hours from Brett's Dance Academy on Charing Cross Road, where she is an instructress. Only twenty-three, Aytoun's bobbed hair and make-up, short skirts and 'low cut gowns' embody the fashionable 'modern girl'. Once part of 'night-club queen' Kate Meyrick's empire, Brett's is one of the shady clubs which exemplify the growing tension between modernity and moral reaction. The heady pleasures of its dance band and pink and gold decor attract pleasure-seekers of all kinds. Aristocrats rub shoulders with 'immoral women, known to the police'. Aytoun's brittle glamour might occasion whispered gossip and envy alike from Jarni's other boarders. Her job is demanding and confounds boundaries between legitimate labour and illicit sexuality; detectives and magistrates struggle to distinguish flirtatious charm from soliciting. Brett's will become notorious after Freda Kempton, another instructress, dies from an overdose of cocaine acquired from the Chinese restaurateur Brilliant Chang.

If Aytoun suggests the fantastic pleasures of mass consumerism, her landlady and housemates confront the cruel realities of modern life. Maisie Reed and Millie Boynton have just been laid off from their work as cigarette cutters in Lambert and Butler's Drury Lane factory. A year later, the dressmaker Lillian Davis is found dead of an overdose of cocaine in the room she shares with Christina Russell. Moving through the 'saloons and lounges' of the West End, Davis had been addicted to drugs for almost eighteen months, Russell tells the coroner. Newspapers attribute the tragedy of Davis' death to the influence of the so-called 'dope king', Edgar Manning – Jamaican jazz drummer and then notorious for kneecapping three men who attacked him outside the Palace Theatre, in nearby Cambridge Circus.[48]

Markets of property and labour and the challenges of finding a place in an unequal city guide the Kittens – like countless others – to Great White Lion Street. They also establish the contours of the area's everyday cosmopolitanism. The 1921 census identifies 11 per cent of Holborn's population as 'foreign': 4652 people, of whom 1296 are from Italy, 635 the United States, 617 France, 354 Poland, and 353 Russia. Since they exclude long-standing Irish communities and Britons born in the empire the figures underestimate the area's bewildering diversity.[49] Born in France, the young Madeleine Gal lives just across Shaftesbury Avenue. She remembers the 'poignant picturesqueness of this little Europe'. Close-knit, even claustrophobic, it is a 'region of a quite different atmosphere, belonging almost to another city'. When they arrive in Seven Dials, the Kittens follow a route traced by successive generations before them.[50]

* * *

The cafe is a shared labour of love. By all accounts, it is also successful. Emily Kitten is a careful bookkeeper, who records monthly takings between £30 and £48 over the years it is open; she estimates there are 20,000 visits in 1926. Soon the Kittens employ a 'college chum' called Blue to help.[51] It becomes part of an expansive network of restaurants and lodging houses run by and for Black and Asian people. Such businesses navigate racial prejudice and the 'colour bar' that determines who can (or cannot) rent a room, eat a meal, nurse a drink, or go dancing across London. When many places are transient – ad hoc dances in a rented hall – the

Figure 1.2 'A sketch of the Kitten's Cafe, from a recent photograph'.

cafe becomes something more secure, providing sustenance and a reassuring welcome for those who make their way to Seven Dials.

In some ways, the cafe takes on the character of its environs. 'Englishmen, Italians, and Frenchmen [are] among [its] patrons', Jim Kitten recalls.[52] A neighbourhood haunt soon attracts visitors from further afield. London is the heart of empire, and its population reflects the bustling docks and multiethnic merchant navy and the rich opportunities for work, study, or organising. Census records suggest around 14,000 people born in Africa or the Caribbean live there. Drawing customers from across the Black Atlantic and South Asia, the cafe becomes what one observer calls a 'resort of coloured men'. For 'seafaring men', Great White Lion Street is a 'place of call when in the Port of London'. They are joined by waiters and porters, students and labourers, musicians and performers – those who make London their home and those there for a time.[53]

Once Jim Kitten had prepared the French 'cuisine' for which the Savoy is renowned. Now he utilises different skills. 'Many lascar seamen [come] there for the curry and rice and native foods which he prepare[s]. Men and women [come] in for tea.'[54] Writers trying to capture London's diversity often focus on its eating places. In Soho, Alec Waugh tastes an 'Oriental flavour' that distils into the scent of a 'street savoured with minestrone'. Intriguing menus mark a cosmopolitan culinary geography that allows the adventurous to eat their way around the world without leaving London.[55]

What is exotic to some is comforting and recognisable to others. The writer Thomas Burke identifies distinct Italian, French, and Russian quarters in Clerkenwell, Old Compton Street, and Spitalfields respectively, with their own social centres, religious and cultural institutions, shops, and restaurants. Each 'builds a country around itself', he observes. For those who eat there regularly, the cafe – like nearby Italian, Greek, or Belgian restaurants – is somewhere to seek familiar tastes, and tongues. Serving a working-class clientele in a down-at-heel neighbourhood, the Kittens anticipate better-known and more upmarket places like the International Afro Restaurant and Florence Mills Social Parlour, opened by Jamaican entrepreneur and anti-colonial activist Amy Ashwood Garvey almost fifteen years later.

'Curry and rice' and afternoon tea – a ritual both domestic and imperial – are the foundation for what becomes a profitable business.[56]

Venues like this matter. Ernest Marke calls them the 'only pleasure for coloured men'. Despite London's burgeoning nightlife, 'very few [dance halls will] allow coloured people in'. Few pubs in Seven Dials will serve Black people.[57] Being turned away from a restaurant or boarding house is equally distressing and radicalising. 'Even in London, the heart of the Empire', observes the Trinidadian socialist and pan-Africanist George Padmore, 'men and women of colour are often ostracised and humiliated in such a way as to destroy whatever early love and affection they might have had for the Commonwealth of which they are supposed to be citizens'.[58] For Padmore and others, their intimate encounters with the 'colour bar' are transformative. Such experiences prompt an assertive new generation of activists to challenge racial prejudice across the empire. For others, they are the impetus to build a refuge in the imperial metropolis.

Politics and profit meld. Efforts to establish student hostels draw in colonial governments, philanthropists, and campaigning groups like the West African Students' Union. Community organising and resistance finds a focus in institutions like the Cardiff Adenese Association and the short-lived National African Sailors and Firemen's Union. At the same time, small entrepreneurs like the Kittens find opportunities. Boxer Frank Craig – 'The Coffee Cooler' – runs a cafe on Bloomsbury High Street, a popular haunt of jazz musicians. During a raid, he remonstrates with police. There was no place 'where these men could go to … [I] allowed them to come [here] for rest and to meet agents.' 'He and his fellow men of colour had no club', continues an unnamed musician, 'and of course they were not allowed to hang about the streets'. Neither Craig nor the Kittens are straightforwardly altruistic. Everything suggests they have a keen sense of their wider responsibilities as businesspeople, though. If venues come and go, moments like this underscore how capital, consumerism, and the small-scale acquisition of property create the precarious social worlds which sustain Black community and politics.[59]

Many customers are passing through, but the cafe is home from home for those living or working around Seven Dials. Friends and acquaintances meet there. It has a crowd of regulars like James Rich, stage manager for productions like *Plantation Nights*, and the musician Laurie French, who often calls in on his way between gigs. In spring 1924, French hires the Adelphi Rooms on Edgware Road for a series of popular all-night dances, selling tickets and advertising 'Jednelles famous Jazz Band' on posters.[60] The cafe becomes part of a recognised social round – a sprawling network of venues, often necessarily transient, run and frequented by Black Britons. Just beyond the Seven Dials precincts are cafes in Denmark Street and New Compton Street, and the Ire Club in Little Newport Street. Further north, behind Tottenham Court Road, are venues like the Wonderful Units Social and Dance Club in Charlotte Street.[61] Here, in Whitfield Street, is the only place that approaches the profile of the Kittens' cafe. Initially the Felix Club and British Colonial Club, it is taken over by Uriah Erskine – Cardiff entrepreneur and boarding-house keeper – around 1923, until a police raid, prosecution, and his early death bring its popularity to an abrupt end.[62]

Much of what we know about these places comes from reading against the grain of what outsiders said or wrote. 'Talk[ing] together in loud raucous tones' suggests the pleasures of catching up with friends; a 'nuisance to the neighbours' is the sound of people having a good time.[63] A 'resort of Black men and white women' carries a salacious charge of sexual transgression, but might just be somewhere couples can gather in peace.[64] The predatory Black or Chinese man is a potent postwar folk devil – dominating how the authorities or journalists see places like the cafe. The venue is perhaps most important to married couples like the Kittens, though. In neighbourhoods like Seven Dials or Limehouse, intimate relationships that scandalise some are part of the fabric of everyday life. Jim and Emily's enduring partnership is not unusual.[65] They welcome others to the cafe, most notably a circle of Sierra Leonean friends that includes the tympanist Frank Obadiah Kennedy and his wife, and W. E. and M. K. Smith – the former a showman with Bostock's travelling shows. Joseph Johnson was interned in Ruhleben and worked with Kitten at Cadby Hall. Now he regularly travels down to Seven Dials from Shepherd's Bush with his wife, Alice, and daughter Pearl.[66] A resort? Jim Kitten is more laconic: 'coloured men who had married white women also visited'.[67]

The cafe's most famous customer – self-styled Abyssinian Prince Ras Monolulu – had also met Jim Kitten in Ruhleben. He visits with his wife, Rhoda: 'They don't call her the princess. She is Mrs Menallooloo', observes Kitten.[68] A racing tipster and hustler, Monolulu's flamboyance – 'voluminous cloak of scarlet cloth embellished with pictures of racehorses and jockeys … pleated white silk shirt [and] balloon like pantaloons' – make him a familiar character on streets and racecourses. Celebrated for his refrain 'I got a horse', he features in newsreels, cigarette cards, and a Regal Zonophone sound recording.[69] Monolulu's 'pride of race' – his trenchant anti-racist and anti-colonial politics – plays out more quietly in the everyday life of the cafe. As they confront a colour bar manifested through insults and catcalls, the hostility of landlords, the populist rhetoric of newspapers and politicians, and legislation on nationality and citizenship, the Kittens and their customers build a world of their own in Great White Lion Street.[70]

Like many places nearby, the cafe can be rowdy. Later into the evening, particularly, people get drunk, tempers fray, arguments turn violent. Emily Kitten is hurt breaking up one fight, though the man later apologises. During a ferocious row, Rita Gilbert – a 'very dangerous woman' – stabs Phyllis Hallbands.[71] Some customers have long criminal records – though in itself that is not unusual – and the cafe is implicated in several court cases that link it to an underworld of organised crime and vice. The Jamaican Cecil Roach has convictions for demanding money with menaces and 'living on the immoral earnings' of his wife and other white women.[72] One evening, plain-clothes detectives follow Laurie French and James Rich from the cafe to Shaftesbury Avenue. Found in possession of opium, Rich – caricatured as a 'dangerous dope-monger' whose 'hypnotic influence' turns women into slaves – is sentenced to six months hard labour and recommended for deportation.[73]

* * *

If the cafe takes on the character of its environs, its popularity, in turn, transforms the area. 'You will hardly take an evening walk around Seven Dials without encountering Black men', observers the writer Arnold Palmer in 1926: 'You might find them in certain pubs, or, less easily, in certain cafes; you are almost sure to see them standing in bulky groups in certain streets.'[74] Cafe and customers are soon visible enough for the Dials to be identified as one of London's 'Black colonies'. The phrase is a journalistic cliché – the stuff of sensational headlines and ostentatious moral panic. It still betrays the paranoid subconscious of empire and marks the Black presence as a troubling inversion of racial order. In London but not of it, the 'Black colony' is dangerously impermeable and a challenge to the institutions of imperial power.

The 'Black colony' is both a material reality and a crude shorthand. 'In the Charlotte Street area of Tottenham Court Road, the cosmopolitan quarters of Soho, and the Seven Dials district live hundreds of black men, mostly smartly dressed and obviously well-disposed with funds to dispense with the necessity to work', observes one newspaper.[75] Some *do* make their home in the Dials. Born in Trinidad and Barbados respectively, merchant seamen Albert Andrew and William Waite board at 82 Neal Street for a time; Jamaican student Lionel de Sylva rooms in Great White Lion Street.[76] Despite their visibility to excitable journalists, census records suggest they are a tiny minority. Most of the cafe's customers come up from dockside hostels in the East End, venture south from Camden's student quarters, or live in nearby rooming districts between Euston and Regents Park, east of Tottenham Court Road, and in Bloomsbury and Hampstead. Seven Dials is a social scene rather than a residential neighbourhood.[77]

There is only one contemporary image of the premises. Published by a muck-raking newspaper on a mission, this 'sketch of the Kittens' cafe, from a recent photograph' watches from a safe distance. All we see is an impermeable shopfront: a closed door, glass panes veiled by drawn blinds, a potted aspidistra, and printed menu. Those who talk about the 'Black colony' often dwell on such boundaries. Magistrates quiz detectives about who can and cannot enter a cafe. Urban explorers stage the dramatic moment when they enter a strange otherworld. The sketch is reflected in Harry Parkinson and Frank Miller's footage of Uriah Erskine's 'notorious cafe bar' in the film *Cosmopolitan London* (1924). Here the distant camera watches a Black man enter with two fashionable young women. There is an intertitle – 'White trash are not encouraged here' – before Erskine opens the door and ushers a woman out. Despite this flurry of activity on its threshold, the cafe remains a facade. In the darkness and shadows beyond are lives unseen, stories untold.

For outsiders, a closed door can be reassuring. It suggests the 'Black colony' can be safely contained and held at a distance. More often, it prompts worry about the 'foreign' worlds hiding at London's heart, where men like James Rich engage unseen in criminal conspiracy. Erskine's is 'entirely a Black man's cafe', observes one detective: 'white men would have the greatest difficulty in entering'.[78] In 1924 the humourist Barry Pain turns to the dangers of the cosmopolitan city. 'London is not English any more than New York is American.' Where others find pleasures to savour, Pain sees an atomised metropolis on the brink of deracination. The 'mysterious Chinaman, the smiling Italian, the wily Lascar and many other races, associating with their own people, retain their nationality', he opines: 'They are in London for their own purposes. But they are not of London.'[79]

Like Pain – an incurious unempathetic outsider – neither the photographer nor the commercial artist crosses the cafe's threshold, let alone looks back onto Great White Lion Street. If Jim and Emily Kitten find time to look around their cafe, they might see familiar faces and its hectic popularity. Staring out, they might watch guardedly for possible hostility from those to whom they will always be strangers. From here, establishing a boundary from the world outside seems necessary to building a profitable business. Teashop chains like Lyons embrace the spectacular possibilities of plate glass. For smaller proprietors like the Kittens, closing doors and drawing blinds creates a shield from the prying gaze of passers-by.

* * *

Seven Dials is already notorious, but its name gains new significance in the 1920s. That the 'Black colony' emerges in a dilapidated 'slum' cements a distinctive sense of place and the growing association between urban decline and racial difference. Politicians, police, and journalists link Seven Dials to the dangers of unchecked cosmopolitanism. The evangelical Public Morality Council singles it out as a moral problem.[80] Those trying to bring order to the Dials become more assertive. Arrests for public order offences often single out Black or Asian men. 'Fashionably, not to say extravagantly, dressed [his] moustache trimmed to resemble the double one in dominoes', Rufus Fennell is a distinctive figure. He is also elusive – variously a chemist and doctor, an actor on stage and screen who appears with Paul Robeson, a mushroom farmer. During the 1919 riots, he emerges as a courageous leader of Cardiff's Black community, organising protests and intervening with local and national authorities.[81] By the summer of 1920, Fennell is in London. Leaving the house of friends in Great Earl Street late one night, he is accosted by a police officer. 'When I remonstrated with him', Fennell later explains, 'he said "I will not have anything out of you, you Black swine."' It is Fennell who is fined for 'insulting words'.[82]

The weight of licensing provisions for gambling, dancing, and alcohol, regulations for the sale of food and drugs, and legislation like the Criminal Law Amendment Act also falls disproportionately on small business owners, particularly if they happen to be Italian, Jewish, Greek, or Black. At times, authorities onsider more concerted action. 'Black Bullies: Yard to Clean up Plague Spots of London' screams one newspaper headline. For proprietors, the growing threat of surveillance and raids – let alone a fine, prison, or losing a licence – makes things increasingly difficult. In this febrile climate, it is inevitable that the cafe – like Seven Dials itself – becomes indelibly linked to crime, violence, and vice.[83]

It is not clear when the cafe first draws attention. It is part of regular police beats by 1923, and often watched more closely. It is no accident that officers invariably focus on the gregarious sociability that spills onto Great White Lion Street, nor that the first prosecution comes after customers gather outside on a balmy autumn evening.[84] At Bow Street Police Court, detectives tell Sir Chartres Biron of watching the cafe after 'numerous complaints from residents'. They see 'about ten Black men and two white women' on the pavement. A 'lady who passed along seemed to be nervous and almost ran past them' – the offhand distinction between loitering 'women' and nervous 'lady' betrays instinctive assumptions about class and respectability. Stepping from the shadows, they arrest the merchant seamen Albert Brafet, Tom David, and Frank Mitchell, the porter William English, and Winifred Dean – who they call 'half-caste' – for 'obstructing the free passage of the footway'. Appearing in court next morning, most are discharged immediately. There is no charge to answer, Biron complains: 'there was no evidence of obstruction, and he could not understand why the people were not told to go away'. Found in possession of cocaine, the Trinidadian Mitchell is less fortunate. It is 'put in his pocket out of spite' by police, Mitchell protests, but he is convicted and sentenced to twelve months' hard labour.[85]

Biron still agrees this is 'a place which the police should keep an eye on'.[86] As scrutiny becomes more intrusive, the Kittens and their customers are in court more often. Jim Kitten is fined £20 for 'permit[ting] disorderly conduct' and 'suffer[ing] prostitutes to meet together and remain' after a late-night raid in June 1924.[87] In January 1927, he is fined £15 for 'suffer[ing] gaming to take place'.[88] There are dramatic flashpoints. Almost fifty people are inside during one raid. When asked to leave, detectives claim, the circus dancer John Moore 'ran amok, behaving like a wild beast … kick[ing] one officer in the abdomen and [trying] to bite his face'. Moore 'usually carried a razor', they say, 'and people in the Seven Dials district went about in fear of their lives'. Evoking racist fantasies of Black primitivism, newspapers inflame concerns about race and immigration.[89]

The same court registers that record Kitten's trials underscore their ordinariness. Official harassment is part of an ongoing struggle between municipal authorities and small businesses. Each prosecution reinforces the assumption that places like this are beyond the mainstream of metropolitan life. It often seems impossible for civil servants and police to see the sailors, students, and musicians who meet in Great White Lion Street. As they fixate on the 'coloured criminals known to have visited this undesirable place', a social hub is turned into a 'haunt' of men like 'William Allen Porter, convicted of drug trafficking and counterfeiting coin'.[90] Suspicion falls on the 'colony' even in cases where race proves irrelevant. When a body is found in an empty Soho shop in 1931, police search the 'Seven Dials area with a view to discovering a coloured man who had been seen with a girl whose description is said to correspond with that of the murdered girl' and visit a local cafe. Legal action and sensational journalism tie the cafe to an underworld of crime and vice.[91]

* * *

In the mid-1920s, for a time, even the most reluctant traveller can wander Britain's far-flung empire without leaving London. Just as jobbing writers turn a short stroll into adventurous global travelogues, so the British Empire Exhibition brings the world in miniature to Wembley. Opening in April 1924, the exhibition grounds house pavilions representing the elements of empire – Canada, Ceylon, and India – and the steel and concrete Palaces of Engineering and Industry. Tutankhamen's tomb sits beside an amusement park and marching military bands – dazzling fakes, cheap thrills, and pageantry. The young John Gray visits with the Better Britain Brigade, though spends most of his time on the 'Giant Racer'. Spectacular and relentlessly forward-looking, the exhibition affirms Britain's role in bringing civilisation, democracy, and progress to the world.[92]

If Jim Kitten is feeling homesick, a short journey on the Bakerloo Line will return him to Sierra Leone. Within the West African pavilion – a 'Walled City' based on Kano, in northern Nigeria – he and Emily might walk through the Gold Coast to the 'Sierra Leone Village'. Here is a barri or rest house, demonstrations of 'primitive' handicrafts, and the raw materials – ginger or palm oil – of extractive imperialism.[93] It is not just objects on display: 'elaborate arrangements' make the pavilion temporary home for 'between 300 and 400 West African natives'. 'As nearly as possible [they] live in conditions prevailing in their own countries', observes one journalist. In the 'Sierra Leone compound … the houses [are] of wattle and daub, with roofs of thatch, lined with felt. The usual native food [is] imported.' Set against the scientific and technological wonders of the Palaces of Industry and Engineering, such deliberate 'backwardness' dramatises Britain's modernity and modernising mission. An ersatz facsimile of a Sierra Leonean village secures comforting myths of empire.[94]

After the horrors of war, the exhibition presents empire as a domestic unit rather than the product of military conquest. Talk of 'commonwealth' and imperial 'family' cannot contain palpable unease. Bloody struggles for self-determination in India and Ireland, the brutal imposition of colonial power, international competition and economic slump, and the violence of 1919 raise the spectre of imperial decline and difficult questions about the limits of belonging. In uncertain times, reimagining Britain's place in the world is inevitably defensive.

Had they approached Jim Kitten, the pavilion's organisers might have avoided importing the 'usual native food'. Within Wembley, Lyons have 'sole and exclusive rights ... to sell and supply refreshments' – with exceptions for national delicacies and branded products like Cadbury's cocoa.[95] Venues like the 'Pacific' or 'Jungle' cafes suggest a rich array of cultures, but behind an exotic facade hides the standardised modern teashop. Entering the 'West Africa Cafe' through an arch of compacted 'mud' means returning to somewhere reassuringly familiar. There is no Jollof rice, but hungry visitors can order 'Cake, 3d. Pastries, 3d. Sandwich, 4d.' – delivered daily from Cadby Hall. A 'native' city built in concrete; a teashop selling mass-produced pastries behind 'mud' walls: a sanitised version of racial difference on sale to white consumers.[96]

Almost twenty-seven million people visit the exhibition before it closes in 1925. They are not all there for the funfair, and its popularity reflects a pervasive fascination with empire and the spectacle of difference – equally evident in the theatregoers flocking to see Florence Mills in *Blackbirds* or hear Paul Robeson sing in *Showboat*.[97] There is a fine line between fascination and fear, though, and cosmopolitan London is more than a commodity. When the Kittens return from Wembley to Seven Dials, their journey shows how the 'foreign climes' beloved of urban guides are also everyday places of home and belonging.

As they make a new life in Great White Lion Street, the Kittens challenge the 'colour bar' that determines where Black and Asian people can meet or eat, sleep or work. The cafe is no utopia. Despite their differences, customers find companionship and decent food. The journey from Sierra Leone – or the Gold Coast or Trinidad – to Seven Dials challenges the racist foundations of colonial rule and questions Britain's imperial power. Wembley's 'Sierra Leone compound' is safely contained, but to hostile observers the 'Black colony' at London's heart seems troublingly out of place. It blurs boundaries; inverts hierarchies that define the British world; provides more evidence that Seven Dials is a problem to address. It will not be long before the Kittens' aspirations bring them into conflict with the rich and powerful people whose ambitions also turn to the Dials. The couple are painfully familiar with the hostility of local police and magistrates. They cannot know that behind the scenes in the corridors of municipal and national power are those conspiring to put them out of business.

2

Monstrous machines

Great St Andrew Street

This is the tale of two windows, separated only by a narrow backstreet, perhaps six metres, all told. The first is an expanse of plate glass, through which light streams into a grand hotel dining room and ballroom. The second – a shopfront, now a cafe – is older, unprepossessing. Small panes in fading frames give up their secrets less readily, screened by a net curtain, handwritten menu, and an aspidistra. From time to time, a stern-faced man stares out at the cafe. Later in the evening, he watches more closely from an upstairs window, light dimmed, half-hidden by drawn curtains. As customers come and go, he scribbles notes as he listens to the raucous laughter, hubbub of conversation, people having fun.

This is also the tale of two men, and the claustrophobic intimacy within which tensions simmer and boil. On opposite sides of a street in Seven Dials two paths cross. In some ways, Bracewell Smith's path here has mirrored that of Jim Kitten: born in Keighley, he worked as a pupil teacher and attended the University of Leeds before moving south to become a teacher for the London County Council. After wartime service with the London Electrical Engineers, Smith began his career as a developer by purchasing the

Shaftesbury Hotel, on the corner of Great St Andrew and Great White Lion Streets. Smith, like Kitten, is a self-made man, returning from war to make his way in the world, seeking opportunities in a peacetime capital reviving after the injuries of the previous years. Smith, like Kitten, is drawn here by ambition and London's property market.

Aspiration and opportunity bring two people to the same street, but differences of class and race, money and connection shape the desperately unequal conflict that will break their lives apart. Smith will become spectacularly wealthy, building a prestigious hotel and property portfolio. He will be a prominent Conservative politician and, after the Second World War, Lord Mayor of London, baronet, and chair of Wembley Stadium and Arsenal Football Club. In the end Smith and Kitten could not have been more different.

* * *

Even at the time, many contemporaries realise they are living through a dramatic moment in the making of modern London. The nervous energy of the war's aftermath seems to echo in the cacophony of building sites and take material form in the skeletons of steel and concrete that rise above the streets. One journalist sought precedent in the reforming zeal of the new London County Council two decades earlier: 'Not since the unsavoury purlieus of Drury Lane … were swept away in the march of progress, to be replaced by the fine thoroughfares of Aldwych and Kingsway, has the process of rebuilding and beautifying the Metropolis been so much in evidence.' Regent Street undergoes 'transmogrification'. Startling monuments of modernity emerge from the old city – offices like Bush House on Aldwych, factories like Carrera's Arcadia Works on Hampstead Road, department stores like Liberty's.[1] Across central London and beyond, cinemas, showrooms, and garages, mansion flats and banks, arterial roads and art deco tube stations reveal a new city bursting from its bounds. A few years later, when the writer Harold Clunn tries to comprehend the astonishing scale of change, he reaches for an even longer chronological comparison: the 'greatest amount of rebuilding that has ever taken place within so short a period of time since the Great Fire of London'.[2]

Frenetic redevelopment is accompanied by intense discussion about what London should become. Books like the London Society's *London of the Future* (1921), edited by Sir Aston Webb, aim to provide visionary blueprints for the capital. For preservationist groups like the London Society, this means rational planning, functional urban zones, greenbelts, and balancing the possibilities of reconstruction against 'conservation of London's distinctive character'.[3] Architect and town planner Professor Stanley Adshead identifies a 'process of ... stupendous change' across central London. Like others, Adshead recognises that the 'erection of popular restaurants, palatial hotels, boarding establishments, municipal housing schemes, Imperial offices, and tubes' brings progress. Optimism is tempered with unease, though. Like the London Society, of which he is a member, Adshead worries that unfettered change threatens to scour the patina from a city 'rich in history and tradition'. The infrastructure of mass culture and speculative commercial development becomes a 'monstrous unmanageable machine', rampaging across old London.[4]

A decade later, optimism will give way to bleaker ideas of inequality and chaos, but in the 1920s, the dreams of a new Seven Dials that animate property developers and entrepreneurial investors are inseparable from efforts to make London modern. Corporate lobby groups like the

Brighter London Society challenge the deliberate approach of authorities, advocating that the 'beautification of the city should come through life and commerce rather than through unnecessary planning restrictions'.[5] As the monstrous machine gains momentum, concern about the balance between planning and commercial development and 'innovation and preservation' intensifies. Fuelled by the irresistible power of capital, it is this machine that squeezes ordinary residents and smaller businesspeople out of Seven Dials.

* * *

Follow the money that flows in and out of Seven Dials and we might understand why a place like this attracts the voracious forces of commercial capital. We might also understand how acquiring a workman's hotel becomes a turning point in Bracewell Smith's growing property portfolio. Although the idea of the 'Roaring Twenties' is retrospective mythmaking, urban redevelopment runs alongside a consumer boom in the heady days after the war. For sure, the abandon with which many return to London's theatres and cinemas, nightclubs and shops, restaurants and hotels reflects a sense of release after the strictures of wartime. It is also – crucially – underpinned by increased leisure time and disposable income for those in work. Satiating the pursuit of pleasure will become a profitable business.

Competition for space and rising property values on London's main thoroughfares prompt entrepreneurs to seek alternative sites for the temples of modern consumerism. On Oxford and Regent Streets, cramped frontages push department stores to build higher. Elsewhere, the overheated property market stretches the West End's bounds, shifting the focus of capital east and into the backstreets of unfashionable districts – often residential and industrial – like Seven Dials.[6] Local politicians worry the area is locked in a downward spiral: decaying buildings and past notoriety deter investors and visitors; property's purchase and rateable value slump; physical decline and economic depreciation accelerate together. For those with money and ambition, there are opportunities here. Tenements, warehouses, and hotels are businesses. Like the land on which they rest, they are also commodities: if 'developed' they become more valuable. That Seven Dials is central and comparatively cheap makes it both attractive and risky.[7]

Plenty of people are willing to gamble. Smith's acquisition of the Shaftesbury coincides with a flurry of speculation around Seven Dials, in which a huge part of the area is sold and bought between 1919 and 1922. Those seeking to acquire property include Covent Garden market traders and the proprietors of small shops and factories.[8] It is the predatory attentions of commercial developers – exploiting what an estate agent calls a 'wonderful opportunity for a speculator or building syndicate' – that will have the most far-reaching effects, though.[9]

In May 1919, the periodical *Country Life* alerts 'investors in high class London real estate' to Seven Dials' commercial potential.[10] The area's appearance in an upmarket magazine's property pages and designation as 'high class' is incongruous, to say the least. *Country Life*'s advice is prompted by the sale of five 'valuable freehold building sites and investments'.[11] 'Close to Long Acre and St Martin's Lane', the lots encompass two of the seven triangular plots around the Dials. They include warehouses, stables, and houses between Shorts Gardens and Great Earl Street; the 'adjoining valuable site' fronting on to Neal Street to the east – a 'commodious block of warehouses and cellars' and six 'dwelling houses' – and the freehold ground rent on The Grapes public house. Just south is the equally 'valuable' triangle formed by Great Earl, Little White Lion, and Castle Streets.[12] While there is no interest in a 'spacious warehouse' occupied by the International Correspondence Schools, the area's eastern quadrant – almost 40,000 square feet of commercial and residential property – sells at auction for the huge sum of £68,750.[13]

Bracewell Smith's journey to Great St Andrew Street is part of this activity. He is not building anew, but acquiring the Shaftesbury is part of the same process of investment and capital accumulation evident elsewhere. The hotel is both massive – built over seven floors with almost three hundred bedrooms on the corner where Great St Andrew and Great White Lion Streets meet – and shabby. Opened around 1910 as an affordable establishment for working people, it soon becomes associated with the labour movement.[14] Labour MPs recommend it to those attending the 1913 party conference; trade union delegations stay there en route to the Western Front in 1918.[15] Despite this trade, the hotel struggles to attract guests and remain profitable during the Great War. Beset with anxiety, manager Joseph Fleck takes his own life in autumn 1917. A doctor links this individual tragedy to the sensation of being forever 'on edge'. In a city at war, Fleck was among 'many people ... suffering from continual worry', in his case 'owing to extra work and difficulties of servants and management'.[16]

Business begins to pick up after the Armistice, but the Shaftesbury's wartime travails and the precarious finances of its owner, Thomas Gordon, make it an enticing bargain. London is returning to normality. Great St Andrew Street is a short walk from the thoroughfares of Shaftesbury Avenue and St Martin's Lane and the West End's increasingly crowded restaurants, theatres, and nightclubs. It is rumoured that Holborn Borough Council has big plans to 'improve' the area around Seven Dials and Drury Lane. August 1919 is a good time to acquire a stake in a hotel like the Shaftesbury. Bracewell Smith goes into business with Thomas Gordon. Registered with a nominal capital of £31,000, their new company Gordon and Smith Limited seeks to 'develop and turn to account' land for hotels, lodging houses, restaurants, and entertainment. As well as the Shaftesbury, they buy billiard rooms across London, including in Frith Street, Soho, and a substantial plot in Upper Tooting Road. The following April, the men register a second company – Central Flats (London) Ltd – to develop luxury apartments across the capital. Smith and his wife Edith move to Great St Andrew Street. There – as Hotel Manager and Manageress – they begin the daunting task of turning its fortunes around.[17]

Figure 2.1 Postcard of Shaftesbury Hotel, London, undated

Smith is in a hurry. Within a few years he has built a reputation as a successful business person and is establishing himself as a leading figure within 'the social and civic life of the borough'. Ambitious and well connected, he and Edith attend civic luncheons as guests of Holborn's mayor, George Harvey. Like Smith, Harvey was born in Yorkshire. Like Smith, he has significant business interests in hospitality: chair of Connaught Rooms Ltd and Burlington Hotels Ltd and managing director of the Aerated Bread Company teashop chain. Like Smith, Harvey is a prominent Freemason. A few years later, the men will become partners when they buy the famous Café Royal on Regent Street.[18] Smith's burgeoning career as a Conservative and Municipal Reform Party politician tracks his older mentor. He is elected to Holborn Borough Council in 1922; he succeeds Harvey as one of Holborn's representatives on the London County Council in 1925; and he, too, becomes mayor of Holborn in 1931. Harvey is MP for the south London constituency of Lambeth; Smith represents Dulwich between 1932 and 1945. Smith's charmed path through Seven Dials shows the intimacy of political and financial power.[19]

* * *

In a very real sense, Jim and Emily Kitten – like many of their neighbours – are in the way. The burst of speculation that follows the war brings new conflicts to Seven Dials. As Smith is redeveloping the Shaftesbury, the growing tensions between capital and people become more visible around Great St Andrew Street. For established companies like the architectural ironmongers Comyn Ching and the sprawling J. Lyons and Co. box factory, the boom creates opportunities to expand into adjoining warehouses and tenements. Smith starts out with £2000 capital; the Kittens have £300 of hard-won savings. Disparities of wealth mean neither smaller entrepreneurs nor residents can compete with the larger developers.[20]

In spring 1920, a developer buys the freehold property at 17 Shorts Gardens. An estate agent describes the building as 'let at low rents to weekly tenants and producing £150 per annum gross'. We might use different numbers: eight households – thirty-three people, aged 2 to 68 – living in fifteen rooms over five floors. We might even give these people names: the widowed washerwoman Mary Durnell, charwoman Eva Picozzi, fishmonger George Clifton and his family. The tenement is their home, not just an investment opportunity.[21] Having acquired several similar properties along Shorts Gardens, the builder Alfred Joyce spends £2000 turning them into commercial premises, then sells them one by one. This is the everyday reality of depopulation, more than the grand schemes and demolition orders of politicians and public health officials. It does not happen overnight, but increasingly those who live or work in Seven Dials are displaced by the monstrous machine of capital.[22]

Council officials recognise the problems this causes. They are often just as exercised by the shadowy figures haunting the property market's margins, however: the disreputable estate agent letting property to inappropriate tenants is another postwar folk devil. Proprietors of small shops or cafes often depend on these vital intermediaries. Seeking premises for what becomes the Caravan Club, Jack Neave and Billy Reynolds approach a 'very helpful estate agent by the name of Solly ... [who] was well known among the Bohemians'. Solomon Faith lives and works with his sons on the fringes of the West End: he lives in Castle Street in the 1920s and has offices in Seven Dials and Soho. It is Faith who finds a basement in Endell Street and handles 'all the technical details between the landlord and the lease and the solicitors'.[23] Months later, a police officer will dismiss him as 'one of the many shady estate agents ... who specialise in letting premises to shady clubs and prostitutes'.[24]

These are recurring concerns. Over winter 1927–28, having prosecuted a caretaker for allowing a house in Castle Street to be used for 'immoral purposes', Holborn councillors consider also taking action against the landlord and letting agent.[25] 'Scallywag agents' prompt another series of 'West End Flat Scandals' in 1931.[26] Sensational revelations around a Neal Street flat linked to the 'White Slave Traffic' prompt the council's solicitor to rail against the unseen influence of 'profiteering agents'.[27] *John Bull* identifies a 'firm of estate-agents, run by a notorious ex-convict' which let the flat to a known pimp: in the West End 'one might find seven shady firms which specialize in letting flats to underworld clients at enormous rentals'. There is little action – landlords are too powerful for that – but it becomes clear that the market alone is an unreliable way to bring order to Seven Dials.[28]

* * *

For a moment, Bracewell Smith's ambitions for the Shaftesbury threaten to founder on the character of its environs. The distance is small, but Great St Andrew Street is not yet the West End. Building a respectable establishment in Seven Dials – somewhere that will attract affluent tourists, travellers, and businesspeople – can seem a Herculean task. For Smith, those difficulties distil into the bustling cafe across the road.

The conflicts of urban development are intense and intimate. From morning until late, the boundaries between the Kittens' cafe and the Shaftesbury's communal areas and rooms overlooking Great White Lion Street threaten to dissolve. Opposite the cafe, the restaurant is open to the street through three huge windows. Guests dining or dancing can see and hear people coming and going or talking on the street outside. Those arriving on foot or by taxi from Shaftesbury Avenue pass the cafe's entrance. In turn, the cafe's visitors might gaze curiously into the hotel's dining room and lobby.[29]

For Smith, the proximity of the cafe and its Black and Asian customers become unbearable. For almost a decade, he and the Kittens live and work on opposite sides of this narrow road. They know each other by sight; they almost certainly exchange words as they pass on the streets. Smith watches as Jim and Emily Kitten arrive in Great White Lion Street and their business booms. Their new life is his problem – even an obsession. The cafe is an 'eyesore', he complains: the 'most disgusting place [I have] ever known'. Frustration turns to anger. How can he make money with a place like this on his doorstep? How can he build his business when 'patrons of the hotel, including Members of Parliament and other persons of the highest standing [are] forced to leave because of Kitten's disreputable clients?'[30]

Smith is not the sort of person to let anyone stand in his way. He is also wealthy and well connected. What happens behind the scenes is unclear, but it is not long before he mobilises others against this threat to his business. He meets senior Metropolitan Police officers at nearby Bow Street station and Scotland Yard. He talks to local publicans and proprietors, encouraging them to complain about the cafe and organising a petition to Holborn Borough Council and the LCC. He exploits his position as an elected politician. Steadily expanding his presence in Holborn Council's work, Smith is soon chair of the Finance Committee and party to decisions that have material effects on Seven Dials and the Shaftesbury Hotel.[31] In summer 1924 he is a member of the General Purposes Committee that grants wine dealer Francesco Russo 'permission to fix pavement light at No. 15, Great White Lion Street'. It seems a small thing, but a single light – next to the cafe, opposite the hotel's restaurant – bespeaks Smith's efforts to protect his guests' sensibilities and ease their passage into the heart of Seven Dials. Bringing Great White Lion Street into the light reveals the indistinct boundaries between commercial self-interest and public service.[32]

Eventually, Smith uses his position within Conservative political networks to take his concerns to the centres of municipal and national power. In autumn 1926, an MP lobbies Sir William Joynson-Hicks, the notoriously intemperate Home Secretary, on Smith's behalf. It must be Dudley Ryder, Viscount Sandon. Smith and the Conservative MP for Shrewsbury move in the same social and political circles; they are brother Freemasons. Follow the money, follow the webs of connection and influence, and the personal and political interests underpinning efforts to make Seven Dials modern start to appear.[33]

* * *

Such lobbying is about more than Smith's ability to turn around the hotel's fortunes. The problem of the cafe is immediate. The stakes are high because this is a critical moment in his attempts to develop his business. It is not immediately obvious, but smouldering tensions on Great White Lion Street coincide with Smith's move to acquire and complete what will become the Park Lane Hotel. Over the first months of 1925, he is the 'prime mover' in a syndicate of Yorkshire businessmen negotiating the leasehold of London's most famous building site. Nicknamed the 'Birdcage', the massive steel frame has stood desolate on Piccadilly, opposite Green Park, since war interrupted a previous generation's schemes. That summer, Smith and his partners, including the staggeringly wealthy Harry Wardman – Bradford-born, prolific Washington DC real estate developer, and union buster – complete what newspapers herald as a 'gigantic deal' and unveil their plans for a 'palatial hotel'.[34] As construction resumes, Smith talks of his fact-finding visits to the United States and ambition to 'make sure that the new building would embody all the most modern American construction, together with the present-day English ideas of comfort'.[35]

The Park Lane Hotel opens in January 1927, just as the conflicts around the Kittens' cafe are about to explode in court. It is a newspaper sensation: the 'most luxurious [hotel] in London'. Its 'modern conveniences' include en suite bathrooms for every room, Turkish baths and hairdressing saloons, garages and sleeping accommodation for chauffeurs, kennels for visiting pet dogs, and 'oxygenised air, changed ten times an hour'.[36] Hundreds of 'distinguished guests' attending the 'Housewarming ceremony' hear how the 'influence of Mrs Bracewell Smith ... has introduced the air of domesticity, by which it is hoped to distinguish the new hotel'.[37] 'Actually', counters the *People*, 'the hotel ... is the outcome of one man's inspiration'.[38]

It is also the outcome of unseen labour and capital accumulation. Smith tells anyone who will listen that he is in the hospitality business, but the Shaftesbury is also a financial asset on which to draw. Acting against the Kittens is interwoven with Smith's need to maximise the value of his assets and accumulate the necessary capital for further investment, particularly as construction drags on.[39]

In January 1927, at the same time as the hotel opens, Gordon and Smith Limited becomes the Park Lane Hotel Limited, with Smith as chair and managing director. A week later, the company acquires the 'leasehold land and buildings ... of the Shaftesbury Hotel'.[40] In March, finally, the company acquires the leasehold of the Park Lane Hotel. From now on, Bracewell Smith will move in very different worlds.[41]

* * *

As the monstrous machine moves across Seven Dials, what does it leave behind? For at least some of those living nearby, the Shaftesbury brings work. Alongside the live-in housekeepers, chambermaids, and porters – people like the young reception clerk Elizabeth Gemmell Smith – the hotel employs a dozen or so people from the Dials. The widow Louisa Simmonds walks the short distance to work from the rooms in Shorts Gardens she shares with her boarder, Bertha Abrams – like her, a still room maid. The lift attendant Thomas Green lives down on Little White Lion Street.

The Shaftesbury also brings visitors to Seven Dials. There are more of them, and they come increasingly from a different social background and further afield than the hotel's original clientele. Shortly after Smith takes over, the 1921 census captures a moment of flux. On census night there are 203 people staying there. Although it is June, 152 of them are men: the hotel is most popular among those travelling for work, not pleasure. The Shaftesbury's origins as a workman's hotel are clear. During the industrial conflicts that roil postwar Britain, it provides somewhere to stay and meet for trade unionists from across the country. Amid the tumult of 1919, when there were 35 million strike days, the hotel had hosted the Joint Negotiating Committee, bringing the National Federation of Employers together with representatives of organised labour.[42]

Two years later, as the 'coal crisis' builds, trade unionists again congregate in Seven Dials. While guests include organisers from the National Motor Fireman's Union in Hull and the National Union of Dockworkers in Liverpool, the largest group is from the Miners' Federation of Great Britain. The lockout that began in April is coming to a head, and officials from the South Wales, Durham, and Lanarkshire coalfields gather in Great St Andrew Street to meet comrades from South Yorkshire and Nottinghamshire. Many write 'out of work' in the census – evidence of the hardship of industrial action.[43] Perhaps the most surprising guest is the charismatic Arthur James Cook: pacifist, internationalist, militant, communist, miners' agent for Rhondda, and elected national delegate for the South Wales Miners' Federation. In a few weeks, Cook will be imprisoned for incitement and unlawful assembly for his role in the dispute. It will not be long before he leads the Miners' Federation through the lockout and General Strike of 1926.[44]

As Bracewell Smith rises through municipal and national Conservative politics, his hotel plays a central role in sustaining the radical politics of the 1920s. The Shaftesbury hosts meetings of the Actors' Association, Chromatic Film Printers, and the National Conference of Hairdressers.[45] Self-styled 'Social Socialists' organise dinners for veteran activists Ben Tillett and Tom Mann 'in recognition of the work they have done for the organisation of unskilled labour since the dockers strike in 1889'.[46] There are moments of startling incongruity. In the autumn of 1925, twelve prominent members of the Communist Party of Great Britain – including Harry Pollitt and Wal Hannington – are tried for seditious conspiracy at the Old Bailey. Cross-examining a detective in court, Willie Gallacher – a leading figure in Glasgow's 'Red Clydeside' – exposes the hypocrisies of undercover officers 'representing themselves as Communists'. 'You are aware that Scotland Yard members have associated with Communists in the billiard room at the Shaftesbury Hotel ...?' he asks: 'I can't say that. I know nothing' is the reply.[47] Two months later, when the London Independent Labour Party meets at the hotel, they pass resolutions on the 'failure of capitalism' and support the National Unemployed Workers Movement. From the 'failure of capitalism' to Communists in the billiard room: it is hard to imagine politics so anathema to the Shaftesbury's proprietor.[48]

In the restaurant and lobby, Gallacher and comrades mingle with very different social worlds. There are teachers and bankers; doctors and opticians; commercial travellers and civil servants. Touring actors and theatrical managers are drawn by the proximity of the West End and the dedicated Rehearsal Room: the hotel is a base and correspondence address for performers like 'Frederick Silvester ... The Premier Equilibristic Manipulator'.[49] London is a global and imperial metropole, and as trade picks up, the Shaftesbury welcomes wine merchants from Italy and woollen wholesalers from the Netherlands. The Brazilian consul is heading to Calcutta. Harry Howard, stationmaster in Kafue, Northern Rhodesia, and William Pyne, Railway Officer from Bombay, have returned to London on leave. It is this commercial and professional middle-class clientele which Smith now strives to cultivate.[50]

If the Shaftesbury's changing character reflects the peacetime revival of commerce and travel, it is driven by deliberate efforts to take the hotel upmarket. Always imposing, the building is smartened up and modernised within and without. Such is the scale of the task that the hotel employs its own painters: father and son William and Edwin Cato live nearby on Neal Street. Following the latest fashions in leisure, a resident jazz band plays for afternoon and evening tea dances. The restaurant is renovated. A postcard sent by a Belgian guest to a friend in Antwerp in July 1931 captures immaculate place settings and pristine tablecloths, the elaborate cutlery of fine dining, a drinks table laden with wine. The plush carpet and dark panelling and furniture bespeak solid respectability. 'Groeten uit Londen' – greetings from London – they write.[51]

Souvenir postcards also show how the Shaftesbury is sold to potential guests. Another postcard – annotated '20–25 Juli 1928' – views the hotel from Seven Dials. Cropped to exclude its insalubrious environs, particularly Great White Lion Street to the left, the photograph emphasises the hotel's grand entrance and striking plate glass windows. A uniformed concierge polices the movement of people in and out from the Dials.[52] New guests receive a specially printed *London Weekly Diary of Social Events*, which includes the latest plays, shows, and films, and a map of theatreland. One visitor scribbles down a sightseeing itinerary – the Tower of London and Law Courts – and the bus route from Hyde Park Corner to Hampton Court.[53]

The Shaftesbury will never rival establishments like the Savoy. Its keynote is solidity, not Society. Like many big hotels, it has a raffish and sometimes illicit edge. Down on their luck ex-officers seek employment; film producers offer acting tuition; impresarios audition wannabes for chorus roles that may not exist.[54] It is a rendezvous for couples of all sorts: chambermaids give evidence and receptionists produce the hotel's register in the divorce courts more than once.[55] Debonair tricksters stroll the bars; opportunistic thieves prowl the corridors; the aftermath's flotsam and jetsam wash up in Great St Andrew Street. 'Must a hotel guest bolt his door as well as lock it?' a magistrate is asked when the auditor Arthur Andrew sues the hotel's proprietors after someone steals from his wallet while he sleeps.[56]

The Shaftesbury is no longer a workman's hotel: Bracewell Smith sees to that, even if old habits die hard and left-wing organisations still meet there in the early 1930s. Demanding appropriate recompense for their creative labour, Associated British Authors and Composers discuss 'the scandalous business of wireless bribery' and challenge the BBC to stand against the music industry's 'racketeering'.[57] In 1932, William Norton, leader of the Irish Free State Labour Party, holds 'secret talks' in the restaurant with Labour politicians Clement Atlee, George Lansbury, and Sir Stafford Cripps.[58] Yet the hotel is now more likely to host the Primrose League, masonic lodges, the Automobile Traders Association, and the St Pancras Conservative Association.[59] In December 1931, Lady Edith Windham and the Victoria Park Toy Dog Association while away the evening dining, dancing, and speechifying at their 2nd Annual Supper and Dance. The five-course meal includes Consommé Volaille, Fillet of Beef with Brussels sprouts and mashed potatoes, and Mixed Fruit Melba.[60]

Stroll into the Shaftesbury after theatres close in the early 1930s, then, and you are more likely to encounter the acerbic *Sunday Times* and BBC drama critic James Agate propping up the bar than delegates from the Miners' Federation.[61] The circumstances are unusual – Britain is at war and most rooms are empty – but the official register taken in September 1939 captures the Shaftesbury's transformation. Most guests are professionals or businesspeople travelling for work – a schoolmaster and olive oil export merchant, a horticulturalist, a surveyor of ships employed by the Board of Trade. This is a different world from the place Smith bought two decades earlier. It is also a different world from the tenements and lodging houses around Great St Andrew Street.[62]

* * *

It is not just the Shaftesbury Hotel that is transformed in the decade after the Great War. Bracewell Smith's property empire grows dramatically. In 1928, his Park Lane Hotel Company buys the Green Park Hotel for £140,000. It is rumoured that each bedroom in this 'super-luxury building' costs £1000 to furnish.[63] A year later, the company acquires the Alexandra Hotel for £140,000. In Knightsbridge, overlooking Rotten Row and Hyde Park, the Alexandra 'caters for an exclusive clientele consisting largely of country people and officers'.[64] In 1929, finally, Smith and George Harvey invest £200,000 in the fashionable Café Royal, then home to London's biggest masonic temple. Together the men 'have done much to revolutionise the hotel industry and to modernize hotel construction', observes one journalist.[65]

Developing the Shaftesbury and reorganising his financial assets is a turning point in Smith's business career. In the mid-1920s, Jim and Emily Kitten and the 'Black colony' are drawn into the efforts of entrepreneurs and developers to remake London in their own image. Seven Dials' stop–start redevelopment is interwoven with the histories of wealthier and more prestigious neighbourhoods like Piccadilly and Mayfair. The conflicts swirling around a backstreet cafe are integral to the arrival of the most opulent modernist hotels of the twenties and thirties. While investing in the Shaftesbury allows Smith to build the capital necessary to leave Seven Dials for Piccadilly, he leaves little obvious trace behind. In 1930, writing in the Society magazine *Britannia and Eve*, the columnist Diana Bourbon can describe the Shaftesbury as a 'quite prosperous hotel'. Redevelopment makes the neighbourhood's inequalities starker, though. A 'threadbare air of shuttered inactivity' hangs in the hotel's environs. Looking around, Bourbon sees the Dials as 'narrow slits of streets of varying degrees of musty non-prosperity'.[66]

Two pressing questions run underneath all this. Who is London for? What might the imperial city of the future look like? At the start of the 1920s, the Earl of Meath imagines a process of 'beautification and development [of London] as the centre of the greater political organisation the world has ever known'.[67] Throughout this process, he counsels, 'let us bear in mind that we should desire to make London a *real home* for the children of the Empire'. Meath's outward-looking internationalism clashes with the idea – increasingly prevalent after the racist violence of 1919 – that 'improvement' might also be a way to decolonise or deracinate London itself.[68]

* * *

Look up, and you might see the future. Stand on the corner where Great White Lion Street meets Seven Dials, keep the Shaftesbury Hotel at your back, and look across the road. You will not find the future in the fading shopfronts and hand-painted signs for refreshments, valet services, R. White's lemonade, alterations and repairs. Nor – despite the hopes of those tempted by the *People*'s football pools – will you see it in the surrealist collage of pasted billposters layered upon a cafe's windows. Earl McCready and Reuben Wright's wrestling match at the Royal Albert Hall, the 'eastern rhythms' of Rina Nikova's Palestine Singing Ballet, and the *Sunday Pictorial*'s serialised life-story of Lupino

Figure 2.2 Corner of Earlham Street and Monmouth Street, 1938(?)

Lane – inspiration for the latest dance craze, the Lambeth Walk: each of these places you in the here and now of 1938.

Look further up, where the streets are changing their names, and the building formed by the triangle of Little

Earl and Little St Andrew Streets juts into the Dials. Look at the advertising hoarding: accommodation to let in the new 'Globe House Seven Dials'; an artist's vision of the same junction from a different vantage point. Something has changed, though: a street corner has been reimagined with the stroke of a brush. Pressing forward like the bow of an ocean-going liner, a modernist colossus of curved glass and metal – 7000 square feet all told – has taken the place of the decaying building that now struggles under the weight of its past and its fantastical simulacra. An ageing tenement foretells its own demise.

Bracewell Smith is a canny businessman, but the hoarding confirms he is not alone in sensing opportunities to make money in these environs. Just as his investment in the Shaftesbury is part of the intense speculation that followed the Great War, so it is tracked a decade later by the Cambridge Theatre Company's purchase of the corner site opposite the hotel. Modern flats and showrooms rise on the streets where Seven Dials looks out to the West End. London's principal commercial property developers tread heavily across the area. Now they are here at the corner where Little Earl and Little St Andrew Streets converge.

Originally owned by the Jane Franks and Sara Marcus Estate, the three buildings that comprise the block are among fifteen 'freehold investments in the heart of the West End' sold by Hillier, Parker, May, and Rowden in spring 1936.[69] If Hillier et al. is known for driving London's suburban expansion, the company that buys the block is equally prominent. Based in Mayfair, H. I., and A. Rubens and its satellites – Raglan New Estates, Raglan Property Trust, the Property and Reversionary Investment Corporation Limited – specialise in acquiring and developing high-end commercial and residential property. Globe House exemplifies the presence of the monstrous machine of capital at Seven Dials' heart.[70]

Except Globe House is never built. It exists as a developer's fantasy, an architect's rendering, a hoarding on a dilapidated tenement. Its only trace is captured by a photographer who finds themselves in the Dials at some point in 1938. The triumphant march of modernity is stymied by powerful vested interests, accelerating material decline, and the start of the Second World War. The machine only reaches so far into Seven Dials' precincts. 'A new building' that will never be is perhaps more revealing of the area's uneven commercial development than the Shaftesbury Hotel.

Even an unbuilt building can still make its presence felt. When Pietro and Marcella Taffurelli and Woolf Lieber gaze on the corner of Little Earl and Little St Andrew Streets they must see something different. They do not need to look up to feel the melancholy of loss – of frustrated dreams and shiny dystopias. Blackened shopfronts and empty buildings, pasted billposters, gaping windows, and a collapsing blind are the corporeal afterlives of long-standing small businesses edged out by the relentless creep of corporate capital.

Woolf Lieber was born in Constantinople; his father, Kalman, in Odessa; his mother, Buny, in Shklow in Belarus. Displaced across a continent, they have been in Seven Dials for decades. Variously a tailor and valet, their businesses move around – they were the Kittens' neighbours for a time – before Woolf arrived in Little Earl Street. Originally from Bettola Piacenza, in northern Italy, the Taffurellis opened their popular refreshment rooms around 1931. They are all the human costs of 'freehold investment' and a developer's grandiose plans. Pushed from the Dials, Lieber rents new premises along Monmouth Street and moves to St Pancras. Pietro and Marcella Taffurelli leave the area. Emptied of people and life – caught in the limbo of planning blight – the block decays slowly. Utopia is not for everyone; development is haunted by displacement; an advertising hoarding can taunt more than it promises.

* * *

In February 1927 – the date matters – the *Sphere* publishes a 'thumbnail interview' with 'London's newest hotel manager'. In this short biography, Bracewell Smith's opulent Park Lane Hotel becomes what his interviewer calls the 'copingstone on his greatest accomplishment'. As narrated here, that accomplishment is built on the intuition, graft, and force of character that have taken a remarkable man from humble provincial beginnings to the centre of metropolitan life.[71]

A self-made man indeed, but Smith makes stories just as much as fortunes. In the late 1920s, every significant career milestone becomes an opportunity to rehearse the life-story first told when the Park Lane Hotel opens. In August 1928, he regales a *Daily News* journalist with what they generously call a 'Romance of West End Purchase'. 'In my early years, I used to lie on the moorland in the Bronte country watching the sun rise and the moon set and dreaming of London', Smith recalls. That 'dream came true in 1908', but it was only after wartime service that he decided to 'strike out as my own master'.

> I started buying and selling houses, making £20 here and £10 there. Success came first, second, and third. I built up one business after another, and when I became interested in the Park Lane Hotel, I determined that it should be the first in

> the British Isles with a bathroom to each bedroom. The staff worked with me gallantly, and in the last six months I made enough profit to buy the Green Park Hotel.[72]

A month later, the *Daily Chronicle* is treated to a more colourful retelling of the story. Returning from the war, Smith explains, 'I wanted to see life, to be free, make money, and be my own boss ... I resigned, and with the money I had ... went in for the hotel business.' The Alexandra, Ritz, and Green Park Hotels, the famous Café Royal: each new property becomes another chapter in a rags-to-riches autobiography.[73] Assiduously cultivated through interviews and press releases, Smith's self-fashioning as a self-made man is every bit as calculating and ruthless as his accumulation of property and power. By the time he dies in 1966, his estate worth over £1 million, Smith has turned himself into a 'twentieth century Dick Whittington'.[74]

There are striking omissions here. Acquiring the Shaftesbury had been integral to Smith's initial accumulation of property and power. By the late 1920s, the hotel has disappeared from his stories of social mobility. When you have made it, there is little kudos – even less prestige – in continuing to associate yourself with a dilapidated slum. Besides, the journey from Yorkshire to Piccadilly seems more dramatic if you skip the Seven Dials staging point.

What Smith and others present as a self-made man's singular autobiography is also inseparable from commercial property markets, London's burgeoning hotel and leisure industries, and the frenetic commercial redevelopment through which the city is made modern in the 1920s and 1930s. This is more than a personal story, in other words. It is not always obvious at the time, but the struggles around the Kittens' cafe are braced by the acquisition of substantial holdings in Seven Dials by corporations and developers.

Despite huge inequalities of class and race, local property markets allow Black, Asian, Italian, or Jewish entrepreneurs to establish themselves in places like Seven Dials. Those inequalities also mean they cannot compete with bigger property companies, let alone the hostile attention of police and local authorities, as they seek to remake Seven Dials in their own image. The ebb and flow of urban redevelopment animates intense local conflicts between residents and business owners, aggressive property companies, and municipal authorities. The emerging fault-lines of the twenties and thirties establish a template for recurring struggles between working-class communities and wealthy gentrifiers and developers. In the end, Smith's advancement will hinge on his ability to leverage wealth, status, and connection to suppress the small business across Great White Lion Street.[75]

The Shaftesbury Hotel's telegraph address is 'Unafraid, West. Cent, London'. Unafraid: one knowing word that acknowledges the area's insalubrious reputation and a respectable hotel's out-of-placeness on Great St Andrew Street. One word that signals an entrepreneur's undaunted commitment to building his business and remaking Seven Dials, regardless of who gets in his way. A telegraph address evokes pockets of development in a place still dominated by decline. Brighter London is patched into the torn fabric of the old city. Seven Dials is not quite a frontier. Still, its tight-knit streets intensify tensions over London's future – the explosive question of who the city belongs to – that will erupt throughout the following century.[76]

3
The local politics of improvement
Shorts Gardens

Autumn's fine rain hangs in the air when Princess Louise, Duchess of Argyll, opens St Giles Buildings. A small crowd has gathered at the entrance to the new model dwellings and mother and baby clinic in Shorts Gardens: journalists, dignitaries in regalia, curious bystanders, mothers and their children – shuffling and uncomfortable in the chill. The road is narrow and the waiting cars and carts and lorries laden with produce stretch up to Endell Street. For those involved in bringing the scheme to fruition – members of the Society for Improving the Condition of the Labouring Classes and Holborn Council – it should be a moving occasion. After years struggling to remedy the 'terrible conditions existing in some Holborn houses', there is finally something to celebrate. 'Oh, Heavenly Father,' says the Bishop of Stepney, offering up a prayer, 'we give Thee hearty thanks that Thou hast enabled us to erect a building for the relief of the suffering of our fellow men, and unto Thine honour'.[1]

Alderman Robert Dibdin is both a councillor and the society's president. Raising his voice above the noise of idling engines and impatient porters, he proudly rehearses the history of a charitable organisation founded in 1844. He reels off details of the scheme: much-needed homes for 140 working-class people, built at a cost of £22,000. Finally, as the crowd becomes restless, the elderly duchess stands to add some words of her own, half-hidden beneath a lady-in-waiting's umbrella. The buildings, she says, exemplify 'that steady, kindly, and wholly individual effort, exactly planned to meet the need it sees and understands, which provides the best and surest ways of dealing with our social problems'. Today, in 1925, the need for affordable modern housing remains 'as great as ever, and even more for the maintenance of family life, for individual happiness, for the harmony and prosperity of the community'. All this is clear from the tumbledown tenements around them and the conflicts that have convulsed Britain since the war. Here, then, is a vital step forward in the march of progress, through which Christian philanthropists and enlightened politicians provide for the citizens of a new mass democracy.[2]

St Giles Buildings can tell us a lot about the local politics of urban 'improvement' in the 1920s and 1930s. After the Great War, an uneasy coalition of planners, architects, municipal authorities, and organisations like the London Society turn to the task of building a modern metropolis. It is in this context that Seven Dials comes to be seen as a problem to solve and an opportunity to enact grandiose visions of the new London. Within these down-at-heel environs, new model dwellings will come to exemplify renewed efforts to transform the area.

For those with such ambitions, the Dials – its fabric and people – is increasingly seen as an anachronistic obstacle to the pressing task ahead. The case for development works through a sleight of hand: calling the 'slum' or 'Black colony' into being as problems to solve – only to justify the steps necessary for their removal. Utopian dreams are invariably punctured by political and financial realities, but the tentative and disputed process of 'improvement' shapes the struggles around the Kittens' cafe. In many ways, the buildings are a tacit admission of failure. By the time they open, the scheme has taken over a decade and an unexpected last-minute intervention to complete. Holborn Council becomes mired in conflicts with business owners, fails to gain support from the LCC and Ministry of Health, cannot afford the costs of construction, and is frustrated by an emerging consensus – among those who have a say in such things – that central London is ill-suited to a residential population.

* * *

Sir George Parker, Holborn's former mayor, dreams of a place that will never be: Five Dials – a plaza as magnificent as Piccadilly Circus. It is commercial London's bustling heart, the meeting point of monumental thoroughfares speeding people and goods across the city. Those returning to the capital after years away will be bewildered: the area is unrecognisable from what it had been. Thirteen acres of 'slums' south of Shaftesbury Avenue have disappeared under compulsory purchase orders and the whirlwind of the wreckers. Where there were 'shops, tenement houses, and warehouses ... in a most unsatisfactory and insanitary state of repair', geometric office blocks gleam in the sun. Where people lived, the streets swarm with white-collar workers during the day and are eerily quiet at night.[3] A tangle of streets and courts has become a planned grid. Extended to include Great and Little St Andrew Streets, the imposing line of St Martin's Lane heads arrow straight from Shaftesbury Avenue to the new Thames bridge at Charing Cross. Little Earl Street and Shorts Gardens connect Cambridge Circus to New Oxford Street and a grand public space before Holborn Town Hall.[4] Progress has 'wiped out' the alleys of old London: Neal's Yard or Little White Lion Street are now only ghosts.[5] This staggering transformation – what boosters call the 'most considerable scheme that has been attempted in modern times towards the improvement of Central London' – cost over £5 million.[6]

No one can accuse Parker of lacking ambition. For years he has identified the 'need for abolishing the slum [of Seven Dials] … and for erecting on the land thus rendered vacant buildings more worthy of a central London borough'.[7] From Holborn Town Hall, gazing down on the city, councillors and planners imagine the area's new future. In so doing, they redraw the map of central London: a tangle of streets and ageing buildings will be swept away, replaced by grand boulevards and towering cathedrals of business, work, and consumption. Parker's dreams take life as the far-reaching plans set out in the Seven Dials and Drury Lane Improvement Scheme (1920).

HELP US ABOLISH THE SLUMS

A sketch of St. Giles' Buildings, Seven Dials, which were opened by Her Royal Highness The Princess Louise, Duchess of Argyll.

Figure 3.1 'A sketch of St Giles Buildings, Seven Dials', included in a Society for the Improvement of the Condition of the Labouring Classes fundraising appeal

The confident speculation of the aftermath means the 'time is now ripe for the proper development of that area known as Seven Dials and Drury Lane ... to provide for the commercial needs of the Metropolis'. And so, in July 1920, Parker's grandiose dreams are presented to press, public, and the London County Council. The rhetoric of slum clearance – fixing problems of poverty and overcrowding – is enlisted to support plans for a grid of wide streets and ten 'island' sites for development. 'Improvement' means easing the movement of goods and people and facilitating the necessary investment to create an upscale office district. 'Improvement' also means making 4500 people homeless. For the scheme's boosters, this is a price worth paying. The 'real object', Parker argues, is to 'make the borough more nearly what it should be in the times to come'. Politicians 'could not afford to shut their eyes to what was in front of them'. The old Seven Dials is to be sacrificed on the altar of municipal prestige, increased rate income, and commercialisation.[8]

Parker and the borough surveyor, E. F. Spurrell, are most prominent in explaining their importance, but these proposals involve a disparate coalition of councillors and interests. Holborn Council's Special Committee includes the estate agent Arthur Slee; Reverend Wilfred Davies, Rector of St Giles-in-the-Fields; Robert Dibdin and his sister Emily Dibdin, a member of Holborn's Maternity and Child Welfare Committee. Parker's Municipal Reform Party dominates, but the committee includes independent voices like Labour councillor William Forster Bovill.[9]

Dreams are always of their time and place. The fantastical visions of the Improvement Scheme reflect growing faith in the possibilities of town planning. It builds on an emerging yet fragile consensus that central London should be remade for commerce and leisure. Its inception – and eventual collapse – are shaped by municipal government's political and financial limits. Crucially, it repackages these ideas as a solution to the urgent social problems that beset Seven Dials. Of these, the housing crisis is most acute. It is clear by 1919 that deteriorating housing and overcrowding in central boroughs like Holborn, Westminster, St Pancras, and Marylebone demand 'anxious consideration'. For the scheme's supporters, alleviating this 'blot on our system of administration' is a ready justification for reducing the Dials to rubble.[10] As they court public opinion, Spurrell talks of 'many houses of an unsatisfactory character, with dark basements looking onto narrow streets' – 'persons ... living their lives under conditions which no authority having the welfare of the people at heart could countenance'.[11] For sure, Seven Dials has changed since the nineteenth century, but there are still 'no playgrounds, gardens, or open spaces': it is 'not suitable for ... the rearing of children'.[12] 'Improvement' is presented as a necessary step in cleansing an ageing slum's 'mean streets' and 'evil reputation' and providing for future generations.[13]

'Notorious Slum to Go' – but you need to call a slum into being to justify your plans for its replacement.[14] It might gesture towards London's housing crisis, but the Improvement Scheme is really animated by an awareness of the depressed value of property and rateable income in Seven Dials. In this calculation – the calculation made by many politicians – an area 'within easy reach of omnibuses and Tube railway services, near Theatreland and on the fringe of an important and valuable area of Western London' is well placed to meet growing demand for 'good building sites'. As London's 'centre of commerce' expands, the

Committee argues that 'valuable land such as exists in the borough ... should be devoted to more useful and lucrative purposes' than providing a home for ordinary people.[15]

In austere times, lavish plans can seem an alluring way out of intractable political and financial crises. The line between ambition and desperation is never clear. After a short-lived postwar boom, Britain is rocked by economic depression, mass unemployment, and the retrenchment of government spending in the late 1910s and early 1920s. For London's borough councils, the effects are desperate. As rate incomes collapse and resistance to any increase in local taxation grows at least some politicians search for quick fixes.

Its boosters never say as much, but this is one way to understand the scheme's destructive fantasies of 'open[ing] up the property for the erection of commercial offices, hotels, and theatres fronting road[s] of the size and dignity of Kingsway'.[16] In establishing a grid of 'island' blocks, the scheme promises to create 'vacant sites [which] would carry high ground rents' and 'considerably enhance' the area's rateable value.[17] The 'small tenement houses, shops with living rooms above, factories, and warehouses, and fifteen public houses' have a 'gross value of £71,000 and a ratable value of £53,000', asserts Spurrell.[18] The *Kensington Post* takes his analysis on face value:

> The proposed demolitions would entail an outlay of about £5,000,000 by way of compensation, but in view of the very eager demand that exists for building sites, it is believed that the land would be quickly taken up, and that palatial buildings in steel, ferro-concrete, and stone, similar to those on Kingsway and Aldwych, would soon be in course of erection. By these means it should be possible to turn an existing rateable value of £53,000 into rateable and site value of £350,000 a year within quite a short time.[19]

'It is believed …', 'it should be possible …': the Improvement Scheme is a confidence game: Parker and Spurrell, sellers of snake oil, promising to bring untold prosperity and prestige to Holborn by unleashing the transformative power of capital.

Holborn Council approves the Committee's plans but add one caveat to the minutes of their discussion: 'any scheme should provide for the suitable re-housing of the displaced population either within or without the Borough'.[20] If municipal boosters and journalists paint improvement's commercial possibilities in bold detail and vivid colour, for those living in Seven Dials the future looks more like a join-the-dots picture. When the committee promises to begin demolition within months of LCC approval they neglect to mention that there are no firm plans for rehousing those 'rendered homeless'. Parker guesses that building new cottage housing will cost £600,000 – perhaps to be borrowed through Housing Bonds. Through the summer and autumn of 1920, residents face an uncertain future in which they are relocated to an unknown 'site to be acquired some four or five miles outside Holborn – probably in one of the northern suburbs'.[21]

The discord between how politicians, planners, and journalists discuss the two strands of the scheme is both revealing and deliberate. It is revealing because it underscores how politicians are preoccupied with harnessing the power of capital to increase property values and rate income. Addressing the housing crisis is of secondary concern to creating a thriving business district. Bracewell Smith's dual position as an elected councillor and an entrepreneur invested in Seven Dials suggests the rapprochement between planning and speculative development. He is not unusual. When new Mayor George Harvey addresses the 'brilliant gathering' at the Connaught Rooms celebrating his election in December 1921, he attributes the borough's success to the political dominance of 'those who had got responsibilities – businessmen and professional men of whom Holborn might be proud'. Like Smith, Harvey has skin in this game. To a complicit audience of council officials and fellow members of the Municipal Reform Party, he acknowledges how 'war has upset the whole equilibrium of society'. The entwining of political power and capital creates strong foundations on which to rebuild, though, unlike 'one borough ... that seemed to be controlled by a trade union' – George Lansbury's Labour administration in Poplar. In this view, there is little distinction between selfless commitment to sound governance and 'economy' and commercial self-interest.[22]

The discord between how the Improvement Scheme's different strands are discussed is deliberate because it seeks to resolve a growing dilemma for all central boroughs. The *Holborn and Finsbury Guardian* notes how Holborn and Marylebone – they might add Westminster – 'have a huge day population and a rapidly decreasing night population. Both are rich, busy boroughs, with an immensely high rateable value, and in both the office and the warehouse is eating up the dwelling houses.'[23] The plaintive annual refrain of Holborn's medical officer of health echoes this analysis: 'although the number of hotels and boarding houses keeps increasing, the borough is becoming less and less residential and more and more important as a business centre'.[24]

In moving to resolve this crisis, Holborn's proposals follow the injunction of Stanley Adshead, Professor of Town Planning at University College London: 'Central London is to-day no place of residence for the masses.' For Adshead – as for organisations like the Brighter London Society – the heart of the metropolis is to be devoted to commerce and consumption. In dismissing the 'masses' – a word dripping with privilege and pejorative codes of class and race – Adshead leaves no future for cosmopolitan neighbourhoods like Seven Dials. There is no recognition that such areas retain significant residential populations. Adshead imagines Seven Dials out of existence, just as the Improvement Scheme contains a vision of modern London which endorses and seeks to accelerate its depopulation by unleashing the forces of capital.[25]

Developers are aware of the rich opportunities here. As discussion of the Improvement Scheme crescendos, the estate agent Rowland Stuart advertises a 'magnificent freehold corner building site' comprising the dwellings, shops, and yards between Great Earl, Little White Lion, and Castle Streets. 'This proposition should prove an exceptionally fine investment owing to the proposed scheme for improving the neighbourhood', observes the advert pointedly.[26] Amid the media frenzy of 1920, only one journalist says the quiet part out loud: 'It is not intended to sanction the erection of residential chambers on the new sites, but to confine the buildings to business premises and suites of offices of approved design.'[27]

The Seven Dials and Drury Lane Improvement Scheme exemplifies wider efforts to make London modern. It is smaller in scope, but its ambitions echo more familiar contemporaneous debates over the fate of Waterloo Bridge. The controversies over whether to replace or preserve a collapsing bridge turn upon the balance between embracing the future and retaining the monuments of the past in London's redevelopment – between efficiency and the reassuring symbols of Britain's past.[28] In the Improvement Scheme, the idea that rational planning and new roads will drive economic development links earlier projects like the construction of Shaftesbury Avenue and Kingsway to the urban motorways and ring roads that characterise planning after the Second World War.[29] In contrast to the tortuous discussions around Waterloo Bridge, the path of 'improvement' is cleared by the axiom that Seven Dials contains nothing of architectural or historical significance worth preserving. This means Parker's plans are not the only version of utopia in which the area disappears. John Murray's proposed Imperial Way envisages the Dials obliterated by a grand avenue leading north from a new Thames bridge at Charing Cross on to Holborn and New Oxford Street.[30]

Despite the giddy editorials and indulgent fantasies, in the end, the Improvement Scheme goes nowhere. Dreams of what Seven Dials might become clash with the realities of municipal government and the area's dilapidated fabric. The difficulties of razing and rebuilding a neighbourhood are insurmountable. It is impossible to reconcile overlapping authorities with jurisdiction over Seven Dials, to salve tensions between Holborn and Westminster councils, the LCC, and central government, and to overcome local opposition. Financial retrenchment makes the scheme unaffordable. The minutes of the council meeting are laconic: 'In view of the many difficulties in the way of carrying out such a scheme at that time, the Committee were unable to submit any concrete recommendations to the Council.'[31] Newspapers are more succinct: the plan is 'shelved in view of the cost'.[32]

Aggrieved and approaching retirement, Spurrell defends his plans to anyone who will listen. For the construction industry, the *British Builder* rails against this short-sighted decision. 'Clearance must come about sooner or later', they argue. More than a sound 'business proposition', removing the 'reproach of this slum area in the heart of London' is a matter of national and metropolitan prestige.[33] Fantasies of urban renewal – particularly the 'battle of London's bridges' – allow councillors to resurrect and again reject the scheme for a time. Until it is finally abandoned in 1926, levelling Seven Dials can sometimes still seem a good idea.[34]

* * *

It is easy to dream when you view a city from above. Walking away from the Dials along Shorts Gardens in the years after war becomes peace, the challenges of 'improvement' are more visceral: dilapidated buildings, an empty plot, and the stench of a basement levelled with 'household refuse ... decayed wood, ashes, bones, old iron, broken pots, fragments of rags, and vegetable mould'.[35] Pressed between vertiginous back-to-backs, the courts here have long been among the poorest parts of Seven Dials. Charles Booth's investigators characterised the block as 'semi-destitute and criminal', noting the stories police and rescue workers tell of its notoriety as a red-light district. Across the road looms Tommy Farmer's lodging house. At its biggest, the house provides 240 beds in 16 wards: it is a resting place for men down on their luck, elderly or infirm, unemployed, living hand to mouth until wards are gradually mothballed after 1934.[36] Perhaps because of this transient population and lack of communal space, perhaps because police are more likely to patrol here, the street and courts are known for gambling, drunkenness, and petty crime. In the first half of the 1920s, it is this unpropitious empty space on the corner of Shorts Gardens and Neal Street that becomes a focus for different visions of what might be.[37]

A decade earlier, there had been houses here, though they were deemed unfit for habitation and demolished when

Holborn Council acquired the land in 1911. The council's proposed modern dwellings with bathrooms and indoor toilets were stymied by the outbreak of war.[38] After the Armistice, the plans are resurrected, but the 'altered conditions of the housing problem' make politicians less certain in their ambition. The site cost £11,000 but pressing ahead is prohibitively expensive. Wavering now will cause 'grave disappointment, especially in that part of the borough' cautions Robert Dibdin, but strident voices demand the land is sold.[39] 'The point to consider was whether Holborn was a suitable place in which to erect working-class houses', argues Alderman Green. For Green, at least, the answer is no: the imperatives of economy mean new housing should be built elsewhere.[40]

It is impossible to separate the weakening of political will from financial retrenchment and the legal constraints imposed by national and municipal government. Asked to inspect four potential sites – including Shorts Gardens – the Ministry of Health's London Housing Board deems them too small and land values too high to justify residential development. Now formally prohibited from borrowing money to build, frustrated councillors recognise the implication: no new housing scheme will be approved in Holborn.[41] The crisis is overwhelming, but by 1920 it is already clear that 'owing to the very high cost of land in the centre of London the council is unable to undertake the erection of housing in its area'.[42]

For almost two years, the fate of Shorts Gardens is bogged down in vacillation and bitter debate in committees and correspondence columns. There are offers from businesspeople and developers. The British Legion seeks permission to erect a hut for ex-servicemen. Locals press for the site to become a children's playground.[43] It takes a conflict of interest and what looks like a *deus ex machina* to break the impasse. Robert Dibdin is a prominent councillor, but he is also a leading member of the Society for Improving the Condition of the Labouring Classes. What happens is never public knowledge, but behind the scenes he brokers a deal. The Masonic Grand Lodge of England have ambitious plans to expand their premises on Great Queen Street, east of Seven Dials. The society owns the adjoining tenements on Wild Court and Wild Street. By the end of 1921, the Grand Lodge is negotiating purchase of these properties with Dibdin. Their conversation is difficult, but the society agree a price of £20,000 if the Lodge also pays to rehouse their tenants. In February 1922, while chairing a meeting, Dibdin 'mention[s] a vacant site in Shorts Gardens as a possible site for rehousing'. When the committee seeks 'to ascertain if the Freemasons would be willing to purchase this site from Holborn Borough Council and hand it to this Society for rehousing purposes', the Grand Lodge agrees.[44]

Four months later, the society approaches Holborn Council with an offer for the site and plans for new model dwellings. 'Amidst laughter', Dibdin tells councillors they are 'to have the work done for them, and at the same time receive a present of £5500'.[45] Perhaps his audience laugh because they know exactly where that gift comes from: many of them are Freemasons, and the council has its own lodge. When councillors first discuss the proposed Masonic development, George Harvey and Sir George criticise the Works Committee's apparent disinterest. Infuriated that the committee's report focuses on practicalities rather than fulsome support, Harvey explodes: the proposal is the 'biggest improvement that Holborn [has] ever seen, and it [is] a disgrace that the Council should appear to be taking no serious notice of it'. Harvey and Parker insist the committee is instructed to confer with the LCC, Ministry of Transport, and the Grand Lodge to establish 'what could be done to support the proposal'.[46] The striking art deco Freemasons Hall – initially called the Masonic Peace Memorial – rises on the enlarged Great Queen Street site between 1927 and 1933. The connecting Connaught Rooms – named after the Grand Master, the Duke of Connaught and Strathearn, and managed by Harvey – is remodelled and extended at the same time. The gossamer threads of power interweave the remaking of Seven Dials with that of grander environs across London.

A humbler building will also rise as a legacy of Freemasons Hall. There are only two modifications to the society's proposed model dwellings. First, the London Medical Mission's centre in Shorts Gardens has closed, leaving no provision for mothers in Seven Dials. At the request of Holborn's Maternity and Child Welfare Committee, the society agrees to build a clinic and lease it to the council.[47] Second, at the society's request, councillors close the public right of way on Nottingham Court, running beside the plot between Shorts Gardens and Shelton Street. The change is ostensibly necessary for the building: it creates a larger yard for children to play and 'accommodation for the perambulators of the persons attending the clinic'. It also allows the council to address long-standing concerns: quiet and secluded, the 'court has been, for many years, a source of annoyance to the authorities by its improper use'. Modern provision for housing and health goes together with older forms of moral reform.[48] Despite concerns that the site is 'overloaded', support for the scheme is 'practically unanimous'.[49]

Overseen by architects C. Westcott Reeves and Alfred Rason, construction begins in summer 1924. A decade's accumulated rubbish is covered with twelve inches of concrete. Modern dwellings rise on the mouldering detritus of the past.[50] When the block opens a year later, it exemplifies the society's commitment to providing affordable housing with 'up to date' conveniences of light, heat, and water. Thirty-seven individuals or families move into the one-, two-, and three-bedroom flats, paying an 'economic rent' of five shillings per room per week. It is not long before rents rise, cracks appear, and paint starts to peel. The society continue to maintain and update the buildings, though: over the following decade they plant trees and install electric lights and a new boiler.[51]

Perhaps the Improvement Scheme's bombastic fantasies also disappear under St Giles Buildings. If the project had not begun before the war and been completed by a philanthropic organisation founded eight decades earlier, it would not have happened. For a moment, though, it is possible to celebrate the triumph of a different vision for Seven Dials. The society commissions an anonymous artist to commemorate the dwellings' opening. It is an advert, of a sort, but there is little bombast in the diptych view from Nottingham Court and Neal Street. Modern London is less visible than the ruled pencil lines upon which the painting is composed. Dwarfed by the five-storey building, the tiny figures peopling Seven Dials – like the horsedrawn cart and porter's barrow – could come straight from the 1880s. We are a long way from the colour and clamour of brighter London, let alone the untrammelled commercialisation and destructive futurism envisaged by George Parker. St Giles Buildings appears as a legacy of the past as much as a glimpse of the future. Here is an older, though no less powerful, utopia: conservative, domestic, quietly aspirational.[52]

* * *

Figure 3.2 St Giles Buildings, Shorts Gardens, Artist's Impressions, 1925

People and politics remake Seven Dials, but it serves some well to attribute its changing character to anonymous and apparently natural 'economic tendencies'.[53] 'Regretful as it is to lose their citizens,' notes a local newspaper editor, 'it is inevitable that they must migrate to other and cheaper areas and rate subsidies merely delay the ultimate end'.[54] There is nothing inevitable about the deliberate choices behind this process. Despite their differences, the Improvement Scheme and St Giles Buildings address the same problems; their fate is determined by the same crises of municipal government. The collapse of one and modesty of another reflect the impossibility of thinking big in austere times. Look closer, and we see the antagonisms of improvement.

The formulaic minutes do not tell you how often council meetings are rushed and bad-tempered. It is not long before the new councillor C. G. L. Du Cann rages against 'short sittings, inefficiency, absenteeism, and the autocratic temper of elderly gentlemen too long exempt from public criticism'.[55] He might have George Parker in mind: even before his plans collapse, Parker is notoriously intemperate, unwilling to brook even gentle dissent. But there is more at work than clashes of personality. Du Cann divides the council into '"Spenders" (who talk economy) and "savers" (who vote for it)'. He counts himself among the 'solid block of fighters against increasing expenditure' – virulently opposing any rate increase and committed to creating space for commercial interests to transform Holborn.[56] Parker is this lobby's paternalistic face, but people like Du Cann are increasingly brash in embracing the consequences of commercialisation and interests of capital. 'No more legislation on housing was wanted', argues Councillor F. W. Loasby against a proposed rent cap: 'The evils to landlords of the present housing regulation were sufficient.'[57]

Du Cann's distinction runs along generational rather than party lines. The pejorative 'spenders' helps to dismiss members of his Municipal Reform Party – people like Robert Dibdin – who try to assuage the injuries of improvement. Dibdin is no radical: he is committed to economy and the Improvement Scheme. His philanthropic work is inseparable from the task of maintaining an organic national community. Model housing projects serve to alleviate the threat of class conflict and 'Bolshevism'. In 1926 – the year of the General Strike – the Society for Improving the Condition of the Labouring Classes appeals for donations through the pamphlet *Strike at the Root of Social Unrest*. 'It is an undoubted fact', observes Dibdin, 'that good housing makes for contentment and individual happiness which lead us along the road to national prosperity'.[58] He is still a consistent and increasingly marginal voice on the council 'against commercializing the borough so that people would not desire to live in it'.[59]

At times, Dibdin's understanding of Seven Dials as a place of home and life, rather than a workplace for a growing 'day population' and playground for those who come out at night, is given a sharper edge. In August 1920, the London Labour Party sends 'a protest to the Holborn Borough Council concerning the grandiose project of demolition of dwelling houses to be replaced by business premises in Long Acre and Seven Dials'.[60] Two years later, the *Daily Herald* rails against the council treating the borough as a 'largely commercialised district run for the benefit of vested interests with little thought for the well-being of those who live in the borough'.[61]

As activists intensify their 'strenuous activity', preserving Holborn's residential status and resisting exclusive ideas of 'improvement' become pressing issues.[62] Leading figures like the communist and internationalist Arthur Field lobby councillors and write to newspapers about 'arresting the depopulation of central London'.[63] The few Labour councillors like author William Forster Bovill use their position to push for new housing. Bovill sits on the Improvement Committee but is a tenacious opponent of attempts to turn tenements into offices or warehouses. After a grasping landlord evicts residential tenants from Vernon Chambers, Bovill chastises the council for failing the 'house-needy community'. At an angry meeting, he fails to overturn this decision: his position, Bovill reflects, 'did not coincide with the ideals of the landlord class, or those municipal enthusiasts who claim that rates should have precedence over the comforts and necessities of human life'.[64]

These struggles allow at least some residents to organise on their own behalf. Joseph – sometimes Jeremiah – Maloney becomes Secretary of Holborn Independent Labour Party in the mid-1920s. Then living at 24 Great Earl Street, his family are long-standing residents of Seven Dials. Maloney is a workman for Holborn Council; his adult son and daughter work in Myers' gentleman's outfitters on Long Acre and Lister's chemists on Great Titchfield Street respectively. They will soon be among dozens of people displaced when their homes are levelled to make way for the new Cambridge Theatre. Trenchant opposition to slum clearance and demands for better housing come from within as well as without Seven Dials.[65]

Holborn remains Conservative, though – so conservative that the library will not carry the *Daily Herald* and Arthur Field can speak of the 'reactionary borough of Holborn'. However hard they fight improvement's logic and effects Labour's influence remains small. The party fails to secure any council seats at many elections in the 1920s, and splinters acrimoniously over the presence of communists. Holborn is dominated by the Municipal Reform Party, and the interests of capital outweigh those of labour. Until the Labour presence on the council grows significantly after 1935 and the Holborn Tenants' Defence League is formed in 1938, an older generation of paternalists is often the only check on the area's commercialisation.[66]

* * *

If different visions of Seven Dials' future are at stake, these conflicts are really about money and power. There are irreconcilable pressures on property and land, and it is impossible to untangle the question of whether it should remain a residential neighbourhood from concerns over local prestige and value. Unspoken commercial interests ghost exchanges in a council chamber. While plans for Shorts Gardens remain undecided, Holborn Council receives offers from those who see a business opportunity. Timber merchant

Reuben Glicksten tries to gazump the Society for Improving the Condition of the Labouring Classes. Born in Russia, based in Stratford, and living in Park Lane, Glicksten's offer exemplifies the possibilities of the postwar construction boom.[67]

There are more concerted efforts to determine the course of development. It is not immediately obvious, but perhaps the market matters most. George Parker dreams of an office district to rival the city, while others strive to absorb Seven Dials into Covent Garden's hinterland. The demand for space to store and sell fruit, vegetables, and flowers seems insatiable. Warehouses and wholesalers have already reached 'north of Long Acre into some very poor class property', observes merchant George Monro – 'enhancing the value of that property', he claims. Shorts Gardens and Neal Street already contain the famous barrow maker, Ellen Keeley, and market firms like Peter Martino's fruiterers. Monro's company has a warehouse in Langley Street. Like many counterparts, he identifies the area 'bounded by St Martin's Lane, Long Acre, Shaftesbury Avenue, and Endell Street' as an opportunity to relieve pressure on Covent Garden and ensure the market's future.[68] Of course, the sale of Shorts Gardens draws interest. Architect H. Spencer Stowell submits plans for a building of steel and concrete that contains a printworks, warehouses, and garage. Development will 'improve this portion of London', he observes. 'A large sum would be paid for the land and so benefit the ratepayers of Holborn … The basement storage is very badly needed by Covent Garden, which must inevitably expand.'[69]

This is a well-organised lobby, and George Monro is a powerful figure – chair of the Propaganda Committee of the National Federation of Fruit and Potato Trades Associations and President of the Commercial Motor Users Association.

As councillors deliberate, neighbouring businesses petition against building working-class dwellings as a misuse of much-needed space. This will depreciate property values, they observe pointedly, while commercial development will increase value and rateable income. Such arguments complement the council's financial ambitions, but the market lobby diverges in how it assesses the Dials's condition. Unable, and unwilling, to recognise the problems caused by the proliferation of commercial vehicles servicing the markets, Monro insists there is 'ample room for further expansion without interference with public traffic'. Drivers, politicians, and beleaguered residents might disagree.[70]

Construction of St Giles Buildings goes ahead, but for decades the power of this lobby and Covent Garden's sprawl drive Seven Dials' decline. Warehouses displace tenements; businesses press for a place of home to be remade for trade. If the market needs space, it is equally voracious for flexible labour. There are good reasons so many porters and sellers of flowers or fruit live in the Dials. Profiting from the irregular rhythms of unloading and loading produce means companies rely on being able to summon labour throughout the day and night. Casualisation and unpredictable and hourly pay means market workers need cheap local accommodation. In 1924, challenging the brutal effects of precarity, 4000 porters affiliated with Ernest Bevin's Transport and General Workers Union go on strike for a guaranteed weekly wage, overtime, and eight-hour day. Newspapers relish the 'amateur' spectacle of well-dressed managers and clerks unloading fruit and vegetables, but the dispute is bitter. While Reverend Wilfred Davies tries to placate strikers, George Monro leads the hardline Employers' Federation rejecting their demands. Colourful clichés of porters dextrously balancing baskets – beloved of guidebooks and filmmakers – belie Covent Garden's exploitative working conditions and uncompromising capitalism.[71]

At least some politicians recognise aspects of these problems. James Claydon is a local butcher, Municipal Reform councillor, and prominent member of Holborn's Housing Committee. A few months after the strike collapses, he vents his exasperation at proposals to replace people with offices or warehouses and rehouse residents in outer London. Idyllic visions of new cottage housing are a pipedream: such houses are neither healthy nor desirable, Claydon surmises, and prohibitively expensive when you add the costs of travel and food and the effects on leisure and family. 'The people who make these propositions forget that there are thousands of workers who by force of circumstances must … live in London'. When Claydon rails against the ignorance of those attending 'a mayor's banquet [or] Masonic Ladies night' he has fellow councillors in mind. As well as those labouring in London's nocturnal economy, 'we have our markets that require workers most of the twenty-four hours'.[72]

Growing concern about Seven Dials' decline cannot be separated from Covent Garden's expansion. The fate of grand plans and modest housing schemes are entangled with controversies around the market's future. While these issues recur until New Covent Garden opens south of the Thames in 1974, local politicians remain strangely oblivious to the market's effects on its environs. In March 1926, a heated council meeting discusses and 'strenuously oppose[s]' a short-lived proposal to move the market to the site of the Foundling Hospital, built in the 1740s by philanthropist Thomas Coram. Bloomsbury's historical precincts must be preserved, councillors argue. 'It would undoubtedly be a drawback to have a large market in or on the borders of their borough', observes then Mayor Warren Coleman: 'it would be detrimental to the residential and quieter parts'. Well-meaning, perhaps – but Coleman's position ignores the market's long-standing and increasingly damaging presence across Holborn's southern border. Seven Dials is too down at heel – its people too poor and cosmopolitan – to be visible as anything other than a social problem or commercial opportunity.[73]

* * *

When Princess Louise opens St Giles Buildings on that autumn day in 1925, it is already clear that Seven Dials will not follow the boulevards of Haussmann's Paris, nor even become a shadow of London's Kingsway. Its problems have not gone away. Rather than enacting grandiose visions of the future, authorities now struggle to manage what seems like inevitable decline. There are fitful attempts to ease the movement of traffic: one-way streets, new streetlights, asphalt instead of the old wooden blocks – quick fixes that can never succeed. Holborn Council proposes widening Shorts Gardens, Little Earl Street, and Little and Great St Andrew Streets; the LCC consider using compulsory purchase orders to turn Monmouth Street into a broad east–west thoroughfare. Such anaemic schemes are shelved when the Second World War begins.[74]

Councillors soon abandon any plans for new housing: heady postwar ambitions amount to nothing more than rebuilding a handful of tenements, including a block on Betterton Street, between Endell Street and Drury Lane. Building anew is exceptional. Instead, the annual reports of successive medical officers of health document their desperate efforts to improve 'dilapidated and insanitary premises'.[75] Officials visit hundreds of houses each year. Where conditions are 'found wanting' – as happens with between forty and sixty per cent of buildings — they insist on repairs, try to make landlords act. Efforts intensify in the late 1930s. Annual inspections fall from a peak of 1000 in 1926 to around 700, but officials are more vigorous in imposing closing or demolition orders on tenements identified as unfit for habitation. Drastic action is unusual: the landlord lobby remains strong and closing orders peak at 41 in 1938. This is still a step change in attempts to tackle the area's problems.[76]

Old buildings deteriorate, but the shift reflects how the LCC becomes increasingly assertive in using powers acquired under the Housing Act (1935) to ameliorate 'slums' across London. In 1937, the council allocates fifty flats in the new Ossulston Estate in Somers Town to rehouse residents displaced from Holborn.[77] A year later, the Public Health Department moves into Seven Dials to 'strike this "black spot" off our list'. As they walk the streets and courts – knocking on doors, climbing stairs, peering into rooms – Dr Andrew Raffle and colleagues begin to delineate the boundaries of a slum clearance area.[78] In the spring of 1938, Raffle summarises their painstaking survey:

> The area around Seven Dials contains many buildings which are congested. Most of the property is very old & the fabrics are worn out. The buildings are usually three or four storeys with shops on the ground floor. Rooms are let out on the top floors. Passages & stairs are dark, & there is an absence of adequate sanitary conveniences.

If the whole neighbourhood demands remedy, some areas cause particular concern. Raffle singles out the environs of St Giles Buildings – two blocks in Shorts Gardens and Neal Street, Nottingham Court, and King's Head Yard. Houses in the yard have already been demolished and adjacent buildings facing the road deemed unfit for occupation. Further intervention is desperately needed, though.[79]

It is not long before progressive zeal is bogged down by jurisdictional conflicts and competing political and commercial interests. In March 1939, Raffle's exasperation with his borough counterpart boils over in an acidic internal memo: Dr J. A. Struthers has 'on more than one occasion been informed of all these points, and the desirability of dealing with all the unfit houses in the neighbourhood'. Incredulous that Holborn will not assume the costs of redevelopment, Raffle is further frustrated by the difficulty of gaining support from business owners and residents. A proposal to extend a clearance area on the corner of Monmouth and Shelton Streets is 'limited by a few other houses, flats and substantial industrial premises on all sides'.[80] Sometimes these conflicts play out within buildings. Raffle glosses his 'category map', which assesses properties for clearance or demolition: 'the importance of the business on the ground floor has been weighed against the conditions of the living accommodation'. The needs of capital can still outweigh those of people living in Seven Dials.[81]

As Raffle soon realises, the politics of improvement is remarkably unchanged from the acrimony of the early 1920s. 'The site of the area is very small', submits his concluding report, 'but situated in a central district rapidly become commercialised to the exclusion of residential property'. His handwritten first draft is worded slightly differently: Seven Dials is 'situated *importantly* in a central district where commercialisation is rapidly expanding at the expense of the residential user'. Proximity to the West End still fuels the fantasies of politicians and planners, and entices developers, theatrical entrepreneurs, and Covent Garden merchants. The slip between residential property and residential users is more revealing than Raffle intends. Making London modern – what he calls 'commercialisation', others 'improvement' – has profound human costs. Perhaps it is inevitable that the report's final edit writes the people out of Seven Dials.[82]

* * *

An unfamiliar figure hurries along Shorts Gardens. G. E. Bartlett is in a rush – desperate to complete his allotted surveys for Sir Hubert Llewellyn Smith's monumental *New Survey of London Life and Labour*. At the entrance to St Giles Buildings, he glances at the plaque marking its opening five years earlier. There are three households on his list here – three cards on which to record occupations, ages, incomes, outgoings, and accommodation. Most people respond, though the barrage of questions must feel as intrusive as the unannounced presence of a well-dressed stranger in their home. Any reassuring illusion of objectivity Bartlett presents in person is tempered by scribbled comments that betray his prejudices. Mrs Keogh lives with her adult son – a Covent Garden porter – at number 13: 'Seem very comfortably built flats, in the very heart of a group of factories', he writes. The elderly Mrs Thompson lives alone on her pension at number 28: 'Police look very well after the widows of deceased comrades', he observes.[83]

Bartlett is as hasty to judge as he is to get through his work. New model dwellings bespeak working-class respectability, but he has already surmised that they are out of place in a street of factories, warehouses, and tenements. From St Giles Buildings, he crosses the street to 33 Shorts Gardens. Perhaps he hesitates before pushing at the door: the place has been a rooming house for years, but its best days are gone. Nine people lived there in 1921, including the Belgian refugees Mary and Jean van Keynbeeck, and Lee Chung and Elsie Radford – born in China and the United

States – who worked at the fashionable Romano's restaurant on the Strand. Now Bartlett records twenty-one people – eight households – living cheek by jowl. On uneven stairs and landings and in cramped rooms he confronts the realities of poverty, poor housing, precarious employment, and an ageing population. There are four elderly widows – one an 'invalid', two living alone. There are sellers of flowers and vegetables, cleaners of offices, backstage West End workers. The Harnells – a stagehand at the Coliseum, his wife, and their five children – share a single bedroom. Bartlett can hardly contain his revulsion. Escaping to the street as soon as possible, he adds a 'general remark' to his card: 'house worse than a coalhole'.[84]

Even as they push for new housing, paternalistic councillors worry that developments like St Giles Buildings will be anomalous. They are right: Bartlett might not realise, but the distance between model dwellings and old tenements dramatises the failings of 'improvement' within a single block of Shorts Gardens. A few comfortable flats are inadequate to the problems facing boroughs like Holborn. Efforts to ameliorate those problems only make things worse. Number 33 is one of the premises deemed unfit in 1938. Closing or demolition orders remove the most egregious tenements but – as this building's precipitous decline shows – reduce the available local housing. By the 1950s, 'dreary and overcrowded tenements' are more overcrowded than ever.[85]

There had been a moment when Seven Dials' future might have been written differently – when it conjured competing visions of what London might be. Here and in the hostile scrutiny of the Kittens' cafe we see the complicity of political and economic power. Conservative politicians are deeply invested in the area, and – for a time – improvement collapses any distinction between urban planning and capitalising on markets in land and commercial property. In the end, the story of the Improvement Scheme is of a future that never was – a utopian plan for a city that exists only in maps. As the realities of financial retrenchment and municipal governance turn dreams to dust, politicians cede the task of making Seven Dials modern to the forces of capital. St Giles Buildings is the sum of planned development in the period – the last new housing built in the Dials until the 1980s. From the mid-1920s at the latest, the politics of improvement is ad hoc and reactive – fixated on past legacies and present crises rather than looking forward. It is not for want of trying, but failed ambitions have lasting consequences.

In the late 1920s, when the Town Planning Act gives authorities renewed licence to dream, politicians and planners have already shifted attention north to the squares of Bloomsbury and the Foundling Hospital. Preservationist groups such as the Foundling Estate Protection Association and Society for the Protection of Ancient Buildings mobilise against the institution's 'threatened destruction'. The Holborn and St Pancras Town Plan goes nowhere but marks Seven Dials' fading from the official gaze.[86] The area is left behind by the march of 'progress'. Holborn Council tinkers at the edge of housing problems, while the LCC builds massive new estates and ribbons of semi-detached speculative development stretch along arterial roads and railway lines. Schools empty and clinics close, while Labour councils in boroughs like Bermondsey and Finsbury make ambitious provision for citizens' health and well-being. Corporate palaces rise on the Embankment and Aldwych, while plans for a rival office district are ignored.

Forgotten or deliberately ignored, the ensuing planning blight is the political context for Seven Dials' decline.

The neighbourhood becomes a place of failed visions, shabby compromises, mismanaged decline – its stagnation evidence of the failings of postwar planning. In 1938, the *Architects' Journal* lampoons 'an overwhelming vision of slums waiting to be cleared, bridges waiting to be built, a green belt waiting completion, [and] "fly-over" crossings in Stockholm but not in London'. Flights of fancy contrast with the mundanities of urban life: remnants of an older city, unplanned and decaying, where movement and modernity grind to a halt. The 'congested corners [and] bottle-neck streets' of 'Covent Garden [and] Seven Dials' are 'crying out for sound and drastic planning'.[87] The same year, the journalist Ivor Brown surveys 'acres and acres of central territory which ought to be valuable, ought to be worthily and handsomely developed' – ought to be 'smash[ed] and scour[ed] away'. It is 'curious and calamitous', they observe, that the 'historic squares of Mayfair are razed' while 'nothing happens to the shabby little streets, the mouldering houses and courts, and the broken shells of ancient stores and warehouses'. Its problems more intractable than ever, Seven Dials remains an abject other, haunting other grand plans and grander places.[88]

4

Libel, law, and politics

Long Acre and the Strand

It takes them less than twenty minutes to walk to the High Court of Justice, but Jim and Emily Kitten might as well have entered another world. On the Strand they pass upmarket restaurants and shops, glittering theatres, and grand hotels like the Savoy, where Jim worked in the kitchens a few years earlier. On the Strand they move through the symbolic heart of empire. As they walk, the couple might glance into a colonial outfitter's or gaze at the High Commissions of the white settler dominions of Australia, New Zealand, and South Africa. It has been a tense journey: a very different version of imperial culture is about to play out in court. The owners of a small Seven Dials cafe – a Sierra Leonean man and his London-born wife – have sued a national newspaper for libel.

Since it opened, the cafe has drawn unwanted attention. Police make it part of their beats through Seven Dials, particularly after dark. Officers stop or arrest customers in the surrounding streets, usually for minor public order offences. They visit the cafe and warn its owners. They raid the premises and initiate formal proceedings. At different times, Jim Kitten appears before the Bow Street magistrate for permitting unlicensed gambling, prostitution, and disorderly conduct. Intense scrutiny of a Black business reflects virulent concerns about racial difference within parts of British public life. Salacious reports on the courtroom appearances of Kitten and others cement the association between Black culture and crime.

This attention will become unbearable. For almost three years, the cafe is subject to vicious attacks by the weekly newspaper *John Bull* – its owners swept up in a campaign against unchecked migration and Britain's 'Black colonies'. *John Bull* poses as a selfless defender of British culture, but neither the newspaper nor its publishers, Odhams Press, are disinterested observers. Publisher and cafe occupy the same urban milieu. On the corner of Long Acre and Mercer Street, Odhams' editorial offices turn their back on Seven Dials, but their printworks, warehouses, and studios straggle north into its heart. Journalists and photographers reporting on the cafe might have regularly passed down Great White Lion Street. They could have walked there in five minutes. There are hints they have talked to well-connected residents. It is not just scandal which floods in and out of Seven Dials. It is subeditors, compositors, stenographers; paper, ink, machinery: modern journalism's essential labour and materials.

John Bull's attack culminates in an article published in April 1926: 'A Terrible Negro Haunt' rails against the 'coloured rascals who infest ... that insalubrious neighbourhood ... around the Seven Dials'. Jim Kitten is caricatured as a dangerous predator – an 'unsavoury looking person' with 'no respect whatever for law and order'. Regardless of citizenship or birthplace, he is presented as an outsider who does not belong. As the West End presses into Seven Dials, hostile policing and muckraking journalism press in on the cafe. This is when the Kittens decide to take a stand.

Suing a newspaper for libel is unusual and brave – foolhardy, some might say. It draws the couple into a controversy over the interplay between culture and politics. *John Bull*'s calculated attack encapsulates the excesses of sensational journalism and growing fears about the relationship between an unchecked press and the citizens of a new mass democracy. The paper often pushes the limits of acceptability, chasing publicity by daring victims to seek redress. Libel law is the frontline in negotiating the interaction between press and public.

Suing *John Bull* is political in more fundamental ways. For the Kittens, legal action is about defending their reputation and livelihood. It is also about defending a vibrant Black business against overbearing pressures. English law is a vehicle for anti-racist politics. Over three days in February 1927, tensions that simmer on the streets of Seven Dials boil over in the imposing surrounds of the High Court of Justice, raising explosive questions about race and racism across the British world. Jim and Emily put their faith in British justice, seeking damages of £1000 and an injunction. Claiming rights that are their due as citizens of empire, they trust that the law is above differences of colour and class. Against a newspaper's vitriol, they offer meticulous evidence of the damage to their business, hard work, and respectability. It quickly becomes clear that what their barrister calls a 'general attack on men of colour' defines both *John Bull*'s malicious reporting and the 'colour bar' deforming everyday life in 1920s and 1930s London.

* * *

IN THE HIGH COURT OF JUSTICE 1926 K/No.309.

KING'S BENCH DIVISION

Writ issued the 19th day of April 1926.

BETWEEN JAMES KITTEN Plaintiff.

- and -

ODHAMS PRESS LTD. and

E.R.THOMPSON. Defendants.

STATEMENT OF CLAIM.

1. The Plaintiff is a Restaurant Proprietor and keeps a small refreshment house, known as "The Café and Restaurant" at 16, Great White Lion Street, Shaftesbury Avenue, London. He is a British subject, born at Sierra Leone, Gold Coast, West Africa, and lived there for 18 years. He then came to Europe and after having been employed in various places, he became the Tenant of the above premises in 1921, and has carried on business there, since that date.

2. The first-named Defendants are the Proprietors Printers and Publishers, and the last-named Defendant is the Editor, of a newspaper known as "John Bull", and they published and printed, or caused to be published and printed, certain libellous matter concerning the Plaintiff, in the issue of the 10th day of April 1926.

Figure 4.1 'Statement of Claim, 1926

Odhams Press and *John Bull*'s successive editors are used to being in court. For a campaigning newspaper, a sensational libel trial has become a shortcut to publicity, political impact, sales, and advertising revenue. There is nothing unusual in their attack on the Kittens. For two decades the newspaper has mirrored the colourful persona of its first editor, Horatio Bottomley. Throughout his various incarnations as financial speculator, Liberal MP, patriotic demagogue, bankrupt, and fraudster, Bottomley remains the self-styled champion of the 'man in the street'. Long after his disgrace, *John Bull* is still outspoken in defending the British everyman. Noisily populist in tone, muckraking and sensationalist in style, it acts 'without fear or favour' in exposing the dangers posed by overbearing political and financial elites, a rising tide of immorality, and the insidious depravations of various 'foreigners'. Readers are becoming familiar with its crusade against Britain's 'Black colonies'.[1]

Such reporting is entwined with tightening immigration and citizenship legislation and frenzied concerns about the dangers of racial difference. 'In recent years ... London has half closed her door to the foreigner', writes F. A. Mackenzie in 1924: 'Those who are here can remain so long as they behave themselves, but they have to report their presence to the police and be registered'.[2] People like Jim Kitten are British subjects, not 'foreigners'. After the racist violence of 1919, though, the message from successive governments is clear: Blackness is a sign of 'alien' nationality, formal citizenship rights mean nothing in practice.

Sensational reporting exacerbates these tensions. Like other newspapers, *John Bull* treats areas like Seven Dials and places like the cafe as exemplifying the dangers of unchecked immigration. Starting in autumn 1923, ten separate articles identify the café, and often its owners.[3] Coverage initially reflects individual court appearances: 'Menace of the Blacks' (July 1924) and 'A Black Betrayal' (July 1925) report Jim's first appearance at Bow Street and James Rich's conviction for 'dope trafficking'. As the furore deepens, such flashpoints coalesce into a more sustained expose. Sober courtroom testimony is reworked as an explosive analysis, which holds fascination and theatrical revulsion in constant tension. In July 1925, *John Bull* calls attention to the 'activities of the coloured rascals who infest the "Black Colony," that insalubrious neighbourhood ... around Bloomsbury, Charlotte Street, and the Seven Dials'. Here, they suggest, 'live hundreds of coloured brutes who do no real work. They impose upon women, blackmail men, lure people to gambling dens or nightclubs or peddle dope'.[4] These are the pejorative stereotypes of Britain's 'Black colonies' – places of crime, violence, drugs, sexual corruption, moral contagion, and disease. For muckraking journalists, places like the cafe are 'meeting places of the dissolute and degenerate Blacks, [which] should be carefully and persistently watched'.[5]

By April 1926, when *John Bull*'s final article revisits familiar places, people, and themes, the tone of reporting has shifted decisively. Where reporters took their cue from the court appearances of men like Rich, having 'lately made enquiries in regard to the tremendous number of black men now in England' they now begin a more ambitious journalistic investigation.[6] Where earlier reports acknowledged the 'difficulty deporting some of these troublesome scoundrels because they are British subjects', they now fix boundaries between race, nation, and legal status.[7] Regardless of birthplace and citizenship, the inhabitants of Britain's 'Black colonies' are 'unwanted aliens'. The hardening of an impermeable colour bar turns men like Kitten into outsiders who do not belong.[8]

For *John Bull*, then, the cafe itself is an unwelcome intrusion. Rather than a respectable business, it 'answers the description of a restaurant'. Rather than a community hub, it is a 'lair' – its owner an animal. A 'rendezvous for coloured criminals of every description', it welcomes the 'most contagious sweepings of the underworld'. Rather than a hard-working businessman, Jim Kitten is seen as 'a disreputable caterer for the coloured rascals who make his cafe day after day a meeting-place for hatching roguery and crime'. 'Aliens of all nationalities are flooding this country', thunders *John Bull*: to stop this growing 'evil' the Home Office must 'check the ever-flowing stream!'[9] In the following century, such inflammatory language will become all too familiar.

The article is melodramatic, but it follows a recognisable playbook – stock in trade for a newspaper notorious for seeking controversy. Journalists and sub-editors are well practised in such overblown personal attacks. 'The average newspaper does not court legal trouble', claims Charles Pilley, *John Bull*'s erstwhile editor: 'it is too costly in time and money, and the publicity of a libel action is a doubtful advertisement'.[10] The frequency of *John Bull*'s court appearances and choreographed coverage suggests otherwise. Lawyers and editors recognise that linking someone to crime and vice and targeting their 'profession or trade' is 'always highly dangerous' – risking 'ruin' or 'marching orders for the editor'.[11] Damages can be considered aggravated if editors use headlines, larger fonts, or posters and placards to dramatise libellous stories.[12] In spring 1926, *John Bull* does all these things: meticulously trying everything possible to provoke its victims into action.

* * *

'A person has a right to the enjoyment of his reputation and of the moral and material advantages to which it may entitle him in his relationships with other people', notes the lawyer W. Valentine Ball.[13] It is this – founding principle of the laws of libel – that allows Jim and Emily Kitten to stand up to *John Bull*. Newspaper editors fret about the law's chilling effects, attributing modern journalism's troubling 'timidity' to fear of being sued. It is more common to consider legal action a vital defence for ordinary citizens facing the harmful intrusions of the press.[14] It is impossible to know what conversations pass between the Kittens and their confidantes over the spring and early summer of 1926. On 8 July, though, the solicitor William Drake duly submits their claim against Odhams Press and *John Bull*'s editor, Edward Roffe Thompson.

It is a brief, dry, and formulaic legal document. Written between the lines, though, is a poignant and desperately moving account of the injurious experience of racial prejudice and a newspaper's wrath. *John Bull*'s attack means Jim Kitten has 'suffered great pain and mental worry ... been injured ... in his character, credit, and reputation, and ... brought ... into odium and contempt'.[15] Reproduced in full, the article of April 1926 maligns him as 'an immoral and degraded scoundrel', whose cafe is 'a rendezvous for rogues and rascals' and 'centre for the association of low class Africans and white women'.[16] Such reporting destroys the Kittens' good name, but its material effects are equally devastating. After April the Kittens' monthly takings collapse from between £30 and £40 to around £20. Little wonder they claim damages of £1000 and an injunction silencing their aggressors.[17]

Most libel suits do not reach court. The process is long and tortuous, cases are ruled ineligible or settled hurriedly by defendants. The Kittens face another problem: their solicitor is suspended then struck off for making false allegations against another solicitor.[18] Even if things run smoothly, the financial costs and risks of action mean handbooks counsel caution: it is safer and more effective, they suggest, to seek informal redress or an apology.[19] For the Kittens, moreover, trusting in British justice requires a further leap of faith. Their everyday experiences of the legal system are encapsulated in being summoned before the Bow Street magistrate, hostile policing, and the penalties of race and class. Bow Street – small, shabby, local – is at least somehow familiar. A libel suit and short walk to the High Court of Justice takes them into radically new terrain. Here their business will be dissected, their lives together exposed to the public gaze as never before. This is why solicitor Edward Wooll stresses the need to weigh the benefits of redress against the dangers of further publicity and reputational damage. Over the coming weeks, the 'anxiety and terrible expense of litigation' will become apparent.[20] That the Kittens *do* set out to the Strand, underscores the extent of their anger, their desperation, and – perhaps – their sense of the importance of taking a stand.

Opening on a Tuesday afternoon, the trial runs over three days in the first week of February 1927. London is unusually cold that week: an anti-cyclone sits over the North Sea, the temperature barely gets above freezing, the city shivers under a sharp east wind. As the Kittens leave Seven Dials and hurry down to the Strand they are bundled up against the chill.[21] Entering the Great Hall to meet their barristers, they see stone figures of Solomon and King Alfred – embodying the justice and wisdom of the law whose protection they now seek. Little can have prepared the Kittens for this experience, though. As they enter the panelled courtroom, their confidence is shaken.

Like Jim Kitten, Ernest Marke was born in Sierra Leone. When Marke enters the dock at Liverpool Assizes on trumped up charges of murder around this time, he is overwhelmed: the 'awesome' spectacle 'frighten[s] the life out of me'. 'The whole scene' was 'what I had imagined the real judgement day would be', Marke recalls. He looks around: 'There wasn't a black face in sight. Dejectedly I wondered what chance I had against all these people when even my accusers were white.' This is the intimidating sight confronting Jim and Emily that morning. As they take their seats in court, and Lord Chief Justice Avory begins to speak, it is not just the cold making them shiver.[22]

As the preliminaries end, the Kittens' barrister is first to rise. Now in his 60s, Edward Holton Coumbe is an unlikely champion: a lawyer and politician, LCC councillor and sometime mayor of Stoke Newington. In 1919, troubled by the putative links between Eastern European Jews and Bolshevism, Coumbe tries to commit the LCC to not employing 'aliens' – even if naturalised.[23] Coumbe's politics are disquieting, but his case against Odhams Press is formidable. *John Bull*'s reporting exemplifies a dangerous racial politics, he argues. Jim 'was a man of colour, but he was a British subject, and the defendants in their campaign against the immigration of undesirable aliens had exceeded the limits of fair comment'.[24] Journalistic polemic creates an unjustifiable caricature. 'Black people visited the restaurant, as did lascars,' Coumbe observes, 'but because of that there was no justification for this attack.' This is a site of community, not a den of iniquity.[25]

While *John Bull* presents men like Jim as dangerous outsiders, Coumbe and the Kittens insist on their rights of belonging and citizenship: while the article is 'a general attack on men of colour and aliens ... Kitten, as a matter of fact, was a British subject'. Britishness matters: Jim has the right to live and work in London, and the licences necessary to run a refreshment house. Citizenship is also a cultural ideal. That is why Coumbe emphasises the hard work, thrift, and domestic respectability through which the Kittens' built their business – saving money from low-paid catering jobs before 'launching out on [their] own account'.[26] The wound incurred escaping from Ruhleben means Kitten's body carries powerful ideas of heroic national service. Coumbe carefully places the Kittens at the centre of ideas of Britishness.[27]

What Coumbe calls a 'general attack on men of colour' exemplifies the 'colour bar' that solidifies after the Great War. Challenging *John Bull*, he ventriloquises how Black and Asian Britons contest racial prejudice and claim citizenship rights more widely.[28] His address echoes the critique of the Coloured Alien Seamen Order (CASO) set out by West Indian and West African seamen in Barry in a letter to the Colonial Office: 'We have never regarded ourselves as *aliens* to Britain in peace or in war ... So long as the Union Jack flies ... so long will we regard the word alien as totally unsuitable.'[29] Delivered in court rather than in writing, we see how the libel trial underscores the stakes of postwar racial politics. These stakes are dramatised by the prosecution of those we might now call community leaders – boarding house keepers and cafe proprietors. In a nearby magistrate's court, two years earlier, 'several coloured men watched the proceedings with interest' as Herbert Muskett sentenced cafe owner Uriah Erskine. When Muskett 'intimated that he would not let the colour question influence him at all' he tacitly acknowledged the resonance of such cases.[30]

The Kittens also reject *John Bull*'s damning depiction of their cafe. Guided by Coumbe, they talk quietly and proudly of the care with which they manage their business and their cosmopolitan clientele. Coumbe calls witnesses who testify to the cafe's good character. Local solidarities of class and neighbourhood run across racial and ethnic lines. Marcel Vautro was born in Holborn, just off Shaftesbury Avenue, though his parents are originally from Lyon. He and his family are the cafe's closest neighbours, sharing a furnished room upstairs. Like the Kittens, they occupy the precarious margins of London's service industries. Vautro is a wine waiter working in the West End. The Kittens are good neighbours: sometimes Vautro hears 'squabbles between customers', but he is certain that the 'establishment was well conducted'.[31]

The most compelling voice in court is that of the musician Frank Obadiah Kennedy. Born in Sierra Leone, Kennedy has been in Britain for twenty-two years. He has made his life there: marrying a white woman, living in rooms in New Compton Street, socialising in the cafes of Seven Dials and Tottenham Court Road. Prior to the war, he toured provincial theatres as a comedian and dancer before finding new opportunities in the jazz craze of the 1910s and 1920s. Like other West Indian and West African musicians, Kennedy joined the renowned Southern Syncopated Orchestra. As a tympanist, he performed in theatres, dance halls, and hotels alongside celebrated figures like American saxophonist and clarinettist Sidney Bechet, vocalist Evelyn Dove, Sierra Leonean pianist Frank Lacton, and Trinidadian trumpet player Cyril Blake. In October 1921, Kennedy was on board the SS *Rowan* when it collided with two other ships and sank in the Irish Sea en route to Dublin. Nine of his fellow band members tragically died; many others, him included, were left badly injured and destitute.[32]

By 1927, Kennedy has known the Kittens for eight or nine years: they are friends, the cafe a regular haunt for him and his wife. 'There had never been any brawls or fights' in that time, he observes.[33] Testifying in court allows him to dismiss salacious newspaper reports and talk movingly of the cafe's everyday importance as a 'meeting place of Black musicians'.[34] Evidence hints at Kennedy's increasingly assertive politics: in 1911, he writes his nationality into a census form as 'Fantee'.[35] Now he patiently explains to his overwhelmingly white audience how there is a 'whole lot of persecution of Black men' in London. Neighbourhoods like Seven Dials and places like the cafe are havens – the 'only place they could go to, as they would not be tolerated in a cafe used by white people'.[36] Little wonder Kennedy values the 'only place he could go without being insulted and sneered at'.[37] Kennedy's first-hand account of how 'persecution' plays out through everyday insults, exclusionary door policies, and official harassment demonstrates how knowledge of the colour bar is both painful and hard-won. Jim and Emily Kitten's place 'was the same as other cafes', Kennedy surmises: 'the only difference was that the police came in and ordered everybody out'.[38]

* * *

Coumbe presents the Kittens' case, but it is the young barrister beside him who gives proceedings wider resonance – though newspapers rarely mention him, and it is unclear if he even speaks in court.[39] Ladipo Solanke's involvement is unlikely, in many ways. Born in Nigeria, educated at Fourah Bay College in Sierra Leone, Solanke has been in Britain since 1922, studying law at University College London. In the mid-1920s, as tensions deepen in Seven Dials, Solanke is beginning his remarkable career as an anti-racist and anti-colonial activist. In May 1926, just a week after *John Bull*'s final published attack on the Kittens, the newspaper *West Africa* reports his call to the bar.[40]

Solanke enters public life during the British Empire Exhibition. Writing to the Colonial Office and West African and British newspapers, he wages a high-profile campaign against the racist spectacle of Wembley's 'West African village'. This ignorant caricature of regional 'backwardness', he argues, fosters damaging ideas of racial inferiority, and does 'serious harm to those of us from Nigeria who are now in London for education purposes'.[41] Around the same time, Solanke becomes a founder member of the West African Students' Union (August 1925) and its publication *Wasu* (1926). Like similar organisations, including the African Progress Union, WASU is a focal point for political activism, challenging the inequities of colonialism and the 'colour bar'.[42] Solanke is the first person to broadcast on radio and record music in Yoruba. In the three months around the trial, he gives twenty talks across Britain. The result is an alternative account of West African history and culture – a powerful 'shadow exhibition' challenging ideas of racial 'inferiority'.[43]

As a prominent member of London's Black elite, Solanke has ostensibly little in common with the rough and ready world of Seven Dials. His diary records unease at the excesses of metropolitan nightlife and working-class sociability. Dismissing those 'practising polyandry among the white girls', Solanke deems a 'high moral life' essential for West Africans in Britain.[44] Reverend Canon A. B. Akinyele, President of the Ibadan Reading Circle, will later praise his 'dignity' and 'simple mode of living, though he has lived over ten years in the centre of English life'.[45] If it is unclear how Solanke becomes involved with the Kittens' case, his presence alone suggests the porous boundaries between social worlds and ties the cafe to the postwar politics of race and empire.

After the trial, Solanke sets out his political vision in *United West Africa* (1927). 'Until Africans at home and abroad ... organise and develop the spirit of the principles of self-help, unity, and co-operation among themselves, and fight it out to remove this colour prejudice,' he argues, 'they will remain hewers of wood and drawers of water for the other races of mankind' – and, he might add, providers of food and entertainment.[46] Self-help, unity, and cooperation: these principles are internationalist in scope, emphasising the need for a common effort to 'improve' society, economy, and polity across Nigeria, Sierra Leone, and the Gold Coast. Although Solanke emphasises the role of educated people in 'taking the initiative in all things', they underscore the importance of cooperating across class lines.[47]

Standing with the Kittens exemplifies Solanke's developing politics. The challenges he identifies are pressing. The Empire Exhibition and *John Bull*'s vitriol distil growing concern about the effects of racial prejudice. New constitutions for Sierra Leone, Nigeria, and the Gold Coast expose colonialism's cruelties.[48] *United West Africa* ends with a clarion call:

> The time has now come when West African nationality must find a permanent foothold in Great Britain. West African individuality must be asserted in this country, West African honour, respect, and glory must be pressed and pushed forward and until it has reached its goal of ambition it may not stop. Progress! I repeat, Progress![49]

Hesitantly – awkwardly – the trial turns an expansive critique of race and empire into a focused defence of a Black business. Solanke tacitly recognises the interests shared by the Kittens' customers and WASU's members. Seeking familiar food and faces, many students might have visited places like the cafe; the rich bonds evoked by Frank Kennedy informed WASU's efforts to open a hostel. Challenging prejudice through libel law is one way to gain 'honour' and 'respect'. Here is another opportunity to establish a 'permanent foothold' in London and further the cause of 'progress'.[50]

Calling attention to a newspaper's racism and the inequities of the colour bar is both an inconvenient truth and a striking political intervention. It is more striking still that Solanke's presence and Coumbe's comments are hardly reported. With few exceptions, newspapers covering the case pass no comment on its political implications. We learn more about what Coumbe says from accounts of how *John Bull*'s barrister responds. The preoccupations of journalists, conventions of court reporting, and lack of trial transcripts almost write a radical racial politics out of the historical record.

* * *

This is not the first time Norman Birkett stands to defend *John Bull* against libel charges, nor will it be the last: the leading barrister of the day is employed on a retainer by Odhams Press. Maintaining a confrontational editorial policy means being well-prepared for such moments. After a decade at the bar, three years as King's Counsel, Birkett is renowned as 'one of the foremost advocates of his time'. Libel is a lucrative part of his burgeoning practice: in 1926 he earns £16,500 in fees, more than double that in 1929.[51]

For an accomplished orator, his task is straightforward: justify *John Bull*'s reporting, establish a platform for their crusade.

Here is the case Birkett sets out: yes, *John Bull*'s articles are 'strongly written and strongly meant' – they are also true. The cafe is a 'plague spot rank with iniquity'.[52] He promises evidence from police and 'residents in the neighbourhood' of the 'disgusting language, the brawls, and the consorting of black men and white women, both inside and outside the cafe'. Yet the cafe's proprietors do nothing, he continues. Their attitude is: '"Let the scum of the earth come in, as long as they are not scum in my cafe," and it follow[s] that any criminal could enter and remain there.'[53] The trial's dynamics turn in an instant. 'In so many cases', observes R. D. Blumenfeld, editor of the *Daily Express*, 'the plaintiff discovers that before so many minutes have gone, the plaintiff has become a defendant'. From now on, Jim and Emily Kitten will feel like they are on trial.[54]

Birkett leads with his prize witness. On Wednesday morning, Bracewell Smith also braves the cold and makes the short journey to the Strand. Smith's appearance is a coup for Odhams Press: every newspaper emphasises his wealth, his ownership of the Shaftesbury and Park Lane hotels, his membership of the LCC and Holborn Council. It also underscores the intimate conflicts that shadow the trial. Grand plans for 'improving' Seven Dials made the Shaftesbury an attractive proposition, but the Kittens are an awkward problem. Visible and audible, the cafe and its customers threaten Smith's investment and ambitions.

Smith is a commanding presence in court. Guided by Birkett, he describes how he has 'kept observation on the … cafe because of complaints [about] the behaviour of the persons frequenting it'. Hotel guests have 'complained of being molested in the streets by groups of Black men'. For several evenings, Smith has watched the cafe: it is 'an eyesore and a disgrace', he insists, his phrasing suggesting how a down-at-heel backstreet must be 'cleaned up'.[55] Testifying in court intensifies the public pressure on the Kittens, but Smith has worked hard behind the scenes to mobilise action: power brings access to local and central government and an audience in newspaper offices. Smith is probably the driving force behind the petition submitted to the Metropolitan Police by local tradespeople, shopkeepers, and landlords. Waiting, watching, writing – Smith's stories of Seven Dials are animated by vested interests and corporate capital. Far from altruistic, his appearance shows how local unease around racial difference might be manipulated.[56]

The trial still exposes the fault-lines and limits of Seven Dials' everyday cosmopolitanism. It doesn't quite work, but Birkett pits the neighbourhood's 'respectable' residents against more disreputable recent arrivals. Those he calls to testify against the Kittens underscore the social and racial codes implicit in ideas of respectability: the dairyman Edward Llewellyn Edwards and grocer Frank Orpin live and work around the corner on Little Earl Street; Charles Mortimer is landlord of the Crown on Great St Andrew Street; Charles Thackeray's boot-making workshop is two doors along Great White Lion Street. For sure, these are residents of long standing, but the absence of any of the Kittens' Italian, Jewish, or French neighbours – often residents of equally long standing – is striking. So is the preponderance of small traders and shopkeepers – those with a financial stake in the neighbourhood – rather than ordinary people.

Thackeray describes 'brawls', 'language ... too filthy to mention', a drunken girl left 'helpless' on the pavement.[57] Mortimer 'refused to serve Black men ... owing to the trouble at the cafe'.[58] John Donkin, superintendent of Shaftesbury Homes technical school, presents the cafe as a threat to the impressionable teenage boys under his charge: 'There were so many brawls that the expression "there is another row at the cafe" had become quite an old saying'.[59] He finishes with a cliché: 'since the cafe opened ... Great White Lion Street was worse than any of the streets in the slum district of the docks'. Smouldering neighbourhood conflicts catch fire in court.[60]

Birkett's alchemy, finally, requires the authority of first-hand knowledge. He concludes by inviting officers from Bow Street police station to share their experiences. Despite his years of service, DS Goddard tells the court, he has 'never seen any place so bad'.[61] Warming to the theme, he tells tales of 'white girls sitting on the knees of black men', 'white girls [who] had called at the cafe and given money to black men', fantastical stereotypes of sexual corruption.[62] It will not be long before Goddard is himself in the dock: arrested for taking bribes from Kate Meyrick, owner of the famous 43 Club, he is caught up in the biggest police corruption scandal of the period. That revelation – if not Goddard's proclivity for kickbacks – is still in the future, and his claims about the cafe go unquestioned. Goddard is echoed by DS Pearce, who describes Kitten's customers as 'Black men of the West End of London and drug traffickers and bullies'. He reels off a list including the counterfeiter William Porter and cocaine dealer Mohamed Ali. Rather than being somewhere to meet and eat, officers imply, the cafe is a criminal rendezvous.[63]

Birkett has readied the ground for this argument. Cross-examining the Kittens, he works to show they knew their customers – including their crimes – and tolerated their disorderly behaviour. Addressing Jim, he asks: do you know

'Gladys Chow, the wife of a Chinaman, but living apart from her husband'? Do you know Randolph Jones, convicted for living on Chow's 'immoral earnings?' What about John Moore, who kicked a policeman in the groin when arrested in the cafe?[64] Kitten acknowledges some of this, but rejects Birkett's maligning of his establishment's character.[65] There is a difference between someone's character and their conduct, Kitten insists: a man might have sold opium in the past, but he 'saw no reason ... why [he] should not frequent his restaurant provided he behaved himself. He would be served if he went to other well-known cafes.'[66] Pressed again, he reiterates the limits to his responsibilities: 'My premises are open to give refreshment to people who behave themselves. I am not supposed to know what a man did in 1925 or any other year'. Kitten is right: licensing legislation enshrines the separation of conduct and character.[67]

Emily Kitten is an equally formidable presence, though Birkett tries to present her as a frail ingenue. You 'had the task of controlling these black men many times', suggests the barrister: you were 'assaulted ... trying pluckily to stop a fight'. Recognising where this is going, Emily rejects the insinuation immediately: she and her husband worked hard together to 'keep the restaurant respectable'.[68] It is Emily who produces the cafe's account books, showing how their takings fell after *John Bull*'s attack.[69] Appearing side by side, the Kittens refute Birkett's characterisation of interracial relationships as mercenary or immoral – they have built a life together for almost ten years – and also distance themselves from the coercive behaviour of men like Randolph Jones. 'Coloured men who had white wives used the restaurant', Jim explains: 'He himself had married "an English lady" ... and had always lived happily with her.'[70] Since their marriage, Emily tells the court, she 'had lived with

Kitten ... and he had treated her very well'.[71] The women they serve are not of 'ill repute'. Where Birkett sees prostitution, Jim Kitten counters 'it may be a white wife calling for her Black husband'.[72] Against the damning prejudices of outsiders, the Kittens tell alternative stories of love and intimacy in cosmopolitan Seven Dials.

It is both astonishing and predictable how Birkett can mould the stories told in court: astonishing because it works; predictable because he speaks from a position of exceptional institutional power. From there, it is easy for a skilled barrister to exploit the moral panic roiling postwar Britain. Newspaper reports link the 'Black colony' to disorder, crime, and violence. For many observers, courtroom exchanges resonate most strongly when they support those connections. That is why journalists fixate on salacious accounts of scenes in the cafe. That is why subeditors are predisposed to frame the case as if the Kittens, not *John Bull*, are on trial. Newspapers are more likely to report detailed evidence against the couple than testimonials in their support. After a long summary of Smith's testimony, *The Times* notes only: 'Further evidence was given by customers at the cafe and by neighbours that the cafe was conducted properly.'[73]

* * *

Darkness falls, a trial ends, a barrister reaches new heights of theatricality. Standing to deliver his closing remarks, Norman Birkett dismisses Coumbe's efforts to make the case about the postwar colour bar.

> there had been an undisguised attempt ... to introduce into the case matters dealing with prejudice against coloured people. Whatever might be the view about the colour question in political or social spheres, the supreme consideration

> in the court was the administration of justice. Mr Coumbe had become so lyrical over the question of colour that he had thought that he was going to break into the words in *Iolanthe:* –
>
> Hearts just as pure and fair
> May beat in Belgrave Square
> As in the lowly air
> Of Seven Dials!
> (Laughter.)[74]

Removing the cafe from the 'political and social spheres' neatly displaces scrutiny from *John Bull*'s reporting. Ignore the euphemistic 'colour question', Birkett tells the jury: focus on the cafe's character.[75]

At best, this is brazen: *John Bull* made the cafe an example in its crusade around race and migration. Birkett's argument works, though: he is a clever barrister, whose silken tongue drips poison. The kindness for which he is known only reaches so far. Time and again, he mobilises connections of race and class to put the Kittens in their place. A court reporter's brackets cannot contain the laughter. Quoting Gilbert and Sullivan deflects charges of racial prejudice. It also conjures a moment of intimacy in a crowded court. The ripple of humour reflects a joke shared between counsel, judge, jury, gallery, and readers who are mostly white: playing the colour bar for laughs, it is Birkett who makes the trial about race.

There is a cruel politics to laughter, particularly when it encourages a knowing sense of privilege at the expense of others. Justice Avory has already shown his eagerness to get in on the joke, so Birkett knows he can get away with it. There is little evidence bearing out descriptions of Avory as 'a dignified and courteous judge who discouraged levity, prolixity, and irrelevance, and who preferred to limit his judicial interventions'.[76] The day before, Jim had described 'most of his customers [as] seafaring people'. Blithely – wilfully – ignorant of the wharves and docks along the Thames, Birkett retorts: 'You are a pretty long way from the sea, aren't you? ... How far from the Regent's Park Canal?' 'I don't know', says Jim, 'but they are all seamen. Some bring their wives with them.' Ignoring Jim, Avory interjects: 'You have not asked him if it is the same wife each time. (Laughter).'[77]

Avory and Birkett's complicity shapes the legal process. In a libel trial it is 'not necessary to prove the good character of the plaintiff', claim the handbooks: 'the law presumes that his character is good until the contrary is proved'. Such smug exchanges suggest how differences of race and class and a hostile judge and jury compromise that ideal. When Kitten insists on his respectability, he confronts the overwhelming weight of newspaper headlines and stereotypes of the 'Black colony'.[78] Observers even laugh when Kitten says: 'all he knew [about the reports] was that *John Bull* had placards bearing the words: "The 'Kitten' and His Mice"'. In laughter, prejudice becomes deafening.[79]

Over three days in court, it quickly becomes clear that the decision to confront *John Bull* is ill-judged. Two cafe owners, whose marriage threatens empire's racial hierarchies, cannot hope to withstand the might of Odhams Press and enmity of the legal establishment. Like other anti-colonial and anti-racist activists, Ladipo Solanke trusted in law's power to effect progressive social and political change. He also came to see justice as a measure of good governance: developing legal institutions is key to Solanke's vision of West African self-determination and 'improvement'. The 'surest test of the soundness of the progress of any nation', he argues, 'lies primarily in the standard of its courts and in the quality of justice administered'.[80] A damaging courtroom encounter shows how inequalities of race and class deform British justice.

Lacking money and connection, the Kittens rely on a disgraced solicitor and anti-alien barrister; Solanke's star is rising, but he is called to the bar only six months before the trial. Odhams Press has its own solicitor – John Monks, who shares offices with the paper's editors and journalists – and retains a leading barrister like Birkett. Inequalities run deeper than access to legal representation. Directing his final summation to the jury, Avory ventriloquises Birkett's performative mockery. We have heard of 'white women … sitting on the knees of black men', he reflects. Coumbe had suggested 'that kind of thing went on at respectable dances between white people', but Avory is astounded: 'I don't know where the learned counsel derives his experience from.' This is more than the dyspeptic rant of someone out of touch with modern life. At the end of a hearing in which race and intimacy are key issues, it is a dangerous steer. Little wonder the jury accepts Birkett's defence without much deliberation: having found against the Kittens and awarding £388 costs to Odhams Press, the foreman asks: 'could nothing be done [about the cafe] except through the good offices of a newspaper?' By then, a great deal has already been done to define the limits of cosmopolitan London.[81]

In February 1927, there are few ways in which the story of the 'Black man's cafe' can be told. In the end, it doesn't matter how much the Kittens insist on the cafe's respectability and their probity. The febrile atmosphere means they cannot distance themselves from salacious cliches of the 'Black colony'. Indelibly associated with an underworld of crime and vice, the cafe becomes a proxy for Seven Dials itself. Jim Kitten has appeared in court for breaching licensing regulations. The cafe is implicated in several high-profile legal cases. Set against the evidence of police and some neighbours, they are problematic subjects around which to rally sympathy and cooperation. Jurors and journalists either do not see, or cannot see, or do not think it matters that a mixed-race couple are seeking redress for the damage caused by a newspaper's racism.

* * *

Jim and Emily Kitten do not just lose their case. After three bruising days they are laughed out of court, humiliated, forced to pay costs they cannot afford. Progressive observers often see libel law as a means for the powerless to defend themselves against an overbearing mass press. It can be, sometimes, but wealth and privilege always determine who has a voice – who can be heard. As the Kittens find to their cost, trusting in British justice was a gamble.

'With the exception of homicidal crime,' observes Edward Wooll, 'no type of litigation elicits such popular interest as … causes célèbres in the form of sensational libel actions'.[82] Although the trial is never front-page news, it is reported widely enough for scandalous stories of Seven Dials to reach across Britain. The muffled furore is sufficient to destroy the Kittens' good name – and, soon, their business. But it never gains the purchase of other cause célèbres around questions of race. A backstreet cafe is not as newsworthy as the British Empire Exhibition. A courtroom address lacks the sensation of an angry exchange with the colonial secretary. Without a public platform and organisational support, the political potential of libel law is circumscribed. It is difficult to generalise from one case, Solanke must realise disappointedly.

The aftershocks still ripple. 'Do you know that "a certain member had complained to the Home Secretary" about your establishment?' Kitten is asked in court.[83] Of course he does not. Two weeks later there is an awkward discussion in the House of Commons. Viscount Sandon, Conservative MP and one-time Assistant Private Secretary to Lord Milner, Secretary of State for Colonies, asks the Home Secretary, Sir William Joynson-Hicks: 'What steps has he taken to avoid in future the state of affairs … revealed in the recent case of the restaurant in Great White Lion Street?' Sandon and Bracewell Smith are members of the same party; like Smith, Sandon becomes an LCC alderman; both are Freemasons. His ostensible concern for public order suggests the entwined commercial and political interests at work in Seven Dials.[84]

In private, the question allows police to demand new unfettered powers to close 'undesirable' venues. Civil servants resist, arguing that licensing regulations and legislation on gaming, prostitution, and public disorder are adequate.[85] In Parliament, Joynson-Hicks observes that the 'premises have received the special attention of the police'. He continues: the 'proprietor has twice been prosecuted and convicted for permitting disorderly conduct and other undesirable activities on the premises, which will continue to be kept under observation with a view to suitable action in the event of any further offences'.[86]

Treating the cafe – like Seven Dials or London's booming nightlife – as a 'problem' of public order is within Joynson-Hicks's comfort zone. He is unsettled, though, by Labour MP Josiah Wedgwood. 'Is the Right hon. Gentleman going to introduce any form of colour bar into this country or make any distinction between blacks and whites?' demands Wedgwood – knowing that the imperial state *does* make that distinction, not least through legislation like CASO. Wedgwood is an indefatigable radical parliamentarian, whose commitment to individual freedom, and antipathy to privilege, makes him increasingly exercised by colonial governance in the 1920s.[87] Before the war he served on the Northern Nigerian and West African Land Committees; he remains a progressive voice on regional development. Reporting on the Dominions and Colonial Affairs Appropriation Bill (1926), *West Africa* notes appreciatively: 'Colonel Wedgwood, as ever, put up stout and sincere championship of West Africanism.'[88] Concurrent with the furore around the cafe, Wedgwood rails against 'that infernal colour bar' in debates over the South African Colour Bar Bill and the East African British Colonists' Association efforts to restrict Indian immigration and voting rights in Kenya.[89]

For Wedgwood, an acrimonious libel trial is inseparable from the struggles of empire. In Britain, people like Solanke and the Kittens challenge the hardening colour bar, claiming the rights of citizenship in court, lobbying authorities, and organising politically and industrially. So do activists across the empire. Supported by the Indian National Congress, Kenya's Indian minority challenge the discrimination they face. In Sierra Leone, a bitter political struggle develops alongside the dispute with *John Bull*. Enraged at a contractual settlement that organises pay and conditions along racial lines, in January 1926 the Railway Workers Union comes out on strike. Supported by Freetown's City Council and a regional relief fund, the strike focuses discontent with the heavy-handed governor, Sir Ransford Slater.[90]

In confronting Joynson-Hicks, Wedgwood deliberately highlights the colour bar's significance and reach. Freetown, Nairobi, London: the locations are not so distant, nor is their prominence in public debate at the same time simply coincidence. In Cape Town, Calcutta, or Cardiff, challenging the colour bar exposes the necessary racism of British colonialism and the empty sham of the Empire Exhibition's rhetoric of imperial 'family'. 'Commonwealth' is impossible when ostensibly equal subjects are treated differently under the law. An institutional commitment to racial equality, Wedgwood implies, is essential to maintaining an empire facing strident demands for self-determination.[91] Joynson-Hicks is evasive – 'that does not arise on this question' – but his bluster belies the trial's racial politics, and the imperial resonance of what Frank Kennedy termed 'prejudice against coloured people'. It is not so far from Seven Dials to Sierra Leone. Nor, it turns out, is a backstreet cafe so removed from the corridors of power.

This is always an intimate story of Seven Dials and its people. For three days, the High Court becomes a stage on which to enact the nature and limits of everyday cosmopolitanism. This is a desperately unequal clash, pitting the Kittens against the power of Odhams Press and Bracewell Smith. Yet under the public gaze, courtroom testimonies – nervous, diffident, angry, impassioned – crystallise both the rich mutuality and suffocating frictions between neighbours with more in common than they might like to think. At stake is a neighbourhood's remaking. Follow the people, the money, the ties of power and privilege: the gossamer binding Smith, Sandon, Odhams Press, Holborn Council, the Metropolitan Police, LCC, and Home Office materialises the ability of the few to mobilise local and national government, popular newspapers, and an array of small traders against the Kittens. 'Cooperation' and remarkable courage allow them to resist this pressure, but what chance did they really have?

Above all, the trial is about the Kittens' reputation – the future of the life they have made together. It is a personal tragedy. Celebrating a verdict of which they are 'distinctly proud', *John Bull* is triumphant and vindictive, rehearsing their attack and damning Jim Kitten's 'mendacity and shamelessness': 'Kitten gets Scratched', gloats one headline.[92] Ordered to pay costs, within weeks the Kittens must sell their stake in the cafe. Having invested several hundred pounds, they receive just £30. Pursued by creditors, Kitten goes bankrupt. Somehow the cafe stays open for another eighteen months. The writing is always on the wall.[93]

* * *

Over the first six months of 1928, two things – apparently unrelated – happen in Great White Lion Street. Clues to the first hide in the registers of the Bow Street magistrate's court. An anonymous clerk records an unusually large number of arrests for public order offences – usually drunk and disorderly – in this tiny backstreet. It is not obvious from the meticulous handwriting, but most of those arrested and fined are Black. Born in the Kissi region of Guinea, the kitchen porter Thomas Gilpin has walked down from the rooms in St Pancras he shares with his German wife, Agnes.[94] Isaac Jackson is originally from Cape Town, but has lived in London since the war. Now 31, he has worked variously as a merchant seaman, musician, and music hall artist. Hiding in plain sight is a dramatic escalation of police activity in the cafe's environs.[95]

Police watch and harass the cafe and its customers; anger simmers in Seven Dials. There is only one occasion when local newspapers make these tensions more widely visible. That February, a year after he had spoken powerfully of the cafe's importance, Frank Kennedy is arrested and fined for assaulting a police officer. Kennedy is talking with friends on the pavement of Great White Lion Street one evening, when a constable orders them to get inside or move on. He stands 'in the doorway to prevent [police] entering' the cafe – another officer alleges Kennedy strikes his shoulder and spits in his face, though witnesses deny this. As Kennedy goes 'inside the cafe and slam[s] the door' growing resentment becomes palpable. Just as the Kittens tried to defend their cafe by suing Odhams Press, now Kennedy goes to court for barring its door against another raid.[96]

The second thing that happens in Great White Lion Street plays out in the financial columns of broadsheet newspapers and the panelled offices of estate agents and developers. Two decades earlier, the Hammond Spencer estate had sold the corner block on which the Shaftesbury Hotel was built. Now they advertise a further 'twelve freehold shops for investment' on the opposite corner: numbers 14–19 Little Earl Street and 12–17 Great White Lion Street. This 'ideal block for future development ... occupies a bold position at the convergence of seven streets'. As if to emphasise the site's commercial potential, the accompanying map is annotated: 'the property is only 100 yards from Charing X Rd. [and] 20 yards from Shaftesbury Avenue'. Thomas Nutley's eel pie house, Declercq's butchers', and the cafe where Jim and Emily Kitten dreamt of a new life are now both a problem – generating a 'low present income of £1174 per annum' – and an opportunity for a bold entrepreneur seeking a 'splendid investment of capital ... for future development'. In July 1928 – four months after first advertised – the block sells at auction.[97]

Except these things are not unrelated at all. Coming just a year after the Kittens are forced into bankruptcy, the sale of a substantial corner block at the heart of Seven Dials at the same time as police renew their efforts to suppress Black sociability underscores the complicity of commercial and

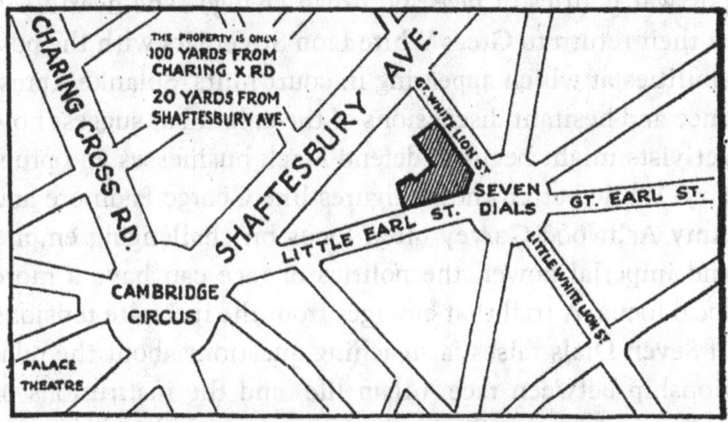

Figure 4.2 'An Ideal Block for Future Development', 1928

political power. Again, we see *both* the overwhelming pressures through which Seven Dials is decolonised and made safe for the monstrous machine of capital *and* the interwoven interests underpinning that process. Nowhere can survive this. By 1930, at the latest, the cafe has gone – replaced by a branch of the Times Laundry Company. From their upstairs room next door, the Kittens see all of this, watching an unwanted future unfold.

In another courtroom, around the same time, another powerful man puts the boot into the Kittens. The Official Receiver dismisses their 'frivolous and vexatious action' as an 'impudent attempt to obtain money'. There are real concerns about the abuse of libel law, but this judgement is wrong.[98] The couple's journey to the Strand is charted by the postwar politics of race and urban change. The heartbreak of their return to Great White Lion Street jars with the possibilities at which appearing in court hints. Solanke's presence and hesitant discussions of the colour bar suggest how activists might begin to defend Black businesses and property. While better-known figures like George Padmore and Amy Ashwood Garvey often focus on challenging empire and imperial power, the politics of race can have a more local focus. A trial that emerges from the intimate tensions of Seven Dials raises far-reaching questions about the relationship between race, urban life, and the institutions of nation and empire. Set out in defiance of overbearing prejudice, here might be a way to make an enduring home in the imperial metropolis.[99]

5
Slumming in bohemia
Great Earl Street

Robert Still jolts awake. It is still early, and the night porter at Tommy Farmer's Lodging House has been dozing at his desk by the entrance. He is sluggish, but slowly roused by the traffic and shouts from the street. Dishevelled and disturbed by the noise, two older men from the ground floor ward join him. They are regulars – an unemployed labourer and kitchen porter who works when he can – so Still lets them follow him as he unbolts the door and peers outside. Following the commotion, the men see an incongruous spectacle. Under the flickering light of the Dials stands the heir to the throne and his rumoured lover, Mrs Dudley Ward, surrounded by a crowd of debutantes, aristocrats, and actresses on their knees searching the ground: 'young women, middle aged women, and men of all ages in every variety of costume, from the blue serge suit and bowler hat of the Prince of Wales to the gossamer evening frocks of Miss Gladys Cooper and Mrs Tallulah Bankhead'.[1]

Mary-Anne Maloney has lived in Seven Dials for decades, but she has never seen anything like this. Now almost seventy, she has moved between tenements in Nottingham Court, Little Wild Street, Great White Lion Street, and Neal Street, before settling into two small rooms with her husband and three adult sons at 33 Shorts Gardens. The air is already warm, light streaking across the sky, as she walks downstairs, hoists her wicker basket, and leaves the building. She is heading to Covent Garden market to choose her blooms for the day.

For almost as long as she has lived in Seven Dials, Mary has sold flowers around the West End. As well as a person, she is a 'type' – a familiar cliché in picaresque tales of London's streets, a colourful presence in the work of photographers and artists, such as Sybil Andrews's linocut *Flower Girls*.[2] Today Mary's routine is interrupted: a couple in evening dress – so out of place they might have stepped out of a Society magazine – ask peremptory questions in accents which cut glass. They are hunting for something. Once Mary understands what, she points the way. 'For several minutes cars ran up and down Shorts Gardens', a journalist will write, 'until some kindly flower-woman directed the leaders to a spot in Seven Dials [where they find] hung on a lamppost a charming drawing of Alice in Wonderland carrying a hog in her arms!' It is June 1924, and the Bright Young People – hectic and half-cut – have arrived, scouring Seven Dials for treasures.[3]

This nocturnal treasure hunt is more than a story of the journalistic silly season. The Bright Young People's exploits are a fixture of newspapers and magazines, eliciting amusement, disapproval, or radical critique. 'Dress makers should rejoice,' one columnist observes, 'for few of the frocks that went to Seven Dials ... will ever see the lights of a ballroom again. A crawl on all fours in that none too clean neighbourhood ... in search of an elusive clue chalked on the pavement, had soiled the majority beyond repair.'[4] Set against the poverty and industrial conflict of the 1920s, such displays of privilege seem distasteful to some. The austere

Sunday Times dismisses these 'weird pranks' as a 'vulgar, noisy nuisance' – contrasting the 'Silly Set's' indulgence to the hard-working people still sleeping. Mischievously reprinting the article under the headline 'Rebuke for the Prince', the *Daily Herald* makes Society's intrusion into the Dials a cause of outrage and protest.[5]

The ripples of this incident pass almost as quickly as the prince's time in Seven Dials. It is a scandal in a minor key – a short-lived spat about the failings of the idle rich. The journey taken by this privileged coterie is freighted with significance, though: the treasure hunt careers between Claridge's Hotel, a Sloane Square coffee stall, the Adelphi Arches, and Seven Dials. More than a route through London, this itinerary marks a dizzying social descent from Society to slum, overworld to underworld, from the centre of patrician culture to the haunts of the homeless and the heart of the 'Black colony'. If the episode is unusual, it underlines how a down-at-heel place of home and work becomes a playground for wealthy pleasure-seekers after the Great War. Seven Dials has long drawn the attention of outsiders, whether animated by a sense of Christian mission or seeking sensation. Now the balance tips from philanthropy to pleasure. The growing number of thrill-seekers who self-consciously cross social and geographical boundaries tells us much about how the area is perceived. It also suggests the affinities between the afterlives of Victorian 'slumming' and what we now call gentrification.[6]

People come not in spite, but because, of Seven Dials' reputation. For nightclub proprietors seeking a venue, artists wanting a studio, or those looking for somewhere to live it helps that rents are cheap, and vacant places are plentiful as the area slowly empties. By the 1920s Soho has lost its edge, while Seven Dials' notoriety lingers. For many, the thrill of slumming – the fun of playing in the dirt – is an inexorable draw. Increasingly, you can experience such delights without leaving home or the cinema. Freelance writers, journalists, and filmmakers turn the area's reputation for poverty and crime into sensation and profit. In print and on screen, through films, guidebooks, novels, and newspapers, it becomes a familiar stop on breathless tours of the underworld. Even when carefully manufactured, notoriety and difference can be commodities to buy, pleasures to experience. If roads and buildings demarcate Seven Dials' bounds, the contrasts between within and without are sharpened by jarring extremes of wealth and rhetoric. New flats and fashionable restaurants like the Ivy studiously turn their backs to the tangle of tenements. These limits are porous, of course, but some writers still claim to sense a change in the quality of the light or taste of the air as they pass from Long Acre or Shaftesbury Avenue into Seven Dials.[7]

Some of the most important cultural figures of the period walk the streets of Seven Dials, then, often at the same time. Artists, writers, intellectuals, filmmakers, and actors come looking for material and local colour. As they wander the city or seek a room of their own, they pass through the area. 'Street haunting', Virginia Woolf calls it, in her reverie on the quest for a lead pencil that takes her through the 'narrow old houses between Holborn and Soho, where people have such queer names' to the Strand in winter's fading light.[8] From Woolf to Agatha Christie and George Goodchild – highbrow literary modernism, middlebrow mysteries, and the trashiest of crime novels – Seven Dials provides a familiar synecdoche for the slum, for the criminal underworld, and for cosmopolitan dangers and delights. Finally, outsiders come in search of a good time in the area's nightclubs and cabarets. In the late 1920s,

Seven Dials fleetingly becomes London's most fashionable bohemian haunt.

* * *

Not all outsiders come to Seven Dials in search of pleasure. For at least six decades, the area has drawn the attention of well-meaning philanthropists. The St Giles Christian Mission begins 'evangelistic and social work amongst poor and criminal classes ... in the notorious Seven Dials and Drury Lane districts' in 1860 – a local 'channel of divine grace and human compassion, lifting shadowed hearts and lives into forgiveness and freedom through Christ's Gospel'.[9] Such endeavours are usually associated with the East End, but their presence in Seven Dials is equally marked. At the French Hospital and Dispensary, opened in 1867 then moving to Great St Andrew Street in 1890, the Sisters of the Order of Les Servantes du Sacre-Coeur provide medical care for 'foreigners' living nearby. From 1888, the National Refuges for Homeless and Destitute Children (later renamed Shaftesbury Homes) provides accommodation, recreational facilities, and industrial and technical training at the intimidating Shaftesbury Boys' Home and Industrial School, on the corner of Shaftesbury Avenue and Great White Lion Street.[10] Ministering to souls, minds, and bodies – the physical and moral improvement of London's poor – is a Christian vocation.

Perhaps best known is the Seven Dials Mission, founded in 1875 and overseen by the Anglican rector of St Giles. The Mission moves from Shorts Gardens to the derelict West Street Chapel and adjacent building in 1887. Built for French Protestant refugees, the place where John Wesley first preached in London, and once home to the Catholic Irish Society, the new premises are a palimpsest of rich local histories. By 1905, the expanded mission contains clubrooms, a gymnasium, temperance societies, and chapel.[11] Its work continues into the 1920s, as a new generation of clergy commits to 'strenuous labour among the poorer classes'.[12] Unsung and increasingly anachronistic, the Mission ministers to souls, solicits donations, and provides sustenance and clothing to those in need. There are Sunday schools, Templar Lodge meetings, and LCC evening classes in the gymnasium. Only once is the peace disturbed: in January 1925, the Mission becomes front page news when the ageing cleaner Joseph Elkin discovers a paper-wrapped parcel of human bones in the vestibule. He thinks the strange gift is a macabre joke by medical students.[13]

These traditions persist in other ways. Many of the councillors concerned in the Improvement Scheme blend this older tradition of good works with modern municipal government; inevitably, they usually live in Bloomsbury. The committee includes Wilfred Davies, incumbent rector of St Giles. Robert Dibdin is a solicitor and former mayor of Holborn, but his father had been long-serving minister of West Street Chapel.[14] At different times, Dibdin himself has been director of the French Hospital and president of the Society for Improving the Condition of the Labouring Classes; at the start of each meeting, Dibdin leads the society's committee in prayers. After her election in 1919, Emily Dibdin, his sister, joins the committee. Following her father into settlement work, Dibdin is a prolific writer for the *Church Missionary Gleaner*, of children's books, and the first history of the institution to which Dibdin senior devoted his life: the *Seven Dials Mission* (1913). Like Norah March, social worker, eugenicist, secretary of the National Baby Week Council, and a fellow councillor, Dibdin's role in the Improvement Plan and Maternity and Child Welfare committee underscores the changing ways in which care and welfare are delivered. Philanthropy and good works live on through people like Dibdin and March and their utopian schemes for making Seven Dials modern.[15]

Yet Seven Dials has no equivalent to slumland priests like Basil Jellicoe, whose radical zeal drives the pioneering work of the St Pancras House Improvement Society to the north. For many contemporaries, mission work seems old fashioned. Christian Socialist Charles Marson rails against the well-meaning but misguided individuals who impose on poorer neighbourhoods. As well as 'ambassadors of the better land', Marson argues, 'the clergy ought to be correcting the unworthy caricatures of the poor which fill ... the ignorant minds of ... [the] plutocracy'. Calling for a radical social inversion, he continues: 'We have missions from public schools and universities to Bethnal Green and Southwark [when] we really need settlements and missions from Seven Dials and Hoxton to Oxford or to Eton.'[16]

* * *

It is fitting that the first attempt to depict Seven Dials on film is about a philanthropic 'slumming expedition'. *The Duchess of Seven Dials* (1920) is also a love story that follows the romance between Lady Irene Worth, 'democratic' young aristocrat, and Reverend Noel Fortescue, the 'penniless' curate tending his slumland parish.[17] Settlement work has brought missionaries into St Giles for decades. Now the London Film Studios and director Fred Paul take cinemagoers into the area's heart.

The cinema is a modern technological wonder, but *The Duchess of Seven Dials* determinedly looks back. Even enthusiastic reviewers acknowledge it is 'old-fashioned, sentimental melodrama'.[18] Gilbert and Sullivan's comic opera persists in the contrast between the 'social extremities of metropolitan life' in Seven Dials and Grosvenor Square.[19] The film echoes the burlesquing of class difference in famous music hall songs like Dan Thomas's *Duchess of Seven Dials* and George Grossmith's *Duke of Seven Dials*. Local histories overshadow this 'romance of London, Past and Present:'

> Slum land, glum land, land of despair and hope.
> Realm of murky dinginess and scarcity of soap.
> You bet yer life some blokes ain't straight,
> Some thieve and booze tween whiles.
> Yet 'ere and there are 'earts of gold
> In London's Seven Dials.[20]

Far from aristocratic, the 'Duchess' of Seven Dials is an elderly spinster living hand to mouth amid memories and caricatures of London's poor – 'villains of the Bill Sikes type' and the unfortunate 'waif'. Noble titles in a notorious slum signal a topsy-turvy otherworld.[21]

Figure 5.1 Scene from 'The Duchess of Seven Dials', 1920

The Duchess's reminiscences – shared with Worth – shuttle audiences between the 1910s and 1860s. The plot unfolds through an 'extended flashback' imagined by Gracie Milton, 'a famous beauty of the old Oxford Music Hall', conjuring spectacular scenes of 'historic interest'. There is a coincidence: Worth's grandfather, the duke, has forbidden her to marry the curate; the 'Duchess' reveals that the duke – her true love – jilted her before their wedding. There is a climax: confronting the duke in Mayfair, the women learn that heartbreak was caused by a duplicitous friend. There is resolution: the duke agrees to Worth's marriage and is reconciled with his old flame.[22] Despite the cliches, the film is well received. The *Bioscope* calls it a 'delightful story of London life' which 'should win universal favour in this country [and is] admirably qualified to represent the British film at its best abroad'.[23]

In January 1921, *The Duchess of Seven Dials* comes home. *Picturegoer* proclaims that 'the real thing in London slums was used as a setting by the London Film Company'.[24] Interested locals can stroll the short distance along Shaftesbury Avenue to the Shaftesbury Pavilion and see themselves and their neighbourhood on screen.[25] Over the next few years there will be similar opportunities, as the Dials becomes a go-to location for production companies seeking a shortcut to poverty and crime. Later in the year, a 'keenly interested crowd' gather as the Broadwest company films there. *In Full Cry* (1921) stars popular British actors Stewart Rome as 'the man of the underworld who inherits a fortune' and Pauline Peters as the 'slum laundress' falsely accused of murder.[26]

Perhaps the traffic of film crews becomes overwhelming. In December 1926, there is a late-night contretemps when 'Police Stop Film Scene in Seven Dials'. As the story develops the stakes rise: authorities 'have banned a scene in the "London after Dark" film series', newspapers report, production is delayed, and a major film might be cut.[27] *London after Dark* is Harry Parkinson's latest venture. Parkinson, a prolific director and producer, is widely admired for 'novelty shorts' like *Wonderful London* (1924). Following a 'young provincial' being shown around by a friend, his new 'piquant tales' offer 'twelve cameos of "Soho", "Mayfair", and other well-known districts', which 'contrast pictures of high and low life in London by night'.[28]

Seven Dials provides an obvious cameo for this project. A name that captures the imagination, it is also less than three hundred metres from Parkinson's studio in Little Denmark Street. Even weighed down with bulky equipment on a cold evening, it takes Parkinson, his cinematographer, and an actor just five minutes to cross Shaftesbury Avenue and set up in an alleyway. Their work is abruptly halted, though: 'to our amazement a sergeant stepped forward and told us we must stop, as we were using a policeman's uniform'. Parkinson protests: the scene depicts the 'history of the neighbourhood and the greater changes for the better' effected by police. It is no use. Having given their names and addresses, the group 'pack up … and return to the studio'.[29] In a much-quoted interview, Parkinson calls such interference 'anomalous' when the government are trying to protect an embattled industry against the might of Hollywood. 'Holding up one of few British pictures' threatens the precarious economy of the nation's film production.[30] Perhaps – Parkinson is a clever self-publicist, who later claims to have changed the law on filming in public by lobbying politicians after this debacle. There are reasons to be cynical about how this Seven Dials stunt draws attention to a new release.[31]

Films like *London after Dark* and *The Duchess of Seven Dials* underline the area's draw. They also show how it is made known to outsiders – through the ubiquitous conventions of melodrama, inseparable from the pathos of poverty and dangers of crime. Such motifs also play out in print. George Goodchild's potboiling thriller *Jack O'Lantern* (1929) follows the eponymous 'terror' into this 'poor district':

> Ten minutes ago, he had jostled with the crowd in Piccadilly Circus, had dodged luxurious limousines, had gazed with cynical and contemptuous eyes on women muffled in sables and bejewelled from neck to fingers. Now he turned a sympathetic eye on the poor mob that were counting their pennies and besieging the stalls in the hope of making wonderful bargains ere the market closed.
>
> Poverty and riches – side by side, half-starved creatures jostling overfed mistresses of bloated plutocrats.[32]

As well as being a synonym for slum, Seven Dials is a shorthand for its people. The ennui of Norah James's *Hail! Oh Hail!* (1929) is different from Goodchild's novel, but both treat the place similarly. Amid the commotion and cubicles of Holborn public baths, James's protagonist Lily wallows in tepid water and half-heard conversations. A disembodied voice cuts through the noise: 'I've got to look for a new room to-day. Had one off Seven Dials, but I left it last night. Stayed out.' I wear make-up because 'fellows like it. You know what I mean.' My family 'think I'm in service and get in at ten each night', but 'I often stay out'.

> How long have you been staying out the way you say you do?
> Oh, eighteen months about. No, two years …
> What's your trade?
> 'aven't I been telling you? I was a waitress before.[33]

Seven Dials becomes a proxy for the tawdry temptations of mass consumerism, the loosening of morals, the modern girl's threatening independence and unruly sexuality.

For seasoned observers, places like the Kittens' cafe are absorbed into this broader spectacle. 'We have the Zoo, and Kew Gardens, and Black men outside the pubs of Seven Dials', observes Arnold Palmer in Society magazine *Britannia and Eve*. 'We can eat French food, and Chinese and Russian and German and Spanish and German food. What inducement is there to travel?' Palmer's instinctive equivalence between people gathering in Seven Dials and the captive animals on display at London Zoo is troubling but suggests how the 'Black colony' becomes an essential stop for peripatetic writers and armchair slummers.[34] It figures in the reminiscences of police officers like Inspector Joseph Broadhurst. It provides a backdrop for celebrated crime writers, including Edgar Wallace's *The Hand of Power* (1927).[35] Graham Greene's *Brighton Rock* (1938) follows Ida from Charing Cross Station up St Martin's Lane:

> her heart beat faster to the refrain: it's exciting, it's fun, it's living. In Seven Dials the Negroes were hanging round the Royal Oak doors in tight natty suitings and old school ties, and Ida recognised one of them and passed the time of day.[36]

For those unable or unwilling to walk the streets, reading offers a safely vicarious urban tour.

* * *

Harry Parkinson comes to Seven Dials to exploit its association with crime rather than cosmopolitanism. Arnold Palmer's hymn to the pleasures of eating in French restaurants or Jewish markets has telling limits. Jim Kitten's curry and rice never figures in guidebooks or the itineraries of the cognoscenti. Nor does the food at local Italian and Greek cafes, which usually serve those living and working nearby. From the mid-1920s, though, more and more outsiders follow the Prince of Wales into Seven Dials. They are drawn by the prospect of excitement, cheap rents and rates, and the number of empty properties. Studios and shady nightclubs, in turn, draw a different crowd into this intimate world. London's literary and artistic avant-garde – deliberately dissident, consciously radical – begin to pass among the waiters, cleaners, clerks, tradesmen, and porters who live and work there. A down-at-heel slum becomes a fashionable urban bohemia.

The West End often spills into Seven Dials: people provide the unseen labour that sustains pleasure-seekers, proximity makes it the entertainment industry's backstage. In the summer of 1919, Serge Diaghilev's Ballets Russes entrances audiences with their new *La Boutique Fantasque* at the Alhambra, Leicester Square – while rehearsing at the Shaftesbury Hotel and storing costumes in a warehouse on Great Earl Street.[37] 'All London has gazed at the Russian Ballet', writes a breathless journalist, 'but only a favoured few enjoyed an informal "breaking-up party"' thrown by Vladimir Polunin, the Russian artist and set painter. It is in a 'lofty studio above a fruit store in Seven Dials that Polunin, his wife Violet, and their friend Pablo Picasso – in London for ten weeks – paint the ballet's scenery; it is there that Picasso draws Polunin's portrait. Columnist, company, and 'people from the social world' scramble 'up seven ladders, past sacks of empty fruit baskets ... to the dim and eerie mystery of the studio, where a forest of painted clothes and hanging ropes loomed mysteriously'. In this ethereal fairy world, perched on 'upturned fruit baskets' and 'feast[ing] on cherries and chocolate', the 'long-drawn melancholy tones of a Russian chorus swept out above the deep alleyways of death-still Seven Dials'.[38]

This select gathering is reflected in more humble businesses. Born in Bollengo, near Turin, Felice Pietro Tapparo has worked as a motorcar fitter and cook and served in the Merchant Navy since moving to London. Around 1921, like the Kittens, he uses his savings to lease the Grapes Inn, on the Dials at 1 Great Earl Street. The Grape Vine Club becomes a popular haunt among 'foreign waiters' and others. Respectable enough to appear in the Post Office directory, it still draws attention. A police raid in November 1924 finds people 'dancing to the music of a concertina'. Tapparo is fined for selling unlicensed liquor, the premises struck off the clubs' register.[39] The landlords find a new tenant, but their tenure is shorter still. In June 1925 there is a second raid on what is now David Cutler's Shaftesbury Social Club. The Russian proprietor is imprisoned then deported. It is not just the Kittens who learn that running a place of entertainment near Bracewell Smith's hotel can be dangerous.[40]

* * *

One afternoon in September 1927, the bestselling novelist Arnold Bennett – famous for his stories of the Staffordshire potteries and recent *Lord Raingo* (1926) – sits at his desk in Cadogan Square and writes to his nephew: 'I'm going out with Harriet Cohen tonight and ending at the Cave of Harmony (new era).'[41] That evening a watchful gossip columnist mingles with the crowds as London's most fashionable bohemian resort reopens in its latest home. They notice 'Arnold Bennett, who ever seems to enjoy gracing with a paternal, pontifical manner these light adventures, [and] Harriet Cohen, the pianist'.[42] Bennett and Cohen are not the only well-known figures on view. For those visiting in person or in print, the Cave's delights are found among its habitués as much as on stage. Newspaper columns read like an avant-garde *Who's Who*: artist Dora Carrington, architect Wells Coates, theatre designer Doris Zinkeisen, actor James Whale, novelists Evelyn Waugh and Radclyffe Hall.[43] 'There were so many interesting people there that one grumbled because one could not see them all', writes a journalist. As they leave, American actress Tallulah Bankhead makes a grand entrance.[44]

Founded by Elsa Lanchester and actor Harold Scott in 1924, the Cave is renowned for such bohemian sociability. For many, it is inseparable from its leading impresario's flamboyant persona. Then at the start of her career as an actress, singer, and dancer – her defining role in *The Bride of Frankenstein* (1935) still in the future – Lanchester's celebrity is striking: darling of critics and audiences and the face of Pond's face cream. Mixing avant-garde culture and politics, the Cave is a stage where Lanchester can perform, a venue for modernist plays and dance, a meeting place for the cognoscenti, and a nightclub where fashionable London can dance. The Cave is formed out of the same desires for pleasure and freedom expressed in the nightlife of Weimar Berlin or Left Bank Paris after the war. 'Bohemian modernism' becomes a 'theatre of experimental selves' where 'dissident forms of morality, creativity, and sexuality [can] be expressed'.[45] For the young artist Kathleen Hale, a member since it opened and later famous for her books about Orlando the Marmalade Cat, the Cave's importance is more fundamental: it has 'really become our life'.[46]

In some ways, there is nothing unusual about Bennett's late-night visit to the Cave. It is a popular spot in his circles, and he is Lanchester and Scott's long-standing avuncular patron. Lanchester once arrives for lunch at Cadogan Square wearing a 'charming' dress home-made from dusters, then refuses Bennett's offer to buy chairs and tables for the Cave, 'preferring the audience to sit on the floor'. Enamoured by such '*original* inventiveness', he decides she and Scott are 'bound to do something good'.[47] The Cave's 'new era' *is* extraordinary, though. After wandering between premises in Bloomsbury and Fitzrovia, Lanchester, Scott, and their new partner Matthew Norgate, Secretary of the Incorporated Stage Society, have arrived in Seven Dials. 'Adventurous Bloomsbury and even the inhabitants of Chelsea' assemble in the unlikely surrounds of the old Grapes Inn at 1 Great Earl Street.[48]

Disdain for convention, the chance to trade notoriety for cachet, and cheap rents bring the Cave here. Like most people seeing this 'tall, narrow building' for the first time, Kathleen Hale is struck by its character and fantastical histories. It is built in 1835, though the vaults are rumoured to be older – even Roman. It appears in George Cruikshank's illustration for Charles Dickens's *Sketches by Boz* (1836).[49] No longer a pub, it had 'passed through a variety of phases until it became a strange store ... open on all days at all times, where one could buy anything from a toffee apple to a bassinette'. Such queer environs are fittingly bohemian.[50]

Not content with the building's ramshackle appearance, Lanchester and Scott turn it into an otherworldly stage for what is to come. They decorate the attic cabaret in pink, yellow, and 'old gold' then create a first-floor dance hall painted a 'very light shade of green [with] rich red curtains'.[51] The artist John Armstrong (who will soon exhibit his work at the Leicester Galleries), works with Hale, making colourful lampshades, and 'paints the bar with castles and roses in the style of the traditional art of river barges'.[52] Most intriguing is the basement, where members can feast on

Figure 5.2 Harold Scott and Elsa Lanchester in the vaults of the Cave of Harmony, 1928

kippers, eggs, and bacon – though it is not 'a cave hewn out of solid rock', as one excitable visitor claims.[53] In an agency photograph Scott and Lanchester pose amid the crumbling plaster, shadowy arches, and incongruous electric cabling – studiedly mannered, jarringly fashionable. 'Feeding in the vaults, with the glamorous and cunningly hidden blue lighting, will doubtless become one of the minor crazes of eccentricity in London', predicts the *Era*.[54]

For a moment it seems moving to Seven Dials is a step too far. Disreputable predecessors bring kudos, but the prosecutions of the Grape Vine and Shaftesbury social clubs have awkward legal consequences. Only at the end of September do Lanchester and Scott realise that the premises have been disqualified from being used as a nightclub. This 'dilemma' has them hurriedly applying to the Bow Street magistrate to lift the ban.[55] Their barrister distances the Cave from the excesses of working-class nightlife. 'Theatrical performances and cabaret shows were given, and the club was used by a large number of literary and artistic people without complaint', he tells Sir Chartres Biron.[56] Biron needs little reminding: there are more intimate connections at work. In August 1928, Arnold Bennett records meeting Biron twice in one week at the patrician Garrick Club. On the first occasion, they argue bitterly: Biron is with James Douglas, editor of the *Sunday Express*, whose vicious diatribe against Radclyffe Hall's novel of love between women, *The Well of Loneliness* (1928), prompts a sensational literary scandal. When Bennett reprimands 'Jimmy', Biron stands up for him. Despite this, the men are on good enough terms to lunch later that week. Within months, Biron presides over the infamous trial that bans Hall's novel.[57]

All that is in the future. When Lanchester and Scott appear in court, though, it matters that their following includes 'prominent members of the literary, legal, and artistic world'.[58] Biron worries about the building's condition but cautiously agrees 'to remove the disqualification subject to certain structural alterations being made as a safeguard against fire'.[59] It is not the last time the Cave's fate is shaped by privileges of club, class, and connection. Local authorities watch Seven Dials haunts intently. Whatever happens inside the Cave, though, it never attracts the same attention as smaller places owned by Italian, Jewish, or Black residents – no matter who dances with who, or what people drink. Rather than through a police raid, the Cave's demise will be a more mundane song of Seven Dials.

When Bennett and Cohen travel to Great Earl Street, they arrive at the cutting edge of avant-garde culture and a media sensation. In its new environs the Cave seems irresistible. 'The newest and most amusing nightclub I've visited reopened this last week', notes the *Sunday Pictorial*'s women's columnist.[60] Kathleen Hale delights in the 'stupendous party' marking the occasion. She is not alone: the crowds are such that 'people became wedged on the narrow staircase and eventually were unable to pass each other'.[61] To display the 'modernities' of twenties Britain, a photospread in the *Graphic* sets the 'new era' alongside Futurist theatre and 'high tea' on an Imperial Airways flight and heralds the return of 'dancing in a dim atmosphere, negligently sitting on the floor in the cause of art and discussing complexes ... until the dawn'. 'Fresh as paint – for a start', reads the caption.[62]

In turn serious and playful, the Cave is defined by a sense of restless possibility. Both a 'new "little theatre"' and 'cabaret nightclub' popular with a 'Bohemian clique', the 'entertainment may take the form of a play or just what comes into the proprietors' heads'. There are one-act plays by leading modernists like Luigi Pirandello, August Strindberg, Georg Kaiser, and Lady Gregory.[63] Moving between tragedy and comedy, Aubrey Ensor's knowing pastiche 'The Perfect Plot' explores how 'JM Barrie, Noel Coward, and Tchekov might treat the same theme' – the 'eternal' love triangle.[64] Noted Society hostess and patron Lady Emerald Cunard sits in the front row, 'wrapped in sables amid the "batiked" beauties of Bohemia'.[65]

Yet Lanchester is the dominant personality. Introduced by his brother Charles – actor and soon to be Lanchester's husband – Tom Laughton is struck how it is 'run by Elsa and her friends as a vehicle for her talents'. The breadth of those talents, which define what Laughton calls the Cave's 'wit and spontaneity', is astonishing.[66] She and Scott scour the British Museum for out-of-print folk tunes, sea shanties, and popular nineteenth-century songs: Scott edits the new *English Song Book* (1926), Lanchester performs the material on stage. Philosopher Cyril Joad is captivated by her rendition of the cloying temperance classic 'Sell No More Drink to My Father' – seeing this 'rage for Victorian songs, sung with mocking derision' as part of a generational revolt against the sentimentality and moralism usually linked with Lytton Strachey's iconoclastic *Eminent Victorians* (1918).[67] On other nights, Lanchester and Angela Baddeley improvise freewheeling 'dialogues between two charwomen called "Mrs Bricketts and Mrs Bubellamy."'[68] Tasked with capturing the Cave's 'Presiding Genius', photographer Gregory Bernard focuses on the stylised physicality of her dancing. Lanchester's silhouetted naked frame is elongated by Bernard's composition and lighting. As her 'expressive hands' contort to create the illusion of a headdress, Lanchester gazes in wonder at her disembodied shadow self.[69]

All this is ripe for mockery, and the Cave draws withering scrutiny. Contemporary historians John Collier and Ian Laing ridicule 'nursery nostalgia' for the Victorian music hall. Their wry description of those 'enterprising young men and women who had recovered, by arduous research in the British Museum, the words and music of "I Like Pickled Onions"' is an obvious jibe at Scott and Lanchester.[70] Stella Gibbons' best-selling novel *Cold Comfort Farm* (1932) goes further. Familiar with the antics of the avant-garde from her work as a journalist, Gibbons casually but brutally skewers the Cave's affectations. Savvy urbanite Flora Poste is introducing country girl Elfine Starkadder to London's delights:

> She proposed that the three of them should visit the Pit Theatre, in Stench Street, Seven Dials, to see a new play by Brandt Slurb called 'Manallalive-O!', a Neo-Expressionist attempt to give dramatic form to the mental reactions of a man employed as a waiter in a restaurant who dreams that he is the double of another man who is employed as a steward on a liner, and who, on awakening and realizing that he is still a waiter employed in a restaurant and not a steward employed on a liner, goes mad and shoots his reflection in a mirror and dies. It had seventeen scenes and only one character. A pest-house, a laundry, a lavatory, a court of law, a room in a leper's settlement and the middle of Piccadilly Circus were included in the scenes.

The offhand dismissal of urban poverty jars, but Seven Dials is not Gibbons' target. Parodying Flora's pursuit of distinction, avant-garde pretension, and the insalubrious surroundings where 'neo-expressionism' finds home, punctures the pomposity of London's intelligentsia. Flora's plans collapse, though: 'Julia thought it would be a much better idea if they went to see Mr Dan Langham in "On Your Toes!" at the New Hippodrome, so they went there instead and had a nice time instead of a nasty one.'[71] The only antidote to theatrical absurdities is mockery and the simple pleasures of a West End revue.

Avant-garde performances exemplify the Cave's vaunted permissiveness. The boundaries of convention are tested within the headiness of the dance floor as much as on stage. Lanchester taunts old-fashioned morality through a 'brilliant sentimental ballad in terms of Freud' or 'Krafft-Ebing Case #74B Zurich', a sketch in which 'a nun called Blankebin spent her time looking for the foreskin of Christ'.[72] The Cave becomes central to elite queer women's social circles. In Radclyffe Hall's *The Well of Loneliness*, Stephen visits 'a species of glorified cellar' – a 'queer little place down in Seven Dials', then becoming 'rather the fashion among certain literary people'.[73] Hall and her partner Una Troubridge are regulars. On opening night, a visitor is 'amused to see Miss Radclyffe Hall assisting Harold Scott by beating the drum and taking a hand at the cymbals. She did both these things very well.'[74] Scott works with the director Edith Craig, who lives in her own queer love triangle with the writer Christopher St John and artist Clare 'Tony' Atwood; poet and musicologist Sylvia Townsend Warner is a member. If it is not apparent at the time, the Cave will be remembered as somewhere same-sex couples might dance. For the fortunate few, bohemia might sustain the remaking of personal relationships and identities.[75]

The Cave is a kind of home for Townsend Warner, but her attempt to evoke the experience of dancing to a Black saxophonist there crystallises its racial and social exclusivity. 'Play, dark musician, play –', exhorts the refrain to her poem 'Caves of Harmony'. Cliches of Black sexuality and primitivism overwhelm the lyrics: the musician's coat and collar are incongruous and ill-fitting, he 'leers' in 'exhaling his melodious delight', an 'angry lion tosses up a bone'. The Kittens' cafe is close enough for the muffled music to carry across the Dials – close enough for the musicians from the United States, Caribbean, and West Africa gathering there to cross to Great Earl Street in seconds. Despite this proximity, the Cave and cafe might as well have been different worlds. Like many others, the Sierra Leonean drummer Frank Kennedy finds *his* home in Great White Lion Street. It is only as performers – the necessary labour to sustain the cosmopolitan spectacle and soundtrack that draws well-heeled slummers to Seven Dials – that people like him are received into the Cave of Harmony.[76]

The Cave's radicalism only reaches so far, then. It is not the Garrick or an upscale Mayfair nightclub, but it remains an exclusive members' club – haunt of the 'intelligentsia', an obtrusive arriviste in Seven Dials.[77] Describing its appeal, the *Bystander* betrays the privilege on which it depends:

> On any Friday night you will probably witness a little masterpiece rendered by masters of their profession. A one act play is sometimes so clever and the innuendoes so fine-drawn that you may only be 'half there' so to speak. But you will be sitting side by social side with the Great – and that is more than enough for most people.[78]

'Most people' will not be allowed or cannot afford to sit beside 'the Great'. Showily radical, the Cave also employs a top-hatted doorman vetting those trying to enter from Great Earl Street. Ostentatious bohemianism it is not so far from the Prince of Wales and the Bright Young People scrabbling in the dirt, after all.

The Cave's 'new era' lasts less than twelve months. 'Poor battered Cave of Harmony', laments Kathleen Hale: when the building is not made safe, it is 'summarily closed down as a fire hazard' in spring 1928.[79] Holborn's Liberal Party move in; earnest electioneering replaces a 'queer little club'. Delighted columnists imagine the unwitting 'smart set' finding 'where formerly there was champagne, there is ink'.[80] Within twelve months, the limited company set up by Lanchester, Scott, and Norgate has ceased to trade.[81] The Cave's afterlives exceed its habitués' misty memories, though. From 1937, it is partially reincarnated through the 'Song and Supper Room entertainment' at Covent Garden's Players Theatre. There Scott creates *Late Joys*, an after-theatre programme of favourites like *The Boy I Love is Up in the Gallery*.[82]

Figure 5.3 Nightclub in Seven Dials, London, 1927–28

* * *

After the Cave, comes the Caravan. Jack Neave and Billy Reynolds are not as renowned as Lanchester and Scott.

Reynolds is long forgotten, while Neave stalks the fading edges of memory. A 'character' of long-standing and minor fame, he was once an unmistakable figure with his lank ponytail and tattoos, broad-brimmed hat and flowing black cloak, walking stick and iron foot. Living precariously on the margins of modernity, Neave is an itinerant hustler, a teller of fortunes and tales, a mystic and phrenologist, an antique dealer, a founder of cults, an impresario of cosmopolitan resorts. In summer 1934 he and Reynolds also open a nightclub that deliberately flouts convention. The Caravan is a basement dive at the top of Endell Street, on Seven Dials' eastern edge. An advertising card, passed hand to hand, invites pleasure-seekers to 'London's only Bohemian rendezvous, said to be the most unconventional spot in town'. For those in the know, the cues hide in plain sight. The Cave's implicit permissiveness had been part of its draw, but Neave and Reynolds go much further. Enlisting the help of 'bohemian artists', they decorate with wall-hangings and carpets, 'primitive' masks, paintings of dragons and gipsy caravans, improvised divans – an ersatz Orientalism brought from Caledonian Road market to Seven Dials. When it is crowded, the dimly lit basement is stiflingly hot, thick with smoke, and heavily scented – perhaps to conceal the overwhelming smell of sweat and piss. It is often crowded: in six weeks, the membership book amasses 2000 names.

The Caravan and Cave bear passing resemblance, but this crowd is very different to the rarefied privilege on display in the venue at the far end of Shorts Gardens. The first names in the book include self-styled bohemian and disgraced solicitor Redvers Grey and the three Reynolds sisters, spuriously claiming the title 'Hon.'. Lawyers, teachers, and accountants make their way down the steps; an

MP is rumoured to be inside. The young John Deakin – then an artist, later Francis Bacon's confidante and a leading photographer – is a regular. Special Branch officers follow Ronald Kidd, suspected communist and founder of the National Council for Civil Liberties, there. In the basement they rub shoulders – often more – with sailors and tailors, decorators and cabinet makers, shop assistants and clerks, penniless street artists, petty criminals, 'convicted prostitutes', painted boys, plainclothes detectives. 'Coloured persons of both sexes [are] among those present', observes one detective. They might include James Rich: once a regular at the Kittens' cafe, Rich is now a familiar presence in such queer clubs. There are impromptu performances, hectic chatter, exuberant couples of all sorts 'dancing to Charlie', kissing and caressing on sofas, fucking in the bathroom. If the Cave enjoys tacit official tolerance, the Caravan gets anonymous complaints and the scrutiny of Holborn Council and the police. 'At the above address', write Endell Street's ratepayers, 'is the Caravan Club, only frequented by sexual perverts, lesbians, and sodomites. It is an absolute sink of iniquity.' After weeks of surveillance, it is raided in August. Neave, Reynolds, and many of their less privileged members end up in the dock at the Old Bailey.[83]

As entrepreneurs try their luck, so a growing number of artists, actors, and others are drawn to Seven Dials looking for somewhere to live. The area has always been convenient for the West End. In the 1920s, the actress Constance Collier runs the exclusive Fifty-Fifty Club with her friend Ivor Novello. Two decades earlier, beginning her career, she rented a 'cosy little apartment at the top of a very high building' in what she quickly realised was an 'unfortunate' location – a 'continuation of the Seven Dials' on Shaftesbury Avenue. In the 'most immoral house in London' drunks slept on the stairs and 'ladies of easy virtue' inhabited the flats below.[84]

From the mid-1920s, more people like Collier arrive. Modern apartment blocks bring a more affluent population to Seven Dials' outer limits. Attracted by affordable rents and a central location, others make their home within the Dials. The preponderance of furnished rooms in subdivided tenements makes the area particularly suited to single men or younger families. Although it is never a rooming district in the same way as Bayswater, there are hints that it might provide a suitable home for enigmatic bachelors, men-about-town, those making their way in the world. Invariably transient, their presence anticipates the gentrification of areas like Barnsbury in the 1950s.

In 1925, the actor and playwright Frank Vosper moves into an apartment at 7 Upper St Martin's Lane, sharing the address with fellow actor Cecil Fearnley. Vosper will be known for the mysterious circumstances of his death: he falls from the transatlantic liner the SS *Paris* in 1937, in an incident involving his partner, Peter Willes, Miss Great Britain, Muriel Oxford, and Ernest Hemingway.[85] For now, Vosper is full of domestic schemes. He covers the sitting room walls with brown hessian, then asks an artist friend to paint the bedroom ceiling. Outsized and outlandish, the 'nude figures sprawling about' mirror the cubist experiments of French painter Georges Braque. What one friend – admirably understated – terms 'very modern and original', is a suitably transgressive interior for a young queer man forging a life in London.[86]

Vosper becomes friends with John Gielgud, just beginning his celebrated career. 'I greatly admired this flat', Gielgud remembers. When Vosper moves out in 1927, he capitalises on the success of *The Constant Nymph* at the nearby New

Theatre, takes over the lease, and leaves home. He is there for eight years, often living with his partner, John Perry. 'There was no proper kitchen, and the bathroom, with a rather erratic geyser, was down a very draughty flight of stairs. But otherwise, the place was charming.' As fame and fortune advance, Gielgud rents the 'large attic upstairs', though its 'windows [are] black with the dust of ages'. His renovations are not as extravagant as Vosper's: he 'paint[s] the floor ... buil[ds] in some cupboards and turn[s] it into a spare room and studio'. Such rooms of one's own are a mark of success and a sanctuary.[87]

The aspiring actor Robert Donat is also in his mid-twenties when he and his wife, musician Ella Voysey, 'decide to try their luck in London' in 1930. As later told to journalists, moving to 22 Little St Andrew Street is a rags-to-riches romance:

> [They] took a three room flat in Seven Dials, right among the street markets. It was grimy and noisy and 'the bugs were awful' but they were happy. They had a wonderful view of a public house and of the floodlit Nelson Column in Trafalgar Square. Both their elder children ... were born there.

As they come and go, the Donats pass the waiters, cooks, and hairdressers living around them. Of course it is noisy: beneath and behind sprawl the machine shops and smithies of Comyn Ching metalworks. The view of Trafalgar Square might be journalistic licence, but they look onto the Two Brewers, Elizabeth Prechner's furrier's shop, and the alley leading to Lumber Court.[88] They narrate this as a turning point in their lives together. Donat is invited to star in the *Count of Monte Cristo* (1934): 'so, Robert and Ella Donat sold their flat in Seven Dials ... and set sail for Hollywood'. In this parable of hard work and personal fulfilment, they return – now with a lucrative MGM contract – several years later to 'an old rambling house high up in the Chilterns, with pinewoods and pastures, and a pony for the children'. By then, the 'grimy' tenement that was their first home is empty and crumbling.[89]

Perhaps the Donats are on nodding terms with the bookish young man down the street, who will become one of Britain's most notable designers. Misha Black is born in Baku in 1910, though his wealthy parents soon move to London. In the late 1920s, struggling to get established, Black works at a design studio and attends evening classes at the Central School of Arts and Crafts on Southampton Row. Around 1929, he and fellow artist, Lucy Rossetti, begin a new venture. They find somewhere cheap – two rooms and a toilet – within walking distance of the Central School. Perched high above a wireless supplies shop, once home to a warehouse clerk and family, Studio Z looks down onto the Dials at 29 Little St Andrew Street. To save money, Black sleeps there. Short-lived but prolific, Studio Z designs posters, exhibitions, window displays, letter headers, and bookplates. When they pause and look up from their desks, Black and Rossetti gaze onto the Shaftesbury Hotel, the old Grapes Inn, and new Cambridge Theatre.[90]

Seven Dials provides the necessary domestic and creative space for artists and designers, particularly those working on the margins because of their age, background, or politics. Black hosts the first meeting of what becomes Artists' International – later Artists' International Association (AIA). His friend Clifford Rowe has returned from the Soviet Union impassioned by the possibilities of socialist culture. They convene a group of like-minded peers from the Central School. James Boswell has recently joined the Communist Party; from a working-class socialist family in Oldham, James Fitton and his wife Peggy are artists and illustrators;

Pearl Binder, daughter of Russian-Jewish immigrants, has also returned from the USSR, and is gaining a reputation for her drawings of the area around her Whitechapel home. Leaving Shaftesbury Avenue, Boswell and his wife climb to the 'top of an old building in Seven Dials' and a studio 'furnished with fruit boxes from Covent Garden'. They are 'greatly impressed because the electric light had been cut off and we sat in candlelight'. In this makeshift milieu, Rowe talks animatedly 'about working in the USSR and the need for painters to organise internationally in support of the working-class movement. It was all rather leftish stuff, and you can imagine how romantic it was.'[91]

A rough-and-ready Seven Dials studio feels an appropriate setting for this political genesis. Left-wing, anti-fascist, ferociously committed to art's democratic potential, AIA translates Seven Dials' association with Chartism for an ominous new world. *Hunger Marchers* (1934), its first publication, captures the struggles of the National Unemployed Workers' Movement. Its first exhibition is in an empty shop in Charlotte Street. AIA gains members – six hundred by 1936 – and momentum as the domestic and international situation worsens. *The Social Scene* (1934) is followed by *Artists Against Fascism and War* (1935). Amid such fervour, it is striking that AIA's activism never addresses the local politics of race, class, and capital that coalesced in Seven Dials a decade earlier.

AIA and Misha Black are just passing through. The official stamps in the identity card Black must carry as an 'alien' track his movements through Seven Dials, Charlotte Street, and Bloomsbury, onto Hampstead and the modernist Isokon building – Lawn Road flats – during the 1930s.[92] A change of address denotes professional success, new personal circumstances, affluence – a journey from the margins to mainstream. In different ways, this same journey is undertaken by many ordinary migrants from Italy or Russia who make the Dials their first home in London. Such transience ensures the traces of gentrification only reach so far. Beyond the dwindling population, what is most strikingis how little has changed by the late 1930s. Once you leave St Martin's Lane behind and walk into the Dials, there are few obviously bourgeois residents. The journalist John Wells lodges in Shelton Street with other single men working in nearby theatres and markets; the commercial artist Leonard Haggerty has rooms on Neal Street. It's not much, and the regress of depopulation and decline seems inexorable. Like the slummers who flock to the Cave of Harmony, people like Black and Gielgud tread lightly, leaving little impress on property markets and the place's character.

* * *

It is always a challenge to capture a place and its people. 'When a well-known and small locality such as Seven Dials is mentioned', observes the *Kinematograph Review*, 'and the period is fixed in the present, extreme realism, rather than melodrama, [is] necessary to produce the illusion of life'.[93] It is equally challenging to avoid melodrama when trying to depict Seven Dials. For a new generation of slummers, enduring cliches and past notoriety are hard to avoid. For philanthropists and pleasure-seekers, and the makers and consumers of culture, that is part of the draw. The realities of poverty and decline, in turn, create the material conditions for outsiders to find a place of repose on central London's margins. Empty spaces, cheap rents, affordable rates, and planning blight are the preconditions of what we call gentrification.

No one can call Mabel Lethbridge typical. Despite her privileged background, her journey to Seven Dials is driven by necessity and she stays longer than most. Having lied about her age – she is only 17 – in 1917 Lethbridge is horrifically injured in an explosion at the National Munitions Filling Factory in Hayes. She loses an ear, a lung, and her left leg. Estranged from family, in constant pain, Lethbridge lives hand to mouth for months.[94] Only when she arrives in the Dials around 1920 can she rest. Welcomed into Jarni's – Nellie Rigiani – Lumber Court boarding house, Lethbridge then rents rooms in Litchfield Street. She sells matches, 'minds the door' for a backstreet 'Thieves' Kitchen', then goes into business hiring stools to theatregoers queuing outside the St Martin's and Ambassadors. The reinvention of this 'maimed war heroine', as what a journalist calls 'Peggy, the pioneer chair girl ... one of the personalities of London theatre-land', is an intimate story of resourceful determination in desperate circumstances. It is also shaped by the colourful characters and ad hoc economies Lethbridge encounters in Seven Dials.[95]

In the 1930s, Lethbridge writes movingly about the care and companionship she finds in Lumber Court. Despite its poverty, the area provides the kindness and warmth that are absent elsewhere in her life. Its inhabitants – costermongers, flower sellers, petty criminals – offer food and shelter when she is down and out, protect her from an abusive husband, take her as they find her. In turn, Lethbridge writes about them as people. Even this most sensitive observer cannot avoid cliché and melodrama entirely. Rather than being invisible, anonymous, or a homogenous mass, though, those living in Seven Dials appear as individuals with names, stories, aspirations, and anxieties. They are mostly rounded characters, not caricatures. 'So much do I love and admire them', Lethbridge writes, 'that I regret I am not born of them, and never have been happier than during those years of match-selling and poverty when I was accepted on the Seven Dials'.[96]

At least some outsiders find in Seven Dials an instinctive welcome and authenticity which they contrast with bourgeois snobbery and artifice. 'These Dials dwellers were my friends', Lethbridge writes. 'To them I was a working-class girl.' Yet their affectionate nicknames for her suggest class differences cannot be wished. Local children call her 'Airy', Jarni tells her: 'they says you've got airy fairy ways'.[97] While the name sticks, it is Lethbridge's refusal to raise her daughter here that marks the limits of belonging. When she becomes pregnant, Lethbridge leaves for the 'respectability' of Victoria: 'The people in the Dials lived in unspeakable squalor and I felt I could not join them.'[98]

Proximity is not the same as intimacy. The growing number of outsiders – even those as sympathetic as Lethbridge – drawn into Seven Dials does little to disturb hierarchies of class and race. The traffic of slummers to the neighbourhood is never as great as that to east or south London, moreover. There are fewer opportunities to minister to the souls of those in need. Local restaurants do not attract diners and guidebooks in the same way as Soho: increasingly popular from the 1890s, almost mainstream by the 1930s. Seven Dials remains somehow unfashionable or hidden. Neither poor nor exotic enough to compel the imagination, it is harder to find in photographs, paintings, and films than Bow or Limehouse.

Yet curious visitors still make their way there, just as they have since the 1840s. Even before a new theatre opens in 1930, the pavements bustle with well-heeled strangers seeking redemption, thrills, belonging. As Jim and Emily Kitten pause from their labours to watch the world go to and fro, they might observe a remarkable array of novelists, journalists, artists and actors, aristocrats, and avant-gardists. They might stare at the outrageous spectacle of wealthy and sometimes well-known bohemians travelling down Great White Lion Street to the latest resort: Elsa Lanchester, arresting red hair and home-made cape; Radclyffe Hall and Una Troubridge, smart in collar and tie; Tallulah Bankhead, haughtily glamorous, instantly recognisable. Returning from work in a West End kitchen, they might unwittingly pass Pearl Binder, feverish with ideas after an Artists International meeting, or Robert Donat, trudging home from another performance at the Ambassadors. It neither lasts nor lingers, but for a time Seven Dials is recolonised as a playground for those who do not quite belong.

6

The ghosts of modern London

Little White Lion Street

Just as the Kittens are locking up their cafe for the last time, a modern wonder rises from the ground across the Dials on the corner of Little White Lion Street. The Cambridge Theatre opens in autumn 1930. The ambitious venture of theatrical impresario Bertie Meyer, the Cambridge is designed by the architects Wimperis, Guthrie, and Simpson with dazzling interiors by Serge Chermayeff, best known now for iconic modernist buildings like the De La Warr pavilion in Bexhill on Sea.[1] Chermayeff's work, particularly, astonishes critics. Without and within, the Cambridge is lauded as a stunning technical and aesthetic achievement and an opulent sensory experience. Little wonder that London's latest theatre is a public sensation.

Standing on the pavement of Great White Lion Street, an artist captures an art deco monument, its gleaming facade and neon signs illuminating the Dials beneath. From right outside the old cafe, they reimagine the theatre as a lighthouse towering over the darkened streets behind. Their radiating pencil lines suggest the beams from a bulb. Here, gathering on the pavement, are the fashionable audiences who now flock to the area. A spectacular building of national and international significance has brought light, order, and modernity to Seven Dials, heralding its emergence as a site of leisure and pleasure at London's heart.

The Cambridge is more than a symbol of the new brighter London. Illustrators and photographers, journalists and critics of architecture and theatre make the building a central character in stories of a down-at-heel neighbourhood's transformation. Chermayeff draws an arresting cover for the opening night's souvenir programme, in which blocks of black, grey, and white and a striking sans serif font form the schematic outline of an engine. Interconnected cogs turn upon the axles of a stylised 'CT' logo. The 'Cambridge Theatre' drives 'The Wheels of Progress'. Modernist graphic design evokes both the theatre's aesthetics and its vital motive force in making Britain modern.[2]

The Cambridge is what the future used to look like. Opening night is heralded by journalists and critics as a formative moment in making Britain modern. Yet the strangeness of a theatre on Little White Lion Street means discussion turns on two unlikely contrasts. First, here is a place of mainstream entertainment in a neighbourhood associated with work and working-class housing. Second, ground-breaking modernist architecture is pressed close within surroundings characterised by decline and poverty.

This version of modern London is haunted by the past. Ghosts stalk Seven Dials; spectral figures cross the stage. In the artist's drawing an uncanny figure, aloof and uncomprehending, watches the strange spectacle from across the road. Opening night is a chance to celebrate utopian visions of what London could be, but the traces of local histories are remarkably tenacious. To explore these contradictions, and how they frustrated Seven Dials' remaking, we might follow in the footsteps of the actors, producers, stagehands, and theatregoers who are now drawn to the area. We might

The new Cambridge Theatre.

Figure 6.1 'Architect's drawing of the new Cambridge Theatre'

walk up to an acclaimed building, take a seat in the auditorium, and watch the productions that filled the stage (if not always the seats). We might also cross the road, imagining how those who live and work there understand the area's transformation. In so doing, the hesitancy, contradictions, conflicts, and limits of postwar redevelopment become clear.

* * *

While everyone who visits the Cambridge in autumn 1930 agrees on its far-reaching significance, how they think about the theatre is rooted in an intensely local understanding of its situation. For owners and architects, advertisers and reviewers, and pleasure-seekers flocking to opening night, it *matters* that the capital's newest theatre is in Seven Dials. What brings Bertie Meyer to Little White Lion Street? This is, after all, an ambitious project, fraught with risk, requiring massive capital investment. While grand theatres like the Ambassadors and St Martin's had been built on Seven Dials' boundaries before the war, their backs were turned to the area, which remained a marginal place at London's heart. Remembering his big break – *London Calling*, staged at the Duke of York on St Martin's Lane in 1923 – Noel Coward parses this into self-deprecating humour. While this was the 'first time I had the pleasure of seeing my name in electric lights', the 'gleaming pink bulbs' were on the 'worst' side – 'visible only to pedestrians approaching from the direction of Seven Dials'.[3] Meyer's decision to venture off the beaten track a few years later reflects pressing financial realities and the hard-minded calculations made by entrepreneurs. The arrival of the Cambridge in a cosmopolitan working-class neighbourhood encapsulates a particular moment in the development of the modern theatrical industry.

The Cambridge is not the only venue built beyond the West End's traditional precincts at this time. By 1929 the *Daily Mail* can identify a 'definite tendency to get away from the recognised amusement centre of Piccadilly'. Clustered around Cambridge Circus, five places break ground during this construction boom, including the Dominion (Tottenham Court Road) and Phoenix (Charing Cross Road).[4] There are compelling reasons for the drift east: pressures of space, and the soaring price of land and commercial property on main thoroughfares which are prohibitively expensive, particularly when developers need to invest in prestige buildings and modern equipment. At the same time, speculative investment shifts towards property rather than theatres. As entrepreneurs seek out cheaper locations, the appearance of theatres in 'rather out of the way places' affords opportunities for profit – and irony: the Phoenix, notes one wag, is on the site of an old pickle factory. Theatrical corporations are drawn to Seven Dials for the same reasons as developers like Bracewell Smith and people like the Kittens: cheap property and a central location.[5]

Theatreland's shifting centre of gravity also reflects the assumption that the private car will become the main way for Londoners to move around the city. At the same time as garages appear across the West End, developers look for accessible sites away from main thoroughfares.[6] Holborn Council worry about congestion, but elsewhere backstreet locations like Little White Lion Street are thought to make access and parking easier. Paradoxically, they also seem a sensible response to the cacophony of street noise. Siting a theatre in Seven Dials, notes one newspaper, is 'conditioned by the desire to get away from the roar of traffic which … is beginning to disturb the audiences in some houses'. Memories of the Improvement Scheme mean developers see opportunities to exploit the area's much-anticipated transformation. Despite its character, Seven Dials is 'clearly earmarked for great redevelopment in the shape of a big new road running through it from St Martin's Lane to Oxford Street'. By 1928 the scheme has been mothballed for several years. It is still too good a chance for canny investors to miss.[7]

The Cambridge exemplifies the changing business of theatre. As proprietors work to keep the West End relevant and attractive, a new generation of ostentatiously modern houses addresses the threat of the 'talkie invasion'.[8] Ferocious competition with expanding cinema and dance hall chains means theatrical capital is consolidated into massive conglomerates. The Cambridge Theatre Company is first registered as a private company in 1931. Credited with a nominal share capital of £11,000, it takes over the theatre and 'adopt[s] an agreement with the Seven Dials Estate Company', which owns the site.[9] Within two years, the company is acquired by Sir Harold Wernher's behemoth Associated Theatre Properties for £400,000. The Cambridge becomes part of a theatrical empire, alongside established places like the Adelphi and Apollo. This is a story about the pursuit of profit and power, just as much as Bracewell Smith's property portfolio.[10]

* * *

Overseen by the contractors Gee, Walker, and Slater, the excavations of Willment Bros Ltd break ground in 1928. For the next two years, curious locals, passers-by, and journalists watch a new theatre rise out of old London. For many, the site presages a new era for Seven Dials. It is massive – covering over 10,000 square feet in the triangle between Little White Lion, Great Earl, and Castle Streets – and at the heart of the Dials. Estate agents call it a 'wonderful opportunity for a speculator or building syndicate', though its 'improvement' is protracted and difficult. The freehold is first sold for £30,000 during the flurry of postwar speculation, then exchanges hands again before the site is cleared and sold once more.[11]

Clearance might be the precondition of development, but its unspoken corollary is the deliberate process of ending tenancies and demolition that levels this corner of Seven Dials. Around a dozen dwelling houses and two shops are emptied of people and disappear into a wasteland of rubble – perhaps 160 residents in just over 40 households. At 14 Little White Lion Street, Mary Ann Cutler chars for Feldman & Co., music publishers, on Shaftesbury Avenue; her husband Joseph is a horseman for a local dairy. Number 9 is home to taxi driver Arthur Dolbear, his wife Ellen, and their son Walter, a cinematograph operator in Wardour Street. Then in her late 20s and a skilled tailoress for an upmarket firm in St James's, the couple's daughter, Daisy, has also moved home: after only two years of marriage, her husband, Francis Bennett, was killed in action in France in August 1918. These are the everyday lives that make way for London's new theatre.[12]

For the theatre's boosters and developers, that is all in the past. Now modernist architecture and innovative construction techniques stand in for the progressive impulses driving the 'wheels of progress'. Rather than taking place in isolation, this is envisaged as the first step in a comprehensive local 'improvement'. Twelve months into the project, a photographer captures a geometric skeleton of girders climbing steeply into the sky. Set against the blackened bricks and uneven sash windows of the neighbouring tenement, the sharp-edged steels and right-angles hint at what is to come – 800 tonnes of steel, all told, painstakingly assembled by the labourers of Redpath, Brown, and Company. Seven Dials provides a ready counterpoint against which to dramatise London's newfound modernity. Light needs dark, order needs chaos, and without Seven Dials the Cambridge drains of meaning. That one of the city's 'smartest and most distinguished theatres … [has] risen on the site of one of its most notorious slums' is a compelling strapline for journalists and advertisers. It is also a convenient euphemism, which elides how the people who lived and worked here have been displaced by the 'monstrous machine' of capital.[13]

In many ways, the idea of the Cambridge as a powerful agent of change is moulded around the building's fabric. Approaching from Shaftesbury Avenue, you cannot help thinking that the architects have simply planted this radical new structure into a streetscape where it does not belong. Designed 'on the most modern principles' to weather the vicissitudes of time, it is 'steel-framed with monolithic concrete shell'. As you step out from the narrow corridor of Great White Lion Street, the daunting scale, assertive lines, and luminescent front elevation create an arresting spectacle on a 'commanding site'.[14]

This futuristic skeleton is just one of the Cambridge's faces. Behind the scenes on Castle Street, a skin of Danehill facing bricks cloaks concrete and steel with the yellowing facade familiar to Londoners. Where its grand entrance addresses the Dials, the Cambridge is dressed in Portland stone. This is the stone of Christopher Wren's London – material proxy for enduring tradition, grandeur, and Englishness. Its use here insinuates the Cambridge into a distinguished architectural genealogy, which includes Sir Edwin Lutyens's Cenotaph, the cemeteries of the Imperial War Graves Commission, and celebrated art deco buildings

Figure 6.2 Foyer of the Cambridge Theatre, 1930

like Charles Holden's Senate House. Portland was never the stone of Seven Dials. That is the point: a deliberate contrast to humdrum brick tenements and warehouses materialises the theatre's astounding ambition. 'The architectural standard, if matched in later buildings at Seven Dials should give the whole district an air of distinction', one newspaper remarks. The aesthetic category of distinction stands in for the process through which a 'slum' is cleared, a cosmopolitan neighbourhood made English once more, a new world called into being.[15]

It is only when you pass through the grand entrance that the wonders of the Cambridge became fully apparent. Set within the bustling Dials, the simplicity of the front elevation focuses all attention on the dramatic central tower. Once inside, it is difficult to know where to look. The vestibule is a portal into another world, brimming with an excess of colour, form, and texture. Executed by Waring and Gillow's Modern Art Department, Chermayeff's decorative schema surges on – guiding your footsteps and awe-struck gaze as it propels you towards the auditorium.[16] Beneath your feet circular motifs in terrazzo marble intimate 'the vortex of movement from this point'. Art deco signs, polished cooper doors, and bronze friezes by sculptor Anthony Gibbons Grinling shimmer under futuristic electric lights. Theatregoers are welcomed with 'Music', 'Drama', and 'Dance' – an 'interpretation of the trend of mechanised development from its human aspect to the robot-like central group'.

It is impossible not to gasp when entering the auditorium. Gazing towards the stage and proscenium arch, the repeated symmetry of concealed lighting and transverse ribs high above and graduated shades of colour cascading down across ceiling, upholstery, and carpets exaggerate the illusion of depth. Walls 'sprayed [with] metal leaf' create a sensation akin to entering Tutankhamen's tomb. Settling into your sumptuous seat – wary of the unfamiliar reclining mechanism – you are struck by the small details. Viewed up close, a reading light and ashtray are as arresting as the cavernous auditorium. Ahead over the stage box are two ornamental reliefs – 'abstract representations' of the West End's rhythms and rituals. 'Matinee: A procession of women in sunshine' gives way to 'Evening: Top-hatted men in an illuminated city'. Amid such enchantments, it is hard to believe Seven Dials is so close.[17]

* * *

For contemporaries, construction of the Cambridge is often seen as an attempt to draw Seven Dials from the West End's margins to its centre. We can see this in how photographers and illustrators painstakingly imagine the modern edifice 'ris[ng] on the slums'.[18] Repeated often enough to become a cliché, they invariably frame and crop the theatre to lift it out of its decaying environs. Light radiates from the central tower, windows become brilliant white bulbs, stone gleams. Motorcars and fashionable theatregoers throng the entrance. This is 'Seven Dials, 1930': no longer a congested junction, but a grand piazza rivalling Piccadilly Circus; no longer a cosmopolitan place of home and work, but a playground for well-heeled pleasure-seekers. At a stroke, an artist's pencil effects the transformation politicians, planners, and developers have sought for a decade. The corollary is erasing any trace of Seven Dials' notoriety – the insalubrious, the dangerous, the cast-iron public urinal.[19]

After the striking photograph of a steel skeleton crawling skywards, it only seems possible to show the Cambridge in complete perfection. Perhaps there are two exceptions. In the first – in Chermayeff's personal papers, and never meant for public consumption – white-coated decorators balance on a precarious scaffolding tower as they paint the vaulted ceiling.[20] In the second, published in the *Stage* in September 1930, a photographer captures final preparations for opening night. In many ways, this is a familiar image, cropped to isolate the theatre from its surrounds. Unusually, though, it reveals the backbreaking work and exploitative labour relations that make London modern. Watched by an intrigued bystander, workmen put the finishing touches to the signwriting and neon lights on the front elevation. Along with the tools and materials that are their stock in trade, they embody the necessary labour that secures the illusion of 'progress'.[21]

Serge Chermayeff's map, drawn for the souvenir programme, crystallises the idea that the theatre is transforming

Seven Dials' relationship with the city. Compressing, stretching, and twisting London's scale and orientation, he moves the Cambridge to the centre of fashionable life and leisure. Seven Dials grows. Its streets widen – approximating the famous boulevards of Piccadilly and Regent Street. An impenetrable 'slum' is opened to the circulation of people, cars, and trains. Annotations emphasise the ease of movement: the 'nearest tube stations' – Covent Garden and Leicester Square; Charing Cross overground terminus; parking in Golden Square – all reassuringly close. Streets are smoothed into sweeping curves, tangled backstreets disappear, the passage of cars is made seamless. A hand-drawn map makes 'improvement' a reality.[22]

Chermayeff does not go quite as far as Harry Beck's iconic map of the London Underground, published three years later. His preoccupations are aesthetic rather than technical, his influences modernist design rather than modern electrical circuits. This is not meant to be a functionalist diagram abstracted from the realities of distance and direction. Chermayeff and Beck's cartography shares similar preoccupations, though. Like Beck and the London Passenger Transport Board, Chermayeff is concerned – imaginatively, at least – with accelerating movement around London. Like them, he creates a utopian vision of a networked city.[23]

Efforts to integrate the Dials into the West End create some bizarre distortions. In the programme, the fashionable Restaurant Frascati – 'dejeuner, dinner, dancing nightly' – appears 'three minutes' walk from this theatre'. Even the fittest pedestrian would have struggled to journey from Oxford Street in less than ten minutes. Drivers are imagined speeding along impassable narrow streets, even though 'evening traffic conditions in

Theatreland are exceedingly difficult for owner drivers', as adverts for Offord's Baker Street garage and chauffeur service admit. The map is a knowing fiction, enticing theatregoers into previously unknown districts. It still tells us a great deal about how contemporaries thought – or were encouraged to think – about Seven Dials and its new theatre.[24]

* * *

Opening night at the Cambridge is a sensation. Bertie Meyer's first show is well chosen to heighten anticipation. *Charlot's Masquerade* is the latest of impresario Andre Charlot's long-running West End revues – a *Who's Who* of London's stage, featuring celebrities like Constance Carpenter and Henry Kendall and the high-kicking Charlot Chorus. Top of the bill is Beatrice Lillie, returning to the West End after several years. The result, notes the *Stage*, is 'a hubbub of excitement amongst what would formerly have been styled the denizens of the purlieus of historic, picturesque Seven Dials'.[25]

Breathless theatre critics pay as much attention to their surrounds as the performances. It often seems that the Cambridge itself – 'an open jewel-casket in old gold' – is on stage.[26] Reviewers delight in the 'modern features' that makes their experience so pleasurable: the *Bystander* singles out 'stall seats [that] slide beautifully … when you want to shift your position'.[27] Careful attention to comfort, lighting, ventilation, and acoustics make the sensory and aesthetic experience of theatregoing 'as near perfection as possible'.[28] Inevitably, the production suffers in comparison: 'If *Charlot's Masquerade* disappointed in a few particulars', observe the *Sunday Dispatch*, 'it was because we were expecting it to match in modernity Bertie Meyer's amazing new theatre, and the equally amazing audience collecting there for the house-warming'.[29]

The Cambridge is also a landmark for British architecture – significant enough to warrant an exhaustive review in the *Architects' Journal*.[30] A familiar crowd of reviewers, columnists, socialites, and theatregoers is interspersed with architects and architectural critics, more interested in the building than Beatrice Lillie's singing. In the mainstream and trade press and among professional architects and those teaching in Britain's universities the response is overwhelming. Professor Charles Reilly, director of Liverpool School of Architecture, includes the Cambridge among his 'Landmarks of the Year'. Favourably compared to work by the architectural establishment – including Lutyens' Westminster Housing Scheme and Giles Gilbert Scott's Cropthorne Court in Maida Vale – the Cambridge is among the 'three chief buildings' produced by the coming generation. 'How far has the modernist movement progressed', Reilly asks? The theatre showed that 'when they allow themselves the luxury of curved forms, the modernists can be as exciting and thrilling as when they stick to their pronounced straight lines'.[31]

'London at last has a theatre to compare with the Pigalle of Paris and the Ufa Universum of Berlin', exclaims the *Observer*. Its interiors 'may claim even to surpass any theatre in the modern world'. Here is 'a remarkable building': a major contribution to the international modern movement and the 'first masterpiece in theatre design we have … produced in the so-called "functionalist" manner'. From without, the Cambridge offers 'very little clue' to the spellbinding wonders within. Leaving the street behind, modern technologies and modernist aesthetics are interwoven with astonishing effect:

> standing on the stage to see the Zeppelin like beauty of the upper auditorium, and then to look at the perfect organisation of the stage machinery, light floats, and colour switching, one does not feel that there is any of that usual inconsistency between the two sides of the curtain.[32]

Appearance and experience, frontstage and backstage: all is perfect harmony.

Above all, the Cambridge is reassuringly *British*. Comparisons to the Pigalle underscore how the building becomes entwined with the transnational politics of cultural distinction. Commentators recognise its influences – the 'peculiar decorative scheme appears to be Teutonic', notes the *Stage* – yet are satisfied that British taste and tradition have tempered the excesses of continental modernism.[33] In the 1920s, the Imperial Society of Teachers of Dance modulate the rough edges and sexualised movements of American dances like the Charleston to create an authentically British ballroom style. White dance bands like the Savoy Orpheans smooth out the syncopated African American rhythms of jazz. Now interior designers create a 'fine example of sane modernity': dextrously blending the novel with the familiar achieves a '*style moderne* which is yet not offensive even to English eyes'.[34] Chermayeff's daring interiors will always be contained within a steel, concrete, and Portland stone shell 'constructed of British materials'.[35]

Few critics consider the Cambridge in isolation, then. Discussion dwells more on urban development or cultural politics than the stage. One building stands in for the changing West End, the vigour of modern architecture, competition between theatre, film, and dance halls, and the resilience of a national culture threatened by brash Americanisation and European cosmopolitanism. One journalist calls it 'the best reply to the talkies I have yet encountered'. While older theatres cannot compete with the cinema's opulence, this 'new house ... give[s] points in comfort to the ... most up-to-date of the talkie palaces'.[36] More excitable observers discern the triumph of taste over ignorance. Exemplifying the West End's resurgence, the theatre is pressed into service in the ferocious 'battle of the brows'. For the *Sunday Times*, the Cambridge 'bespeaks sophisticated entertainment. It can never be the herding place of the aghast'. Woven into the opposition between 'sophistication' and the 'herd' are pervasive assumptions about social class and cultural distinction. Discerning theatregoers are set against the excitable masses flocking to the cinema. A purpose-built theatre, an imposing building, and sumptuous interior distance it from the trashiness of commercial mass culture.[37]

In Seven Dials, this competition between stage and screen plays out in microcosm. In May 1930, as the Cambridge nears completion, prolific director Maurice Elvey announces construction of Britain's first talkie studio further down Great Earl Street. Elvey is best known for successful films like *Hindle Wakes* (1927) and *Sally in our Alley* (1931) – the romantic comedy in which Gracie Fields makes her screen debut. If, like Meyer, his latest venture makes the most of cheap commercial property, it also builds on a significant cluster of expertise and infrastructure that has emerged around Seven Dials. Elvey must have known the area. Before the war he directed silent features for the Motograph Film Company, based at Motograph House, two minutes from the Cambridge at the junction of West Street and St Martin's Lane. From 1913, as well as Motograph, the building's studios, vaults, offices, and screening facilities accommodated ventures including the Phillips film company. Between 1926 and 1928, the pioneering inventor John Logie Baird's company Television Limited rents a top floor studio. Baird demonstrated how to broadcast moving images in Frith Street, Soho, but it is from Seven Dials that television pictures are first transmitted from London to New York.

Compared to the Cambridge, Elvey's audacious initiative offers a very different vision for the future of the culture industries. The studio can film in colour as well as with sound, using cutting-edge technology patented by the Raycol British Corporation. Despite the company's boosterism and grand plans – too grandiose, suggest *Truth*, concerned that investors were being duped – only one feature-length film is made using the Raycol process: *School for Scandal* (1930).[38] Company and studio had disappeared from Seven Dials by 1932, but the area remained integral to the business of film production and distribution. Renamed Film City House, the West Street building is still going in the late 1930s. It is joined by the Film Transport Company, based in Shelton Street, and – significantly – the British outpost of the massive Metro-Goldwyn-Mayer pictures, whose offices and private theatre are at 19–21 Tower Street from the late 1920s. As well as competing for audiences, theatreland and the burgeoning film industry jostle for space in central London.

Above all, opening night is a social event – a *Society* event. Since the 1860s, journalists, writers, and filmmakers have scoured Seven Dials for material. For at least a decade, daring slummers and self-conscious bohemians have been drawn to its nightlife. With the arrival of the Cambridge, Seven Dials momentarily goes mainstream. Watching the great and good arrive, even the most world-weary reviewer is unexpectedly 'breathless'. A casual bystander 'would have seen the most amazing collection of celebrities in Europe. Lady Louis Mountbatten, Edgar Wallace, with long cigarette holder, Michael Arlen, with a cynical smile, every well known stage star in London, authors, playwrights'. Aristocrats, novelists, men-about-town: no wonder the *Sunday Dispatch* was 'startled'.[39]

In the short term, at least, Seven Dials is successfully incorporated into the West End. The Cambridge follows the rhythms of Society – becomes part of the fashionable philanthropic round. Somewhere that had invariably fallen within the purview of court reporters now features in 'Court and Society' columns. Gossip columnists watch Princess Beatrice and the Duchess of York arrive at matinees in aid of the Winter Distress League.[40] Glossy magazines allow readers to gaze as 'Lady May Cambridge, great niece of her Majesty the Queen, took the part of Queen Victoria at the Children's Victorian Court Matinee'. Just seven years after May's uncle had scandalously crawled in the dirt, Seven Dials has been made safe for a new generation of royals.[41]

For optimists, here is compelling evidence that 'times are changed in Seven Dials'.[42] When Jim Kitten first appeared in court in 1923, the fear that made a woman pause before passing the cafe preoccupied police and journalists. By 1930, a cheerful young woman's appearance outside the Cambridge personifies the area's newfound respectability. The *Daily Mail*'s bemused 'Onlooker' watches the 'arrival of a gallery first nighter ... 31 hours before the curtain rises'. 'You have a most amusing time watching people going by', she comments. If this nonchalant 'pioneer' exemplifies how the 'American craze for record breaking has already reached this country', she also prompts civic pride. 'That an unescorted woman can do that in Seven Dials', formerly 'one of the most dangerous places for harmless people to pass', bespeaks the dizzying pace of 'progress'. Such comments studiously ignore the frenzied panic of the past decade. In such comforting stories of London made modern, the putative safety of a woman walking alone at night is a powerful fiction.[43]

Amid this whirl, the paradox of a new theatre in an old 'slum' is a constant refrain. Whether it prompts irony or incomprehension, humour or historical analysis, whimsical nostalgia or satisfaction, the starting point is the same: opening a venue like the Cambridge somewhere like this makes no sense. 'That it should have appeared in Seven Dials, of all places, is one of those curious anomalies which London delights in', concludes the *Observer*.[44]

* * *

Despite the giddy rhetoric and utopian dreams of developers and planners, no one followed where the Cambridge Theatre led. For at least five decades, the theatre was haunted by the failure of the Seven Dials and Drury Lane Improvement Scheme. Opening night celebrated the area's newfound modernity. It was hard to sustain the conceit that it marked a radical break with the past, however.

Look closely, and the building itself betrays the tensions between past and present. In the auditorium, Chermayeff's interiors clash with the landscape artist and Royal Academician George William Leech's staid painting of bygone Seven Dials. On the massive safety curtains gliding across stage, where all eyes converge, Leech daubs a thick veneer of history on modern technologies and fire-retardant materials protecting audiences and workers.[45] Bastardising contemporary obsessions with aerial photography, Leech imagines soaring above Seven Dials. From his dizzying vantage point, the dials become a clock face with seven hands marking passing centuries, rather than hours. Beginning in 1330, the result is a fascinating 'resume of London history'.[46]

Leech's aim is not historical verisimilitude – far from it: there has never been a turreted castle or grand civic buildings here. Instead, the device conveniently allows him to imagine the 'wheels of progress' driving the 'Glorification of Seven Dials'. The Cambridge becomes an 'emblem of the emergence of the district from its ancient reputation'.[47] Local histories are deliberately open-ended: painted in outline only, futuristic skyscrapers rise from the triangle between Little White Lion and Great St Andrew streets. As the modern metropolis reaches into Seven Dials, audiences are asked if the theatre is a turning point or conclusion.[48]

Neither, some answer – and not just the cynical or critical. Opening night's 'lyrical ecstasy' is an easy target for *Tatler*'s mockery:

> No mention of fried fish ... to interrupt the ambience of romance! Well, what matter? Hats off to anyone who can find romance ... in Seven Dials. Let us rejoice that beauty is now where formerly was none. Someday, when a wiser and a richer Parliament sweeps away the slums, our great-great-grandchildren will point to the old Cambridge Theatre and say: 'This was the first oasis ... *palmam cui meruit*'.[49]

For sure, the Cambridge *is* beautiful. It is also a gauche newcomer, ill-fitted for its environs. 'Let he who merits the palm possess it' – a fertile oasis amid arid surroundings, the Latin suggests. There is a ready olfactory contrast nearby on Little Earl Street: Paul Leibovitch's fried fish shop, which theatregoers walking from Cambridge Circus might have passed. Sceptical about the significance of *this* moment, *Tatler* still takes it for granted that gentrification will eventually remake central London. It might take generations, but progressive politics and capital's 'monstrous machine' will inevitably bring order and 'romance' to Seven Dials.

What do those who lived and worked in the surrounding streets make of this? What do Paul Leibovitch or Emily Kitten or any of those dismissed as the 'denizens' of Seven Dials think of the theatre planted in their midst? Leibovitch and his wife Antoinette live in Stoke Newington, but their shop has been there for years. Like everyone else, they watched and listened for two years as the neighbourhood was consumed by the din of a colossal building site. Now an overbearing building – an alien interloper, different in scale, appearance, and purpose to everything else – has appeared. Now they watch as a thousand or more theatregoers roll in and out each evening (and some matinee afternoons) like the ocean's waves. Remember the illustration: a solitary figure across Little White Lion Street contemplates the extraordinary sight of fashionable Londoners arriving at the Cambridge. Lines in black pencil suggest surprise and the sartorial codes of class – a cap and short jacket; the open road dramatises the chasm between worlds.[50]

These are not the sort of people who contribute to the *Sphere*. No one who lives in Seven Dials writes a gossip column in the *Daily Mail*. For now, at least, the enigmatic figure remains silent. We might speculate, though – assembling the fragments of evidence, taking our cue from a nagging sense of the theatre's out-of-placeness. Tickets for the dress circle cost as much as ten shillings and sixpence. If you are willing to chance it without a reservation, you can get into the cheap seats – the upper circle – for two shillings.[51] That isn't extortionate, but it makes the Cambridge prohibitively expensive for those working on the service economy's precarious margins, whose weekly earnings are counted in shillings and pence. If the auditorium is unaffordable for many locals, there are parallel barriers between theatregoers and the eating places and drinking haunts they pass en route. None of the restaurants and bars advertising in the programmes are local. An adventurous few might have called into Leibovitch's shop, eaten at Giuseppe Sterlini's dining rooms, or had a drink in the Bunch of Grapes on their way there or back. For most theatregoers, journeying in from homes and hotels elsewhere in London or beyond, a night at the Cambridge is probably accompanied by dinner or dancing somewhere else in the West End.

Within Seven Dials, then, the Cambridge is a spectacle to witness, not something to experience. Or, at best, work not pleasure defines its significance. Proximity to central London meant those working in theatres and music halls had found cheap accommodation in nearby tenements and rooming houses for decades. It is not an abrupt change, but after 1930 the new theatre consolidates the area's importance as a place of work and residence within the theatrical industry. The West End's backstage infrastructure sprawls into local workshops and warehouses – the theatrical costumier Morris Hyman in Castle Street, theatrical stores in Tower Street, next door to Metro-Goldwyn-Mayer's offices.

Census records, directories, and surveys suggest a growing number of stagehands, scene shifters, theatre dressers, ticket agents, stage managers, actors, dancers, and music hall artistes find accommodation nearby. Among the eight people living cheek by jowl across the four floors of 31 Neal Street are the theatrical producer David Isaacs, theatrical agent Phillip Hindin, and stagehand George Beardsmore. Not all of them work at the Cambridge, of course. It still seems the theatre's local resonance is shaped by markets in labour and residential property.[52] Viewed up close, the 'wheels of progress' do little more than widen a growing geographical and temporal divide between the area's longstanding status as a place of work and home and its newfound popularity as a playground for the well-to-do. Whether they are set down and whisked away by car or hurry towards the light from stations beyond its bounds, the distant strangers drawn to Seven Dials rarely linger.[53]

In the end, the contradictions and limits of Seven Dials' remaking are most visible as the incongruity of a prestigious building in Little White Lion Street. Photographs, drawings, and maps make it impossible to escape how the Cambridge remains an island of stone, steel, and straight lines in a tangle of blackened brick and decaying tenements. If the new theatre is a lighthouse, its beacon only makes the darkness beyond more impenetrable. Ominous and mysterious, the warehouses and tenements of Little White Lion and Great Earl Streets inevitably appear in outline – bereft of form and people, a menacing background for fashionable theatregoers and a fashionable theatre. An impermeable border runs along the line between light and shade. Modernity is a facade, the dissipating light too weak to penetrate the shadows.[54]

* * *

In the hubbub around the Cambridge, there is no hint that Seven Dials had recently been known as London's 'Black colony'. Journalists acknowledge its notoriety, but either place this in the distant past or rework it as picturesque clichés of bygone London. The result is a whitewashed version of Seven Dials, which conceals the area's contemporary history. The ghosts of the 'Black colony' still haunt the Cambridge. Jim Kitten reappears as a crudely drawn apparition on stage, rather than a local resident or business owner. From musical comedies to melodramas of empire, theatrical productions betray the racist subconscious of the 1930s.

The Cambridge opens with the spectacular *Charlot's Masquerade*, a 'charming revue' which wows critics and audiences and is filmed for British Pathé's *Eve's Film Review*.[55] It is written largely by Ronald Jeans, Andre Charlot's long-time collaborator. Known as 'one of the West End's most reliable sources of undemanding, expertly crafted social comedy', Jeans takes his cue from the theatre and brings musical revue up to date.[56] The show is a period piece in other ways. In 'The New Education', Jeans turns his craft to the 'influence of the American Talkies' on 'English home life.[57] In the 1920s, commentators worry about the damaging effects of new forms of mass culture on British society. Where pessimists saw untold dangers in Hollywood, jazz, and the Charleston, Jeans finds rich humour. Laughter comes from the cruelties of racial difference. The 'effects of negro drama of the Porgy-cum-Hallelujah type on Mayfair' become a parodic domestic comedy.[58] Publicity photographs show the cast falling to their knees, bodies and faces unnaturally contorted, hands raised in ecstasies of devotion. By caricaturing Black performance styles, Jeans suggests how ridiculous Britons might become if they do not guard against the influence of African American culture. It is the disquieting juxtaposition of Mississippi and Mayfair – byword for patrician Englishness – and Lillie 'bursting as a Society woman into a negro-spiritual, "Everybody talkin' about the Carlton ain't goin' there"', that makes white audiences laugh.[59]

Jeans' writing carries the same prejudice that shapes the struggles around the Kittens' cafe. Here is a warning about the erosion of racial boundaries and dangers of cultural corruption set to music, choreographed as dance, and played for laughs.[60] It is not so far from Seven Dials' streets to the West End stage, everyday realities to exaggerated performances, *John Bull*'s vindictive sensation to Jeans' 'witty' sketch.[61] Such ideas are an intimate part of metropolitan culture. 'Two of the very best items of the revue are imported from America', note the *Daily Mirror*, 'but there is *a brilliant English idea* showing the influence on family life of the negro drama'.[62]

The ghosts of the 'Black colony' reappear in 1935, when the Cambridge revives the hugely successful *White Cargo*.[63] Set on a Gold Coast plantation, this 'play of the primitive' explores the scandalous relationship between a plantation manager and 'vicious half-caste', Tondelayo. Rather than ruthless beneficiaries of empire, white planters, missionaries, and administrators now appear as its victims.[64] Tondelayo is played by character actress Olga Lindo: in this 'red-hot drama of the tropics', observes one newspaper, Lindo 'in a chocolate make-up, is the dusky vamp'.[65] One minor character provides opportunities for Black actors: Charles Keene reprises his role as 'native servant' Jim Fish, though reviewers rarely mention him and he appears last in cast lists.[66] Born in Antigua in 1877, Keene had lived in London for decades, working in the West End and provincial theatre. His wife, Gertrude, and three children were all born in Britain.[67] A decade earlier, Keene might have kept company with actors and musicians like Frank Kennedy in the Kittens' cafe. Now he comes to Seven Dials to perform on its stage, not to socialise in its meeting places. A decade earlier, men and women from Sierra Leone, Nigeria, and the Gold Coast made a kind of home in Great White Lion Street. Now these places are brought to the Dials as the exotic setting for a 'drama of the white man's lot in tropical Africa'.[68]

Although Bertie Meyer promises a modern theatrical spectacle, he is also quickly forced to look back to keep audiences coming into Seven Dials. In summer 1931, Archibald de Bear's 'omnibus entertainment' *At the Sign of the Seven Dials* revisits the eighteenth and nineteenth centuries. Following generations of slumming writers and filmmakers, de Bear seeks to 'make capital of the district in which the Cambridge is situated'.[69] 'The Seven Dials' is the tortuous name for an ensemble cast and an entertainment 'indigenous to the locality in which it takes place'.[70] Yet de Bear reduces an unruly cosmopolitan history to comedic stereotypes and cliched costermongers – striking from the picturesque outfits created by the Covent Garden costumiers B. J. Simmons. Renowned for their authentic period costumes, Simmons' designs – a balladmonger, policeman, and girl – show how a new revue strove to create nostalgia for the old London.[71]

De Bear's most pointed essay in local history is a 'dialogue with music interludes':

A to B, Renee Gadd, H. Saxon-Snell and Betty Stockfeld in "The Sign of the Seven Dials," the new entertainment at the Cambridge Theatre.

Figure 6.3 Scene from *At The Sign of the Seven Dials*, 1931

> Miss Betty Stockfield, and Miss Renee Gadd, as two fashionable young women of the hour straying into that old scene of squalor and violence, the Sesven Dials, now in process of further transmogrification, hold discourse with the oldest inhabitant, who deplores the absence of murders and fights, and resents the intrusion of beauty, order, and smartness which are relatively so dull.[72]

Finally, the uncanny figure from the artist's illustration takes life on stage. Photographs show the veteran H. Saxon-Snell lecturing the 'bright young things of the present day' before art director Clifford Pember's 'tableau curtain'. Reimagining Seven Dials from above, Pember again creates a sanitised version of streets through which audiences had just walked.[73] Vivid contrasts between youth and age, cloth caps and cloche hats, exemplify a magical 'transmogrification'. No surprise a bewildered Saxon-Snell 'wonders what the old Dials are coming to'.[74] If theatregoers laugh at the intergenerational incomprehension, the joke needs the comforting recognition that the 'absence of murders and fights' should be welcomed, not mourned. Safe in their seats, they enjoy a story of progress in which the Cambridge is both set and protagonist.

The idea that there has been a break with the past does not work, however. The 'oldest inhabitant' is a very present reminder of what had been. Whether arriving on foot or in a motorcar, once you have left St Martin's Lane behind, there is little 'order and smartness' to see en route to the Cambridge. Savvy theatregoers might wonder how profound progress had been. Darkened streets, deteriorating tenements, and empty buildings evidence the area's continued decline, just as much as the surveys of public health officials.[75]

By 1931, all this is just too familiar. *Sign of the Seven Dials* is a cynical mass market knock-off of Elsa Lanchester and Harold Scott's knowing music-hall nostalgia – a pallid imitation of the real thing. Reviews are excoriating. Old-fashioned, bereft of spark and intellect, the revue is more appropriate for a seaside matinee than the West End – no competition for the Co-Optimists, wowing crowds nearby.[76] Of the 'musical entertainment', observes the waspish *Sunday Times* critic James Agate – perhaps writing his copy over a drink in the Shaftesbury Hotel – 'one would only say that piers have seen worse, and piers have seen better'.[77] Things get worse. De Bear tells journalists that 'he ceased to be associated with it after its first performance'. Dismissed by its director, derided by critics, then shunned by audiences, the show is pulled after five nights.[78] A month after opening, the company cut their losses and sell the set, costumes, and curtain.[79] An embarrassing commercial failure is a neat metaphor for the limits of 'improvement'.

It is symptomatic that the most striking photograph of George Leech's safety curtain plays havoc with the linear stories of urban redevelopment that become commonplace in 1930. From the upper circle, looking down to the stage below, a photographer tries to capture the auditorium's audacious scale. Placed at the bottom right corner, Leech's visual history is framed by the dazzling proscenium arch. The effect is both stunning and unnerving. Unnaturally elongated by the vertiginous vantage point, the repeated lines of vaulted ceilings, curving seats, and chrome rails create the illusion of a mechanical shutter or eye in motion. Reminiscent of Cyril Power or Sybil Andrews's linocuts of London's underground, the safety curtain becomes a vortex that compresses and distorts the passage of time. Boundaries between past and present swirl and blur. Time and place are in perpetual motion.[80]

* * *

Ghosts walked Seven Dials through the 1930s, called into being by the searching light of a new theatre, animated by obsessive retellings of local histories, dramatised by the decay that leached across its environs. That the Cambridge could be made to exemplify the making of modern London depended upon its striking distance from those surrounds. Whatever they thought about its architectural merits and historical significance, contemporaries invariably dwelt on the incongruity of a modernist cathedral of culture on Little White Lion Street. Where optimists found a prompt for comforting fables of leaving a disreputable past behind, dissenting voices saw the contradictions of 'improvement'.

The excitable confidence of opening night was short-lived. Although the spectacular failure of *Sign of the Seven Dials* was unusual, over the next decade many productions struggle to attract audiences and run for just a few days or weeks.[81] To remain viable, the West End's wonder relies on regular film screenings. Colonised by trade shows, the Cambridge becomes somewhere London's film industry launches its latest releases. They include documentaries like *Baboona* (1935), filmed in East Africa by 'famous explorers' Martin and Osa Johnson. *Kinematograph Weekly* praises the aerial footage of Mount Kilimanjaro and a 'thrilling sequence [in which] natives armed only with spears chase the dreaded and dangerous rhino out of their territory'.[82] Screenings also include 'non-commercial' events sponsored by organisations like the International Brigade Dependants and Wounded Aid Committee (1938). Counting Eleanor Rathbone and J. B. Priestley among its patrons, the committee is run by Charlotte Haldane from ramshackle offices on nearby Litchfield Street. As the Spanish Civil War intensifies, local markets in culture and commercial property again allow the radical internationalist politics of the Artists International Association to find a home in Seven Dials.[83]

Such events are a far cry from the exultant visions of 1930. When the Cambridge opened it was still just about possible to believe in similarly utopian schemes for making Seven Dials anew. Somewhere that ostensibly exemplified capital's transformative power became a cautionary reminder of the dangers of hubris. It was soon clear that the 'wheels of progress' would not turn full circle. Writing in support of a proposed national theatre in South Kensington in 1937, George Bernard Shaw dismissed the 'morbid taste in sites' among those 'clamouring for another theatre in the slums of Leicester Square or Seven Dials'.[84] The whimsical *Sign of the Seven Dials* belied the area's persistent notoriety. While de Bear's revue lamented the decline of theft and violence, court registers and newspaper reports showed how such concerns endured. Nostalgia for a picturesque rookery sat uneasily against efforts to address the problems of poverty and 'slum' housing.

Jim and Emily Kitten were there when the Cambridge opened: they would live in sight of the theatre for another decade. Intimate histories of Seven Dials were woven into the theatre's fabric, but the recent past – their past – was largely erased, even as scenes in productions like *Charlot's Masquerade* bore the imprint of colonial encounters. After the catastrophe of the libel trial the 'Black colony' disappeared from public view and popular memory. White visitors were now more likely to see racial difference on stage than on the street. When the pioneering choreographer and dancer Katherine Dunham wowed audiences at the Cambridge with her West Indian Ballet in 1952, there was no recognition of the rich lives and bitter struggles that had gone before.[85]

7
Names and histories
Little St Andrew and Little Earl Streets

In 1924, reflecting on the quickening pace of change evident on the streets of central London, the journalist and author of *London Scenes* (1920), William Titterton, observes: 'Seven Dials may shortly be given a new and fashionable name, now that the district is shedding its thieves in favour of restaurants'. Such sentiments are not uncommon in the years after the Great War, when Seven Dials becomes subject to the ambitions of politicians, planners, and property developers and their utopian fantasies of what the city might become. If Titterton is attuned to the process through which London was being transformed, he also recognises the importance of naming. That office blocks, eateries, and grand boulevards are poised to displace a decaying slum, he suggests, makes the old associations of 'Seven Dials' dangerous. Almost thirty years earlier, the area's respectable residents had petitioned the St Giles Board of Works demanding that its name be changed. Now Titterton again presents the meanings that cling to a name as ill-suited to the pursuit of profit, prestige, and pleasure. It would take a radical break with the past to secure the area's newfound status. To make London modern, first you had to unmake Seven Dials.[1]

Titterton might have had in mind a recent sharp exchange of letters in the *Holborn and Finsbury Guardian*. Over winter 1920–21, politicians from Holborn, Westminster, and Marylebone become embroiled in a public disagreement about what to call the junction of Oxford Street and Tottenham Court Road. For Holborn's elected representatives, the proposed St Giles Circus is unacceptable. In December 1920, Arthur Chapman, avowed 'lover of topography and ... place names', and leader of Holborn Conservative Association, writes to the editor about this 'unfortunate name'. Chapman is worried about confusion with the better-known church of St Giles, Cripplegate. More problematic, are deep-rooted memories of the 'St Giles slums' of the past – the 'evil reputation' that 'clung to Seven Dials throughout all its history'. Optimistic that the 'last slums ... will be swept away' by the Seven Dials and Drury Lane Improvement Scheme, he nonetheless concludes: 'I cannot think that the people of London will willingly allow that a name which must become a household word amongst them should have such associations.' The fine sounding 'Bloomsbury Circus' is more fitting.[2]

Chapman draws a stinging response from Arthur Field, communist, internationalist, and secretary of Holborn Labour Party.[3] 'There is scarcely a mile of London town that has not some ancient scandal attached to it,' Field points out. Besides, the slums of St Giles are long forgotten. Chapman's prejudice means bad history is also bad politics. Seven Dials' problems cannot be removed at the dash of a pen. 'Burying ... St Giles under Bloomsbury will not whitewash St Giles', nor will a new name conjure a 'University or ... Hotel District' from the ether.[4] Chapman insists on the last word. 'How little the St Giles slums are forgotten', he observes, 'may be judged by the fact that in the last few days London has seen an elaborate American cinema film entitled "The Duchess of Seven Dials".' It is distasteful, at best, that a popular film connects 'the highest of titles with the most degrading associations'.[5]

Titterton will be proven wrong in predicting the renaming of Seven Dials, but over the next two decades the question of what to call a neighbourhood and its streets never really goes away. To understand why – and what is at stake in these protracted and often bad-tempered conversations – we might turn to an intense local controversy over plans to rename Little St Andrew Street. Playing out in the late 1930s through overwrought petitions, angry letters, and tense council meetings, a short-lived furore exacerbates tensions within and between Holborn Borough Council and the London County Council and pits long-standing local business owners and residents against what appear to be distant authorities. Reading between the lines of dry committee minutes and placing the dispute within a snapshot of a particular street at a particular moment in time, allows us to glimpse the different ways in which Seven Dials was understood in the twenties and thirties – by planners and politicians, for sure, but also by those ordinary people who make their lives there after the Great War. Above all, the episode underscores the power of a name to carry stories about a neighbourhood's past. For the proposal's local opponents, the problem is that the new names suggested had far-reaching and damaging consequences in the present. If some observers see injury in the name St Giles, it is an unimaginable absurdity that somewhere might be called after Seven Dials.

* * *

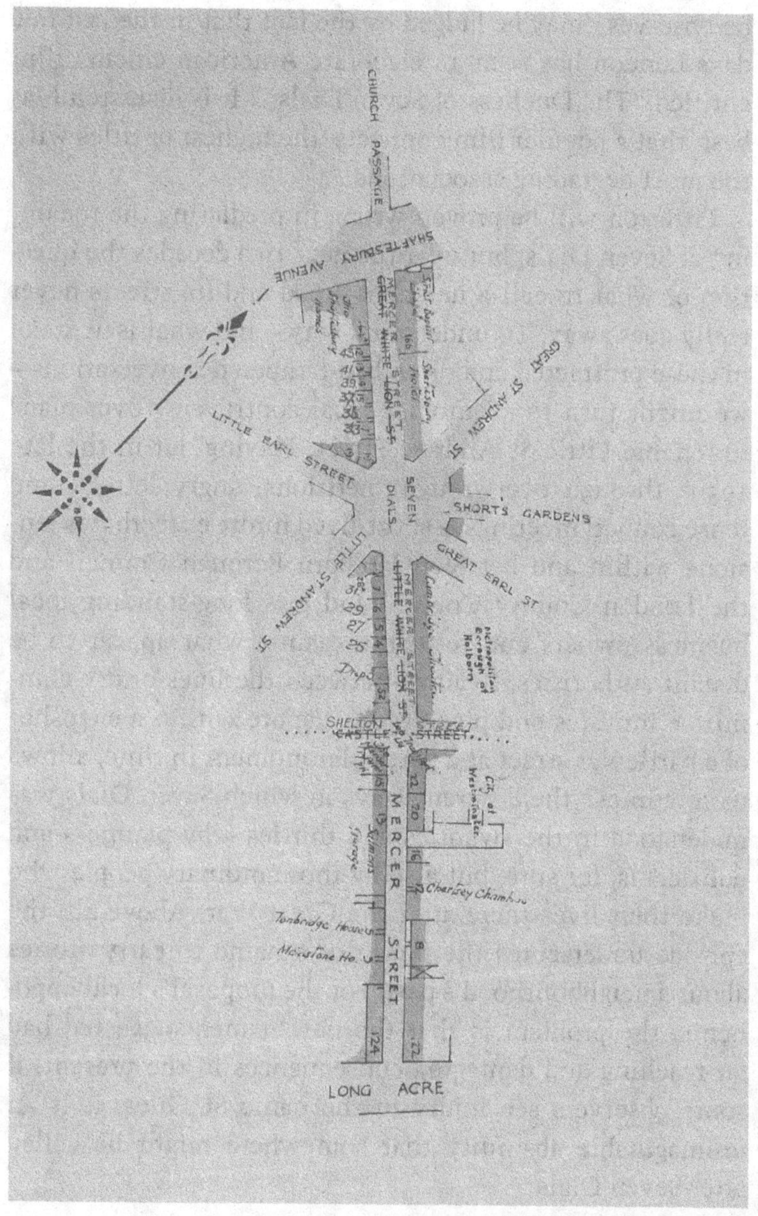

Figure 7.1 ~~Great White Lion~~ Mercer Street, 1938

The polemic over Little St Andrew Street belies its mundane bureaucratic origins. In 1934, the LCC begins an ambitious review of London's street names. For five years, the Street Naming Subcommittee and the council's superintending architect, Edwin Wheeler, work methodically to rationalise the mishmash of names that had accreted over centuries. The 'simplification of nomenclature' aims to speed the movement of people, post, goods, and public services like the Fire Brigade around London. As well as removing names duplicated across boroughs, the subcommittee tackles the unnecessary complexity created by the prefixes 'Upper', 'Lower', 'Great', and 'Little'. If these modernising impulses are metropolitan in scope, they are channelled and – sometimes – challenged by intensely local understandings of geography and history.[6]

The process starts in July 1934, when Wheeler is asked to identify problematic street names: his report, submitted the next autumn, lists several thousand.[7] While Wheeler proposes alternatives in each case, the subcommittee recognises the sensitivities of local opinion. At least to begin with, their approach is open and consultative. Residents on affected streets are notified of proposed changes and invited to respond. Officials hold conferences with borough councils, continuing to consult and seek alternatives where they disagree.[8] The subcommittee meets Holborn counterparts on 10 October 1935, and exchanges letters and reports regularly over the coming years.[9] As the consultation drags on, though, it must seem that the mammoth task is being ground down under the weight of petitions, letters, and editorials. Objections are usually generic – short notice, potential confusion, 'unnecessary and expensive'.[10] From Little Earl Street, the secretary of Home and Colonial Stores argues: 'the present name ... is old established ... any change of name would confuse the buying public'.[11] Yet Wheeler's proposals are mostly unproblematic. In Seven Dials, Castle Street is incorporated into Shelton Street and Little and Great Earl Streets into the radial thoroughfare of Earlham Street with little public comment.[12]

The renaming of Little and Great St Andrew Streets proves incendiary, however. In summer 1936, the unsuspecting Wheeler serves notices of their proposed incorporation as 'Seven Dials Street' to ninety-six residents and business owners.[13] This is a routine bureaucratic process, but what follows is a dramatic and widely reported 'Seven Dials protest'. Those who live and work in the streets mobilise against the proposal. A concerted campaign of letter-writing, petitioning, newspaper briefings, and deputations ratchets up the pressure on the LCC. As the dispute continues, the accumulating correspondence and lengthening paper trail left by fraught committee meetings reflects the time the proposal absorbs. Perhaps the most protracted renaming case in Holborn, it takes eighteen months for the protagonists to finally reach an agreement. Dry formulaic committee minutes struggle to contain the strength of raw emotion swirling around 'Seven Dials Street'.[14]

Why was this proposal so provocative? William Titterton might have overestimated the pace of Seven Dials' transformation, but he grasped how names, histories, and geographies are bound together in how Londoners make sense of their city. For the Bright Young People who go slumming on the streets and the self-consciously bohemian avant-garde who flock to the Cave of Harmony, shady nightclubs and drinking haunts, and the neighbourhood's studios and furnished rooms, Seven Dials' notoriety can be a powerful draw and compelling selling point. At least some of the publicity around the opening of the Cambridge Theatre trades on the area's shady reputation. For theatrical impresarios and some theatregoers, the name Seven Dials itself possesses striking power, investing everyday activities – eating a meal, seeing a show – with the frisson of transgression, of dangerous encounters with other classes and 'races'. Safe under the streetlights or in a luxurious auditorium, white consumers can reimagine a short walk from Shaftesbury Avenue or St Martin's Lane as a slumming adventure.

At the same time, Seven Dials was overburdened with the weight of the past. A byword for disorder and crime, its name threatens local prestige and obstructs its ability to attract pleasure-seekers to the neighbourhood. In June 1930, shortly before the Cambridge Theatre's grand opening, newspapers report a hurried last-minute change of identity. 'This house was at first to have been called the Seven Dials Theatre, but it was found that well-to-do theatre-goers imagined that to be somewhere in the East End, instead of a few yards off Charing Cross Road.'[15] Imaginatively placed nearer Whitechapel than the West End, the anticipated confusion of prospective visitors from suburban London and beyond marks Seven Dials as out of place. Unlikely, even troubling, the idea of a Seven Dials Theatre unsettles the geographical knowledge that shapes the movements of theatregoers across London and their decisions about which venues to visit. 'It may have been the disparaging suggestion of the address that brought to nought the plans', one observer concludes.[16]

This is why 'Seven Dials Street' causes such fury. By the time Wheeler reports in December 1936, he has received twenty letters and a petition signed by fifty-two people 'objecting to the proposal'. Beginning with their 'grave apprehension' at the proposal, the petitioners explain:

> 'Seven Dials' still carries with it a very unsavoury name in London, the provinces and abroad. The various guidebooks to London refer to the name and its associations in a manner that is not likely to ensure confidence in business.

Still the past weighs heavily on Seven Dials. The stories that stick to a name disrupt both the LCC's attempt to modernise London's streets and the viability of local commercial concerns. Correspondents separately 'characterise the new name as the worst that could have been selected'. An enforced move to 'Seven Dials Street', they argue, would be 'detrimental to their business'.[17] Taken aback at the strength of feeling, Wheeler concludes: 'the Committee will doubtless not desire to proceed with the name' having 'regard to the opposition which the present proposal has aroused'. The subcommittee asks Holborn Council to suggest alternative names, and – unusually – consider 'receiving a deputation from the petitioners'.[18]

Rehearsing debates that crystallised around the short-lived 'Seven Dials Theatre', those with the most intimate perspective on Little and Great St Andrew streets reject the proposal outright. No longer a placename, for them 'Seven Dials' is a totem of urban decline and danger. Slummers and advertisers had long traded on these links. Now, however, local campaigners identify such 'unsavoury associations' as a threat to the reputation of the area and its businesses. Overflowing with meaning, 'Seven Dials' is a repository of stories so powerful that it derails the onward march of modern commercial development.

* * *

It is not enough to know why so many people rejected 'Seven Dials Street'. Understanding what was at stake means also knowing who they were and where they were writing from – thinking about the people and place in which the protest took shape. For the London columnist of the *Edinburgh Evening News*, the outcry evidences a changed Seven Dials. 'Can it be that snobbery exists not only in Belgrave Square but "in the lowly air of Seven Dials"?' Seen from afar, the answer is yes: residents of Little and Great St Andrew Streets were 'objecting to the Dialish association being rubbed in'.[19] But this analysis is wrong. Frustratingly, the original document does not survive in the LCC archives. We know the petition 'represent[s] the occupiers of all the shop and business premises in the streets', though, and from here can piece together the unlikely coalition that forms in the late 1930s.[20] Far from ambitious developers or arriviste gentrifiers seeking to stamp a newfound kudos on the area, most of the signatories are residents, small shopkeepers, and business owners who have been there for years. Enmeshed in the cosmopolitan community that strove to make their lives in Seven Dials, they act at a moment when the streets teeter on the brink of crisis.

By 1936, anyone who lives or works in Little and Great St Andrew Streets must feel beleaguered by the quickening pace of urban development. Stepping away from the surrounding West End, even simply walking down the street is an arresting everyday reminder of how it is being left behind by the making of modern London. Densely packed with warehouses and factories, vertiginous tenements towering above shops, cafes, and workshops, Little St Andrew Street is dismal, shabby, and dilapidated. The renaming dispute unfolds at the same time as growing alarm within the LCC and Holborn Council about the street's decline. Public health officials explore the possibility of making it a 'clearance area' under the 1936 Housing Act. This runs alongside a long-planned street-widening scheme to address

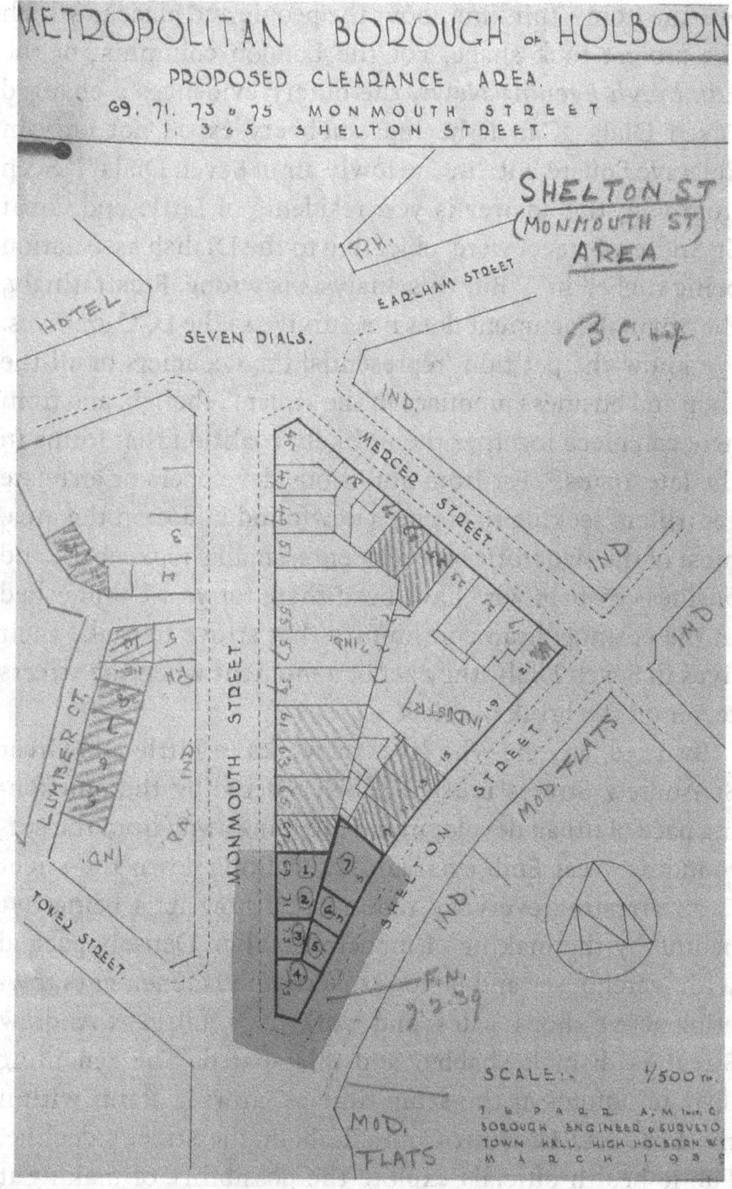

Figure 7.2 Proposed clearance area: Monmouth Street and Shelton Street, 1939

traffic congestion by effectively making Little and Great St Andrew Streets an extension of St Martin's Lane. It is also prompted by the terrible housing conditions officials find in the courts and tenements. After surveying the area in 1938, a large block on the corner with Shelton Street is marked unfit for habitation. Three other blocks are considered 'borderline'.[21] Holborn's Medical Officer of Health comments: 'although fairly substantial, the properties are old, worn out, back-to-back, damp and show other defects justifying early clearance action'. Struggling to address these problems through closing orders and clearance, officials lament the obstacles created by the modern flats and 'substantial industrial premises on all sides'.[22]

As across Holborn itself, the residential population of Little and Great St Andrew Streets falls sharply in the 1920s and 1930s. It remains home to a significant working-class population. Living precariously on the margins of metropolitan markets in housing and labour, this is the same polyglot world that had defined Seven Dials since at least the 1890s. Often recent arrivals in Britain or London, they are drawn – much like Jim and Emily Kitten two decades before – by cheap rents and proximity to the hotels and restaurants of the West End. This comes at a cost, though. In 1939, a council official lists the 'chief defects' of the block on the corner with Shelton Street:

> Back-to-back, no yards, badly positioned and not readily accessible water closets (many in basement), absence of proper light and ventilation, weak disrepaired floors and ceilings, old worn-out fabric and severe R[ising] D[amp].[23]

We might put the people back into these buildings. At 14 Little St Andrew Street, a disparate group of ageing residents – living alone or sharing a single room – crowd together in a four-storey tenement. They include the housekeeper

Lilian Wolbough, barmaid Elizabeth Scandling, unemployed Elizabeth Grice, master chimney sweep Henry Doe, and general labourer Thomas Nichols. Often families who have been there for years occupy the lower floors, with a shifting population of older or single people passing through the upstairs rooms. Next door at number 16, the Wilkinsons share a bedroom, parlour, scullery, and small yard. Father and son work for Schoerling's in Holborn as a whip finisher and messenger; the daughter is a shop assistant for an Oxford Street draper. Above them, at the top of the house, live an elderly pensioner and Covent Garden porter.[24]

By the late 1930s, the streets are more cosmopolitan and transient than ever. While many people leave central London after several years, the area remains home to significant Italian, Belgian, French, and Jewish populations. These long-established communities are joined by a growing number of Greek Cypriots – mostly, but not entirely, younger men. Demetrios and Polymenia Kissia rent 12 Great St Andrew Street, then sublet rooms to their compatriots. In 1939, there are seven others in the house, including two kitchen porters, a driver, hairdresser's assistant, and builder's foreman. Panagista Stasou is a dressmaker, Jane Crumpler – the only resident born in London – a cleaner. Up and down the street there are few obvious signs of gentrification: the actors Douglas Freear and George Smyth-Beale live at numbers 1a and 35 respectively; the intriguing artist's model Phyllis Osborne – rumoured to have been a co-respondent in actress Dorothy Dix's divorce – at number 46.[25]

This is the milieu in which local traders and business owners live. There are notable exceptions. Comyn Ching architectural ironmongers' sprawls along Little St Andrew Street. Bracewell Smith retains his interest in the Shaftesbury Hotel as his hotel empire and political career go from strength to strength. By 1936 he is no longer mayor of Holborn but has become MP for the wealthy constituency of Dulwich. Given all we know, it is likely that Smith, particularly, draws on his connections in the LCC and Conservative Party to orchestrate opposition to 'Seven Dials Street'. For the most part, though, those who sign the petition or write to the council are neither wealthy nor well connected. Far from it: Little and Great St Andrew Streets remain a world of small shopkeepers and manufacturers, tradespeople and artisans, cafe owners and publicans, serving people from nearby tenements and workplaces. Often – though by no means always – they reside above their workplace. Many of them have lived and worked in Seven Dials for decades.

In that strange reverie that comes to those who spend hours scanning street directories and insurance maps, we might imagine something more of Little St Andrew Street and its environs during the day. Skilled craftspeople carving and gilding, making fishing tackle, repairing shoes and leather bags; A watchmaker from Austria, tailor from Constantinople, furrier from Warsaw; Adolf and Toni Ungar, from Krakow, whose hairdressing salon has been there since the war; drapers, milliners, and outfitters, making and selling handmade clothes for customers increasingly seduced by the cheap mass-produced fashions available in the West End; fruiterers and fruit essence merchants squeezed out of Covent Garden seeking cheap warehousing; the tumult of workshops making tarpaulins and picture frames, moulding and metalwork; picturesque older trades – those for which Seven Dials has been known for decades: Leon Paul's armoury and fencing academy; Dominco Di Salvo's handmade ballet shoes; the bird dealer Cecil Isaacs. Everywhere people and goods – coming, going, loading, unloading, buying, selling.

And then the places of repose. Tiny cafes, dining rooms, and pubs filled with those drawn by familiar food and familiar voices – news and the gossip of friends and acquaintances near and far. The Two Brewers Pub, Taffurelli's refreshment rooms, and Secondolfi's cafe have been there a while. Xenof Vassilion's cafe is a recent arrival, though its owner has lived on Neal Street since 1933. It is a sign of the growing number of Greeks living nearby building a home from home, just as those from Italy or Sierra Leone had done before them. The old and new jostling together: artisan traditions of long standing joined by the makers and sellers of wireless parts and gramophones, electroplaters, benders of coils and tubes. A few doors down from the family run tobacconist George Smith and Sons, the precision manufacturing of Neophone Engineering Ltd. In many ways, these are people just like Jim and Emily Kitten, making a living on the margins of modern London.[26]

These are also the people for whom 'Seven Dials' was an insurmountable problem rather than a saleable brand – who put pen to paper to express their anger at being forcibly relocated to 'Seven Dials Street'. Powerful local elites can still define 'improvement' on their own terms. Rather than clinging to tradition, though, many ordinary residents – particularly those small shopkeepers and business owners invested in the neighbourhood – want to be rid of the name Seven Dials and its associations. Intense local opposition to renaming gives voice to the pent-up frustrations of decades. Among those who had struggled to make good in a down-at-heel neighbourhood, a keen sense of the damage inherent in a name is sharpened by an overwhelming feeling of being left behind. Renewing the 'Dialish association' threatens the ability of small businesses to attract the customers and investors on which their future – the future of Seven Dials itself – depends. As the cacophony of development envelops the neighbourhood's bounds, as its transient residential population collapses, as buildings are emptied, boarded up and demolished, and as the spectacle of decline accumulates, the LCC's insensitive and high-handed proposal feels like the last straw. Ordinary and contentious, defensive and deep-felt, the politics of renaming is intimately bound up with the history of a place and its people.

* * *

There is another way to make sense of the opposition to 'Seven Dials Street' – and so to use the street naming controversies to better understand the area. Although the Little and Great St Andrew Streets petition has vanished, there are other petitions from Seven Dials in the LCC archives. Creeping in sideways from those sources, we might fill the spaces left by those we have lost. Lumber Court is a clutter of tenements, boarding houses, workshops, and yards, squeezed into the triangle between Little St Andrew, Little Earl, and Tower Streets. Here is Seven Dials in microcosm: the most congested and run-down part of the neighbourhood, its 'badly arranged' back-to-backs are marked 'unfit' and for demolition in the late 1930s.[27] It is also particularly notorious. A young dressmaker, Lillian Davis, dies in the room she shares with a friend after an overdose of cocaine in 1922. During a feverish moral panic, the inquest links Davis's tragic death to her hectic lifestyle and the 'coloured man' – later named as Edgar Manning – with whom she was often seen in Seven Dials.[28]

Formally, the court does not come under the subcommittee's remit. Public awareness of its work still affords opportunity for an unsolicited petition in November 1937:

> We, the Undersigned, being Owners and / or Occupiers and ratepayers hereby make application to your Council to arrange for and to take the necessary steps to change the name of the permanent way or court now known as Lumber Court, Little St Andrew Street ... to Tower Court or some other suitable name.[29]

If the reasoning is not explicit, like elsewhere in Seven Dials the proposed change suggests yearning for a break of present from past. The petition is submitted by Theodore Wechsler – solicitor, Holborn councillor, and recently elected Municipal Reform Party member of the LCC. Wechsler's mediation echoes the connectedness of local political and commercial elites that defined Bracewell Smith's career. At the same time, the typed petition encapsulates the radically different histories that converge upon Seven Dials.[30]

Nine signatures and two sheets of paper contain the vestiges of the area's industrial past. They include the director of Edward Deverill Ltd, whose business as oilman, colourman, and drysalter has been on Little Earl Street, adjoining the court, since the 1890s. Now the heady chemical stench of oils, paints, and glues is hemmed in by the bustling crowds and bright lights of the West End. The equally heady delights of mass consumerism play out on the fringes of Seven Dials. So does ferocious competition between London's theatres and the cinema's modern wonders. The petition is signed by the managing director of the Ambassadors Theatre, opened on West Street in 1913, and secretary of Metro-Goldwyn-Mayer Pictures, whose offices and private theatre has been at 19–21 Tower Street since the late 1920s. While both businesses deliberately turn their back to Seven Dials, neither can ignore it completely: the Ambassadors stage door opens onto Lumber Court.[31]

Like Seven Dials, both Lumber Court and the petition are shaped by the claustrophobic intimacy of different worlds – even different cities. Off stage, pressed within the main roads, is an indeterminate space between work and home, leisure and pleasure, modern mass culture and an older working London. It seems that the petition is started by the builder's labourer Henry Moss, who has lived at 10 Lumber Court for at least two decades. Along with his wife Susannah, a cleaner, and daughter Joyce, an 'office girl', he will be there until the 1950s. Like Moss, most of the signatories reflect the ordinary cosmopolitanism of Seven Dials: here are tradespeople and small shopkeepers, like the long-established butcher Robert Portwine and Catherine Barty, whose Danish husband is a Lyons chef and has lived there for decades. Ermina Gorrora shares rooms with her husband Giuseppe and brother-in-law Livio, both skilled terrazzo mosaic workers, in the boarding house where Nellie Rigiani – Jarni – had reigned two decades earlier.

Perhaps the most suggestive signatory is Simon Slavin. Then in his late fifties, Slavin and his family live at 6 Lumber Court, though his boot repairing workshop is round the corner on Little Earl Street. Simon and his wife Rebecca, both born in Belarus, married in Mile End then moved to Tower Street before the Great War. By 1921 they were in the court, sharing a five-room tenement with their daughter, five sons, and two lodgers. The oldest son, Louis, worked as Simon's assistant before going into business as a gramophone dealer – renting the shop next door. Two years after the petition, the family have moved again. Simon takes larger premises on the busier Monmouth Street. If work remains in Seven Dials, home is now a big, terraced house in Stoke Newington. Woven through these fragments of family history is a story of work and aspiration – the striving after respectability that shadows the petition to rename Lumber Court.[32]

The petition works: Tower Court is born in July 1938.[33] Following the archival traces of this non-controversy shows how street renaming could mobilise a temporary coalition of convenience within the demotic yet unequal world of Seven Dials. None of the waiters, labourers, or seamstresses who live in the court add their names to the petition; most signatories are residents or businesspeople of long-standing rather than more recent arrivals. Yet the pressing task of extricating the area from its past collapses the distance between concerns over corporate prestige evident in the intervention of American multinational companies like Metro-Goldwyn-Mayer and the everyday hopes and dreams of those small shopkeepers, artisans, and entrepreneurs who made their lives in and around Lumber Court. Take time to know who they were and explore the world they inhabited, and we might hear the voices of at least some ordinary residents – glimpse the flickering outline of their visions of what the area might still become.[34]

* * *

There is one final vantage point on the 'Seven Dials Street' fracas – the ripples of an earlier dispute between municipal authorities and the costermongers who ply their trade in Little Earl Street. Like the more famous Berwick Street in Soho, Seven Dials is known for its bustling colourful street markets. Evidence of growing nostalgia for a bygone city, Cassell's *Pictorial London* (1906) includes a photograph of a 'familiar sight' – 'an open-air market, attended by dwellers in the surrounding streets and courts'.[35] Just as the proximity of Covent Garden means residents make their living selling fruit, vegetables, or flowers around the Dials well into the 1930s, so the long-established Sunday market attracts around two hundred stalls every week, many of them Jewish traders from the East End.[36] Archibald de Bear's ill-fated revue *At the Sign of the Seven Dials* (1931) will try (and fail) to trade on these picturesque associations. Yet it is also around this time in the late 1920s that the LCC and other local authorities become exercised by the disorder of London's markets, now diagnosed as a 'problem'. As they work to 'improve' the area, Holborn Council follow the LCC in seeking to take control – first, requiring that all traders are licensed and then, taking the 'drastic step' of refusing licenses for Sunday trading.[37]

The result is a 'long drawn-out battle' between traders and Holborn Council. For those who work in places like Little Earl Street, Sunday markets have gained the weight of custom.[38] Supported by papers like *John Bull*, which rails against 'callous' legislation leaving the costermonger 'a faint shadow of his former self', traders organise to protect their livelihood.[39] A deputation to the town hall is rebuffed, with the Deputy Mayor noting that 'the people who trade in the Holborn marketplaces on Sundays are not Holborn ratepayers'; even so, he concedes that 'it is a fact that the market is for the benefit of the poor of the borough'.[40] Despite these setbacks, costers like Joe Gornstein and the colourful Mrs Day, then in her nineties, continue to trade. Facing this resistance, council officials begin to prosecute and fine unlicensed stallholders.[41]

Simmering tensions come to a head in spring 1929, when traders combine to fund test cases brought against the council by George Clifton and Napthale Rosenbloom – the latter after being summoned for selling ladies jumpers from a stall in Tower Street.[42] Invoking the precedent of the 'well-known Petticoat Lane ... in a Jewish Quarter', the traders in

Seven Dials – 'now largely the residence of quite poor people of foreign origin' – take their case for licensing Sunday trading before the Bow Street magistrates. Newspapers relish the irony that this attempt to modernise the spaces and times of market trading is rejected because of ancient statute law: the Lord's Day Observance Act, 'passed in the reign of Charles the Second', is the 'rock that the innovators finally split upon'.[43] Undaunted, traders announce a dance at Caxton Hall to fundraise for an appeal. 'Many more of the older school of costers will attend the dance', notes a journalist, including 'Mrs Emma Palmer ... [a] veteran coster, with nearly half a century's experience of street trading'.[44]

While newspapers pit 'innovators' against traditionalists, the 'battle' over Sunday trading is more ambiguous. Council officials press ancient laws on Sabbath observance into the service of making Seven Dials modern. Their vision of 'improvement' marginalises older customs of entrepreneurship and shopping – the picturesque costermonger, beloved of guidebooks – which traders fight to preserve. Long-forgotten now, the politics of a London street market crystallises competing ideas of who Seven Dials belonged to.

* * *

In the late 1930s, residents and business owners from Little and Great St Andrew Streets temporarily make common cause with Holborn Council. Facing the potential disaster of 'Seven Dials Street', concerns over the commercial effects of losing public 'confidence' mesh with the council's fixation on maintaining property values, rateable income, and civic pride.[45] The 'strong opposition' recorded in the minutes of February 1937 comes also from official quarters. Unnerved by the strength of local feeling, the LCC backtrack.[46]

The peculiar politics of renaming becomes entangled with the progress of urban development and the challenge of fashioning usable local histories. Each suggested alternative to 'Seven Dials Street' presses an idealised past into the service of a particular vision for the future. In their petition to the LCC, business owners argue that Little and Great St Andrew Streets should be incorporated into an extended St Martin's Lane. In so doing, they echo plans first presented a decade earlier and symbolically move the street into the heart of the West End. While the subcommittee dismisses this as unworkable, they invite local councillors to suggest alternatives. Five months later, Holborn Council notes that the 'portion of Shaftesbury Avenue within this Borough was formerly known as Monmouth Street, and it has been suggested that this name should be given to Great and Little Andrew Streets.'[47] Reviving the 'old form' ties Seven Dials to a mythologised premodern and aristocratic past: Neal's estate, councillors suggest, was laid out on land around the Duke of Monmouth's townhouse.[48] In February 1938, when the LCC notify ninety-seven households and businesses of the revised proposal, there is just one objection. Monmouth Street comes into being.[49]

By summer 1939 the renaming process is coming to an end. Mindful of the imminent deadline for publishing the new *County of London Street List*, officials hurry through the final stages 'as a matter of some urgency'.[50] Despite countless protests and bad-tempered disputes, the Street Naming Subcommittee can take stock of its progress: in four years it has given thousands of streets new identities.[51] Newspapers which had tracked the acrimony around 'Seven Dials Street' now draw on official briefings to mark the project's outcome. With the new Monmouth Street, an unnamed 'LCC expert' tells journalists, the 'celebrated

Seven Dials have gone: it used to be a test of memory to repeat their names, but by July 1 all the streets will have been newly christened'.[52]

For at least some observers, re-christening streets is a worrying break with the capital's rich heritage. In January 1936, the preservationist London Society asks 'that … consideration may be given to the historical connections of street names'.[53] Councillors had anticipated such concerns, allowing names to be retained 'owing to their antiquity' or where there was 'intimate association of trade and commerce'.[54] In practice, though, such sensitivity cannot alleviate fears that an older city was being rationalised and enumerated out of existence. Swapping old street names for new postal codes runs alongside the pell-mell redevelopment of a modern metropolis. Shadowing such concerns are growing efforts to document and protect the imperilled remnants of bygone London. The London Society's commitment to the 'jealous preservation of all that is old and beautiful' is tracked by the work of the Society for the Protection of Ancient Buildings (1877) and the Georgian Group (1937). It is reflected in the three volumes of St John Adcock's monumental *Wonderful London: The World's Greatest City Described by its Best Writers and Captured by its Finest Photographers* (1924–26). It takes captivating new form in Harry Parkinson and Frank Miller's short films: in whimsical shorts like 'Dickens' London' and 'London Old and New', *Wonderful London* captures both the wonders of the modern age and a city's vanishing buildings and traditions.[55]

Perhaps inevitably, Seven Dials rarely figures in laments for the lost London. When Parkinson and Miller *do* film there, they use the neighbourhood as a setting for a short on the criminal underworld rather than documenting the everyday lives of its people.[56] Concerns over a vanishing name are invariably voiced by people who do not live there. 'Seven Dials is a name compact of charm and romance', notes the *Observer*, 'and it is a pity that ... the last names of the seven streets have vanished.'[57] Oliver Penton, a company secretary living in Surrey, includes Seven Dials with Pimlico, Battersea, and Islington as places of which 'one hardly ever hears' these days. Exercised by the 'prospect of historical local names being ignored, or even forgotten', Penton bemoans how London's past was being 'slowly smothered'. To outsiders, the significance of renaming Seven Dials and its streets is neither apparent nor important.[58]

What is at stake in the sharp exchanges of the late 1930s? Like the 'battle' over Sunday trading in Little Earl Street, the furore around 'Seven Dials Street' is never a conflict between traditionalists and modernisers. Instead, we can see a battle between different visions of what progress meant and who London was for. The politics of naming is impassioned and zealous, detailed and fraught. They might have disagreed about what a place should be called, but all the protagonists recognise the power of a name. Appellations like 'Seven Dials' or 'Monmouth Street' carry the sticky residue of the past, but also have material consequences in the present and future. Symbolism and sentiment are sharpened by local understandings of identity and place and their political and commercial value.

The Labour activist Arthur Field grasped all this as early as 1920, during the spat over what became St Giles Circus. Field denounced 'local suppression of the honourable appellation of St Giles in favour of 'Bloomsbury Circus'. If Conservative councillors wanted to 'make a real bid for the favour of the "Snobocracy"', Field wryly observed, they 'ought to have plumped for "Croesus Circus"'. Suppressing the name 'St Giles' was akin to the proposed demolition of a working-class neighbourhood in the Seven Dials and Drury Lane Improvement Scheme.

> The slums of St Giles! Mr Chapman deplores them, but sees only one remedy, the 'schemes now before the Borough Council (if ever they mature)'. May we breathe the sincere prayer that these schemes will not mature, but will be strangled before arriving at maturity? The curing of unsatisfactory working-class and small-business areas, by the simple process of destroying them and substituting streets of offices, is a process of destroying residential London to benefit 'The City' and finance.[59]

There is something astonishingly familiar in Field's anger at the course of urban development and the exclusionnd inclusion of what we might now call gentrification. 'Improvement', they called it, but who got to choose what to change and how? 'Improvement' schemes revealed the power of political and financial elites to shape London. 'Depopulation' was the modern city's prerequisite and the cruel reality of utopian visions for Seven Dials. Protesting against this emptied city, Field and others offered an alternative rooted in home and work, not leisure, pleasure, and capital. Dismissing the Improvement Scheme, Field argued that the 'slum question' should be answered through the 'organised repair and remodelling of the existing properties [and] the enforcement of existing legislation'. In so doing, he anticipated the work of housing activists, community groups, and preservationists in the second half of the twentieth century. Shaming Holborn's Conservative politicians, Field demanded 'some sign of repentance for proposing to expel the working-class and small-trader vote from St Giles, by their accursed "improvements"'.[60]

Throughout the 1920s and 1930s, we see time and again how a simple name could encapsulate the tensions and conflicts through which London was made modern. Opposition to 'Seven Dials Street' showed that the politics of naming was inconsistent and unpredictable, never mapping straightforwardly onto differences of class. In the 1930s, it was the LCC and Holborn Council who initially tried to revitalise a placename indelibly marked by past notoriety. While the ensuing protest involved well-connected developers and multinational corporations, it also mobilised the same 'working-class and small-trader vote' for whom Labour politicians had advocated in 1920. There was a common logic to Field's campaigning and the Little St Andrew Street petition: ordinary residents trying to protect their livelihoods against overbearing local authorities and developers. It was the same logic that prompted Jim and Emily Kitten to sue *John Bull* and the Odhams Press for libel.

* * *

In autumn 1936, along with thirty-two other households and businesses, Jim and Emily Kitten receive notice that the LCC proposal that Great and Little White Lion Streets are 'renamed as Pyefield Street after the Cock and Pye Fields upon which the Seven Dials was built'.[61] Although most residents accept this change, an 'objection [is] received from a firm of engineers who own all the houses in Little White Lion Street'. The director of that company – almost certainly the architectural ironmongers Comyn Ching, whose workshops and stores sprawl along the street – asks 'whether if a change must be made could it not be to Mercer Street' – the name the road took across the boundary into Westminster.[62] In this case, money talks: after further consultation, the subcommittee agrees that 'incorporation be extended to include Mercer Street and ... this latter name be applied to the whole line of street from Long Acre to Shaftesbury Avenue'.[63]

The proposed Pyefield Street hints at a pastoral moment before Seven Dials was laid out in the 1690s, though its full name is too prurient for modern tastes. Mercer Street evokes rich traditions of artisanal production and mercantile self-governance. In reclaiming these respectable lineages, both names work to conceal the poverty and political radicalism of the nineteenth century. Strikingly, they impose a sanitised and deracinated version of the past on cosmopolitan Seven Dials, effacing the presence of generations of working-class migrants who have made their lives there. Once again, the minutiae of committee minutes and newspaper letters are shot through with stories of politics and money, then and now, marginalisation and belonging, and the capacity of names to carry meanings into the present. On 1 January 1938, almost two decades after moving to 15 Great White Lion Street, the Kittens wake up at 37 Mercer Street.

Denouement: Full circle

Mercer Street

Now the dials have turned full circle, and the place where we began is no longer there. Great White Lion Street is gone. A cafe has been replaced by a branch of the Times Laundry Company on Mercer Street, now shabbier than ever: a once rich past, white-washed.

As another war begins, Jim and Emily Kitten still live in the upstairs room where they moved, full of dreams, almost twenty years earlier. Every day they pass their old place as they walk to and from work in the restaurants of the West End. Every day reminds them of a life that had flourished – and then been destroyed. All around, they see people who had given evidence against them in a courtroom on the Strand, and watch as the Shaftesbury Hotel is transformed, and the Cambridge Theatre rises from the ground. All around, everything else slowly falls apart. Each year, the past weighs more heavily on Seven Dials. Bricks blacken and buildings lean; doors and window frames rot and stick; paint lifts and floorboards sag; warehouses, workshops, and houses empty of life. More buildings are condemned, boarded up, and demolished. The melancholy of loss, the anger of being pushed aside: this is what 'improvement' feels like for those left behind.[1]

On 18 October 1940, Jim Kitten dies in Leavesden Emergency Hospital. Emily is by his side. Almost twenty-three years since they married during the fretful period of the Great War, the couple part in an asylum repurposed in expectation of mass civilian death, as air raid sirens scream and bombs begin to fall. The shadows of that earlier war are long. A doctor lists the causes of Jim's death: 'shock', 'dilation of stomach', 'carcinoma of elbow in an old war wound'. Ruhleben internment camp had been a staging point in his journey to Seven Dials. If the dull pain from being shot did not stop him working, like the memories, it never went away. It worsened in the years before his early death, aged 51.

Grief leaves little trace in the archives, but three years later, in June 1943, Emily Kitten remarries at St Pancras Registry Office, in a small ceremony witnessed by her older sister. Her new husband is also widowed: then in his early sixties and a merchant navy storekeeper, James Tucker had been one of the Sierra Leonean men interned with Jim Kitten. Three months later, Emily Tucker steps on to Mercer Street and closes the door of number 37 for the last time. She and James will live in a flat on Gosfield Street, in what people are starting to call Fitzrovia, until Emily dies at the Middlesex Hospital in 1962, aged 63.[2]

* * *

It is not quite the case that the 'Black colony' disappeared with the Kittens, but its presence in Seven Dials was short-lived. The term was rarely used by the 1930s, when the centres of Black culture shifted to places like the Shim-Sham nightclub in Soho, and north to Camden and the area around the West African Student Union hostel. After the Second World War, the Dials' recent past was almost forgotten.

Almost, but not quite: in the late 1940s the Ministry of Works proposed using the Shaftesbury Hotel as the British Council's new residential centre for colonial students, then arriving in Britain in growing numbers. The Labour cabinet rejected the premises as unsuitable; the Hans Crescent Colonial Centre opened in Knightsbridge in 1950. At the same time, the housing market shaped different geographies of community and politics for successive new generations of migrants, focused on places like Notting Hill, Brixton, and the East End.[3]

In little over a decade, the 'Black colony' appeared and then vanished. That world was hard-won. It was built upon the labour and savings of people like the Kittens and the commitment – shared with customers – to negotiate the 'colour bar' and make a business and a home in the imperial metropolis. It took shape in the face of intense scrutiny, police harassment, and the enmity of at least some neighbours. In the end, it would be the rapprochement between political and commercial elites that determined what happened around Great White Lion Street. Markets in commercial and residential property that brought the Kittens here also drew the attention of well-connected developers. The rise and fall of the 'Black colony' tracked the 'monstrous machine' of capital as it moved across Seven Dials.

The label was coined by muckraking journalists, though – those with an eye for sensation and the power of a well-turned phrase to enrage and scandalise readers. In this sense, the *idea* of the 'Black colony' was a creation of the moral panic around race, empire, and the limits of belonging that shook postwar Britain. It was a phrase meant to do work. Like the 'slum', the spectre of the 'Black colony' was conjured up to justify its removal. Such ideas shadowed efforts by politicians, planners, and developers to remake

Seven Dials in their own image – the process that some called 'improvement', and we might term decolonisation. While the Kittens' journey to the High Court of Justice *was* extraordinary, their lawsuit against a national newspaper

Figure 8.1 Shops in Mercer Street, 1956

reflected a simple but potent desire: to make a living, a home, and a better life. All those things hinged on protecting the reputation of their business and the rich connections it sustained – and was sustained by. Losing the cafe was a personal tragedy. It also exemplified how wealth and power could displace rich cosmopolitan communities. In the decades to come, that process would play out time and again.

* * *

The giddy optimism with which politicians and investors imagined a new Seven Dials in the 1920s was also short-lived. As the pace of change quickened, a place and its people were increasingly left behind. The collapse of the Improvement Scheme had lasting effects: politicians looked elsewhere, planning blight settled on the area, imagined futures were foreclosed. Speculative developers and spectacular developments always drew attention, but neither the Shaftesbury Hotel nor the Cambridge Theatre created the promised momentum. Utopian visions for Seven Dials, moreover, contained little space for people. However much they disagreed about how the future should look, politicians, planners, and developers all assumed that working-class residents and small businesses would make way for big capital and commercial development. In slightly different ways, the entrenched power and sprawling warehouses of Covent Garden market strengthened the torpor that hung over the area. In the end, the grubby reality was that Seven Dials emptied of people as its buildings decayed and were condemned.

Patrick Abercrombie and J. H. Forshaw's *County of London Plan* (1943) is best known for its radical proposals for reconstructing the capital, but it also captured Seven

Dials' condition after two decades of hesitant and haphazard change. Too small and marginal to be identified by name, the area nonetheless haunted Abercrombie and Forshaw's analysis of London's problems and future. Hundreds still lived there, but it was no longer formally defined as a residential neighbourhood. In treating the area as either part of the West End or an industrial and warehouse zone, planners again wrote the people out of Seven Dials. Implicitly, at least, the Dials demonstrated the failings of postwar planning and unfettered commercial development. It shadowed the argument that 'unplanned expansion disturbs the balance' of urban life. As an example of the 'central slum clogging development and traffic flow', it confirmed Abercrombie and Forshaw's suggestion that an area's 'depressing character' deterred developers.

Against this chaos, Abercrombie and Forshaw proposed to reorganise central London into functionally distinct economic units: the 'Shopping, Business, Restaurant and Amusement Area known as the West End', 'Theatre and Cinema Land', the 'Soho Restaurant Area', and the 'Covent Garden and Long Acre district'. For Seven Dials, the logical end point of these proposals was clear: it would be levelled and rebuilt to meet the needs of the new London. Yet it was never more than an afterthought in Abercrombie and Forshaw's thinking. The area's future would be determined by rationalising the flow of traffic around the metropolis and by ambitious plans for better-known neighbours like Soho, Bloomsbury, and Covent Garden. Acknowledging that moving the market south of the Thames meant 'near-by working class housing accommodation ... may well disappear' was as close as they came to recognising Seven Dials existed.[4]

* * *

Figure 8.2 Vacant Site in Earlham Street, 1975

And then there is nothing. Demolition crews leave an empty space where there were once shops, homes, a cafe. Absence describes the triangle between Earlham and Mercer Streets. Linger and you might glimpse a phantom – imagine the buildings back into the outline of hoardings, brickwork shadows and scars, adverts for Dry Sack Sherry and Player's No. 6 cigarettes. Across the way, the Taffurellis' tearooms and Woolf Lieber's shop have vanished beneath a petrol station. Globe House, once a futuristic vision in glass and metal, has melted away. Ghosts of a city that no longer existed – a future that had not come.

* * *

After the Second World War, Seven Dials' decline was precipitous. It was exacerbated by Covent Garden's uncertain future and the ever-present possibility of demolition. By 1957, the area's bleak condition was urgent enough to be discussed by the Society for the Promotion of Urban Renewal and used as a case study for town planning students at Regent Street Polytechnic.[5] By 1970, housing activists and preservationists estimated that 90 per cent of the area's residential properties had been empty for at least four decades.[6]

When Nicholas Saunders – 'hippy, capitalist, guru, grocer', and author of the legendary countercultural guidebook *Alternative London* (1970) – arrived in Neal's Yard in 1974, he found a 'filthy backyard overrun by rats and used by tramps as a lavatory' and 'buildings [which] looked derelict with windows broken or boarded up'.[7] Saunders was part of a new generation of outsiders following Elsa Lanchester, Harold Scott, and Misha Black to Seven Dials in the sixties and seventies. Often self-consciously dissident or working in the arts or creative industries, they took advantage of vacant buildings and cheap commercial property. Designers, architects, and publishers, Beatles' manager Brian Epstein, and Monty Python's Michael Palin and Terry Gilliam had offices or studios nearby. The Roxy Club, centre of London's punk scene, was in a warehouse in Neal Street. Inspired by Copenhagen's Freetown Christiania, Saunders turned an old banana warehouse into a thriving alternative emporium, including a wholefoods warehouse, bakery, and what would become Neal's Yard Dairy and Monmouth Coffee.[8]

The question of what to do with Seven Dials came to a head around 1970. Covent Garden market moved south to Nine Elms. The Greater London Council proposed the area's comprehensive redevelopment: reminiscent of the Improvement Scheme's destructive futurism, Covent

Garden and Seven Dials were to be razed and rebuilt.[9] Sixty years earlier, the LCC's mammoth *Survey of London* (1914) concluded that 'little of architectural interest now remains in the district of Seven Dials'. After the Great War, organisations like the London Society focused on protecting the Foundling Hospital and Bloomsbury rather than their impoverished neighbour. Now residents and business owners, housing activists, and preservationists mobilised as the Covent Garden Community Association to protect the area's historic fabric and future.[10]

On their own terms, these efforts were successful, culminating in a public inquiry (1971), Seven Dials' designation as an Outstanding Conservation Area (1974) and Housing Action Area (1977–84), and the listing of around two hundred buildings by English Heritage.[11] Residents and activists worked with property owners and local authorities on ambitious plans to regenerate the area through 'active conservation of the built heritage'. The Housing Action Area Committee encouraged new housing and brought vacant homes back into use. Dilapidated commercial and domestic buildings were restored rather than demolished, most notably through architect Terry Farrell's sensitive post-modern redevelopment of the Comyn Ching triangle. After a long campaign by the Seven Dials Monument Charity, a replica of the original sundial pillar returned to the centre of the Dials in 1989.[12]

* * *

Seven Dials today is full of modish boutiques, bars, and restaurants. It bustles with wandering tourists and Londoners, compressing the indulgent pleasures of global capitalism into tight-knit gentrified streets. Once known for its ageing residential population, it is now a haunt of young people from across the world. Once full of small shops, eating places, and workshops, it is now a 'destination' dominated by big brands and chains. A cosmopolitan working-class neighbourhood – a place of home and work – has become the upmarket consumerist playground first imagined by politicians, planners, and developers over a century ago. They would be surprised to see so much of the area's fabric intact – astonished by the new developments squeezed into the courts and yards. The overbearing affluence would still warrant satisfaction at a job well done.

It is not that long since Seven Dials was a synonym for poverty and 'slum' housing. Such was its damaging power to speak of the character of a place and its people, that politicians and businesspeople strove for a utopian future in which Seven Dials was expunged from the map. In the end, of course, Seven Dials did not disappear. It has become a brand as much as a place, however. As central London has been repackaged as instantly recognisable neighbourhoods, each with their characteristic pleasures and possibilities, so its name's meaning has altered. In this economy of smoke and mirrors, Seven Dials ironically stands in for fashionable consumerism and a carefully constructed urban aesthetic – what Shaftesbury Capital, the area's biggest landowner, describes as 'shopping, dining, and theatre between Covent Garden and Soho'.[13]

Seven Dials' transformation over the past fifty years has been remarkable. The area is often seen as a model of sensitive economic regeneration through 'active conservation' and community engagement. The Seven Dials Trust observes:

> Mostly unknown and in a state of dereliction when the Covent Garden market moved in 1974, Seven Dials was brought back to life largely through the dedication of the

> Seven Dials Trust, working in partnership with the local authorities and landowners for nearly forty years. Together, the partnership virtually re-invented a lost neighbourhood through a long process of urban renewal embracing social and private housing and new businesses.[14]

When photographers walked the area in the early 1970s they captured the streets of somewhere on the brink. Follow in their footsteps today – compare the austere emptiness of their images with what you see before you – and the signs of 'renewal' are everywhere.[15] The streets are busier, brighter, and more colourful now, though their pattern and many buildings are familiar. In other ways, though – in the character of a place and its people – Seven Dials is unrecognisable.

* * *

It is hard to escape the past in Seven Dials. Much of the area's character comes from the distinctive intimacy of its streets, the scale of its buildings, and the tangible presence of at least a simulacrum of a bygone city. Here is what publicists call a 'one-of-a-kind destination hidden in the bustling heart of London. Set at a slower pace, the roads within Seven Dials are an escape from the busy streets of the city'. That Thomas Neale's unusual layout has survived means exploring can seem – or be made to seem – like a qualitatively different urban experience: stepping out of London, stepping back in time.[16]

The cues for that experience are everywhere – from the pavers beneath your feet to the corridors of immaculate restored buildings you pass through. Based on the heraldic crest of the parish of St Giles, the Golden Hind emblem used by the Seven Dials Trust and Shaftesbury Capital is ubiquitous: bollards, bins, and street name plates; tasteful banners and hanging signs: 'Seven Dials, London: est.1690'.

As if looking backwards, each street name plate recalls its previous incarnation: the plate on the corner of what was Great White Lion Street gets the old name wrong. Street History Plaques and People's Plaques installed by the Seven Dials Trust rehearse the area's fascinating history and celebrate notable people and places. Telling stories about the past is a powerful tool of contemporary place-making.

It can be hard to get much sense of the area in the 1920s and 1930s from all this. Public heritage and popular histories dwell on Seven Dials' seventeenth-century foundation and the picturesque world of the eighteenth and nineteenth centuries. The reinstated 'iconic Sundial Pillar' – a focal point that was not there for most of the neighbourhood's history – is a remarkable example of the invention of tradition, and how that process privileges some histories while excluding others.

There are exceptions. The Cambridge was listed in 1999 as a 'rare, complete, and early example of a London theatre adopting the modern, expressionist style pioneered in Germany during the 1920s' and remains as prominent as ever.[17] A few People's Plaques – those marking John Logie Baird's 'first experimental television transmissions' or John Gielgud's old flat – recall the decades after the Great War. Against the Cave of Harmony's physical evanescence, a plaque on the Grapes Inn immortalises 'Elsa Lanchester's club for London intellectuals'. If the period is remembered at all, then, it is through the privileged outsiders who passed through Seven Dials on their way somewhere else – those for whom it was a playground or temporary refuge. The everyday cosmopolitanism and bitter conflicts of the twenties and thirties have simply vanished. A proposal to mark the site of the Kittens' cafe was rejected several years ago: 'intriguing story but could be considered controversial'.[18]

Whose stories do we remember, and whose do we forget?

* * *

I have found no surviving photographs of Great White Lion Street in the 1920s and 1930s. While photographers captured the scene looking north along the street in 1913 and 1956, there is no equivalent for the forty years in between. Postcards of the Shaftesbury Hotel are cropped so the row of buildings where Jim and Emily Kitten lived and worked remains just out of view. There was once a photograph: a pencil 'sketch of the Kitten's cafe', drawn 'from a recent photograph'. A crude rendering of an image captured to further a newspaper's vicious crusade is our only glimpse of a world long gone. A missing photograph, a place on the edge, a view obscured by intruding outsiders: apt allegories for the place of the twenties and thirties in histories of Seven Dials, and the area's place in histories of modern London. Seven Dials' history encapsulates how London itself was transformed in the twentieth century, however. The tensions that coalesced here in the decades after the Great War were moulded by the capital's contemporaneous remaking. The struggles played out in court in 1927 anticipated the contours and conflicts of Britain's twentieth century.

Seven Dials is no longer in decline – no longer on the margins of urban life, as it was for much of its history. Here, at least, the desperate crises of poverty and precarity, exploitative landlords and employers, and overcrowded and insanitary housing that marked the decades after the Great War are a thing of the past. Those problems were shifted elsewhere rather than solved, though, just as capital and consumerism displaced a richly cosmopolitan world from London's heart. Perhaps the die was already cast by the 1970s. Viewed over the course of a century, however, it is hard not to think that old buildings and characterful streetscapes have been preserved at the expense of people. Little wonder these songs of Seven Dials play in a minor key.

Walk through Seven Dials today, and the questions asked a century ago feel more pressing than ever. Then politicians sought to impose their grandiose visions on a run-down neighbourhood and the 'monstrous machine' of capital transformed central London. Now property portfolios expand, global brands and businesses compete for space, rents and prices rise, and the quickening pace of gentrification makes Seven Dials ever more exclusive. Particularly since the 1990s, when earlier gentrifiers like Nicholas Saunders worried that Neal's Yard was being 'cleaned up', development has been driven by real estate investment trusts like Shaftesbury Capital. What kind of city do we want? Who gains – and who loses – from this version of urban life? Who can you see as you look around, and who has been pushed to the margins? There is a fine line between bringing a neighbourhood back to life and making a place a commodity – turning streets and courts into privatised spaces for the privileged few. Pause for too long in the Comyn Ching triangle, and a uniformed security guard might appear and move you on, even if you are an ageing white historian taking a break from exploring.[19]

The 1920s and 1930s were a decisive moment in this shift, when the paths to different futures still sometimes seemed open. At times, alternative visions of Seven Dials – of London – appeared with startling clarity. The Kittens' libel suit hinted at how law might be used to challenge a racist 'colour bar', resist the course of development, and make a home in the imperial metropolis; and at the potential of solidarities which crossed boundaries of class and race. Market traders organising against the suppression of Sunday trading, and ordinary residents, shopkeepers, and businesspeople campaigning around proposed new street names fashioned different local histories, rooted in custom and tradition, to envisage Seven Dials as a place of commerce and craft. Most strikingly, Labour activists and residents, often finding common cause with paternalistic Conservatives, rejected the logic of urban 'improvement'. Instead of offices, department stores, and speeding traffic they demanded a future in which Seven Dials remained a place of home and work. The call to renovate rather than demolish homes rings down the years.

Such alternative futures were invariably defensive and peripheral. From the late 1920s, at the latest, it was clear they would have little immediate influence on the progress of 'development'. Seven Dials' postwar fate might always have been overdetermined by its central location, the growing pace of commercial redevelopment at its bounds, and the complicity of Holborn's political and corporate elites. It would not always happen this way. For a time, in the 1970s, the Covent Garden Community Association reinvigorated the grassroots activism, mobilisation of small traders and businesspeople, and emphasis on home and work that we glimpse in earlier decades. Over the past century, such modestly utopian yet powerful visions of what London might become have been repurposed to meet the challenges of different places and times. We might need them more than ever now.

In the end, this book is not really about a libel trial or Seven Dials – at least not solely. It is about the making of a modern city and the unevenness, exclusions, and conflicts of that process. It is about the politics of urban life, and the unequal terms on which Britons could participate or share in the gains of a changing postwar world. It is about the significance of the 1920s and 1930s in shaping forms of modern life that, for better and worse, we have come to take for granted. Above all, *Songs of Seven Dials* is about the power of the stories we tell of the past – now and then – to shape a better present and future.

Notes

Introduction

1 Rebecca Preston and Andrew Saint, *St Giles-in-the-Fields: The History of a London Parish* (London, 2024); Adam Crymble, 'The Decline and Fall of an Early Modern Slum: London's St Giles "Rookery", *c.*1550–1850', *Urban History*, 49 (2), 2021.

2 Charles Dickens, *Sketches by Boz* (London, 1836), chapter v. For the illustration see https://collections.vam.ac.uk/item/O682143/seven-dials-print-cruikshank-george/. Douglas Jerrold, *London: A Pilgrimage* (London, 1872), 158.

3 LSE, BOOTH B 354: George Duckworth's Notebook, Police District 2 (1898), https://booth.lse.ac.uk/notebook/booth-b-354; Charles Booth, *Life and Labour of the People in London* (London, 1902–3).

4 W. S. Gilbert and Arthur Sullivan, *Iolanthe; or the Peer and the Peri* (London, 1882).

5 Agatha Christie, *The Seven Dials Mystery* (London, 1929), 38, 40.

6 Alan Stapleton, *London Alleys, Byways, and Courts* (London, 1924), vii, 67–8; Stapleton, *London Lanes* (London, 1930).

7 Jane Shaw, *Octavia, Daughter of God: The Story of a Female Messiah and her Followers* (London, 2011).

8 I acknowledge my intellectual debts to: Hakim Adi, *African and Caribbean People in Britain: A History* (London, 2023); Adi, *West Africans in Britain, 1900–1960* (London, 1998); Caroline Bressey, 'Imagining the Black Cook in Victorian London', *London Journal*, 48 (3), 2023; Bressey and Gemma Romain, 'Staging Race: Florence Mills, Celebrity, Identity, and Performance in 1920s Britain', *Women's History Review*, 28 (3), 2019; Kieran Connell, *Multicultural Britain: A People's History* (London,

2024); Kennetta Hammond Perry, *London is the Place for Me: Black Britons, Citizenship, and the Politics of Race* (Oxford, 2016); Marek Kohn, *Dope Girls: The Birth of the British Drug Underground* (London, 2003); Minkah Makalani, *In the Cause of Freedom: Radical Black Internationalism from Harlem to London, 1917–1939* (Durham, 2011); Marc Matera, *Black London: The Imperial Metropolis and Decolonization in the Twentieth Century* (Berkeley, 2015); Panikos Panayi, *Migrant City: A New History of London* (London, 2020); Susan Pennybacker, *From Scottsboro to Munich: Race and Political Culture in 1930s Britain* (Princeton, 2009); Carina Ray, *Crossing the Colour Line: Race, Sex, and the Contested Politics of Colonialism in Ghana* (Ohio, 2015); Gemma Romain, *Race, Sexuality, and Identity in Britain and Jamaica: The Biography of Patrick Nelson, 1916–1963* (London, 2017); Rob Waters, *Thinking Black: Britain, 1964–1985* (Berkeley, 2018); Waters, *Colonized by Humanity: Caribbean London and the Politics of Integration at the End of Empire* (Oxford, 2023).

9 On London: Stephen Inwood, *City of Cities: The Birth of Modern London* (London, 2011); Jerry White, *London in the Twentieth Century: A City and Its People* (London, 2008); John Davis, *Waterloo Sunset: London from the Sixties to Thatcher* (Princeton, 2022). On Seven Dials: 'A Brief History of Seven Dials', *Seven Dials Renaissance Study*, https://sevendialscoventgarden.study/background/a-brief-history-of-seven-dials; 'Seven Dials – Its History', *Seven Dials Trust*, www.sevendials.com/history; David Hayes, *Victorian Seven Dials* (London, 2004).

10 I am indebted to Stephen Brooke, *London 1984: Conflict and Change in the Radical City* (Oxford, 2024). For broader histories of London: Alison Light, *Forever England: Femininity, Literature and Conservatism between the Wars* (Abingdon, 2013); Judith Summers, *Soho: A History of London's Most Colourful Neighbourhood* (London, 1989); Frank Mort, *Capital Affairs: London and the Making of the Permissive Society* (London, 2010); Judith Walkowitz, *Nights Out: Life in Cosmopolitan London* (New Haven and London, 2012); Simon Danczuk and Daniel Smith, *Scandal at Dolphin Square: A Notorious History* (Cheltenham, 2022); Francesca Wade, *Square Haunting: Five Women, Freedom, and London Between the Wars* (London, 2020); Rohan McWilliam, *London's West End: Creating the Pleasure District, 1800–1914* (Oxford, 2020). Cathy Ross, *Twenties London: A City in the Jazz Age* (London, 2003).

11 Mrs Robert Henrey, *An Exile in Soho* (London, 1952), 170. LA, GLC MA SC 01 210: Seven Dials, Holborn, map signed by

AB Raffle (10 May 1938); LCC Medical Officer to Valuer (18 May 1938).

Chapter 1

1 TNA, HO 144 22301: SDI Frankton to Superintendent (19 February 1927); Superintendent Morton (19 February 1927); TNA, J 54 1951: James Kitten versus Odhams Press (February 1927); 'The 'Black Man's Cafe' Libel Action', *The Times*, 9 February 1927; 'Negro Cafe Owner's Libel Suit', *Guardian*, 10 February 1927; *Kelly's Post Office London Directory* (1926), 331, 322.

2 'The 'Black Man's Cafe' Libel Action', *The Times*, 9 February 1927; TNA, J 54 1951 (February 1927).

3 Matthew Stibbe, *British Civilian Internees in Germany* (Manchester, 2008).

4 Israel Cohen, *The Ruhleben Prison Camp: A Record of Nineteen Months Internment* (London, 1917), 115–16.

5 TNA, FO 425 602: List of Civilian Internees at Ruhleben (1915); Stibbe, *British Civilian Internees*, 59–60, 105.

6 Cohen, *Ruhleben Prison Camp*, 115–16.

7 TNA, FO 383 71: Prisoners, Germany (1915).

8 TNA, FO 383 187: Prisoners, Germany (1916).

9 TNA, HO 144 22301: SDI Frankton to Superintendent (19 February 1927).

10 TNA, FO 383 211: Provision of certificates of internment at Ruhleben Camp (7 November 1916); Board of Trade, List of Merchant Seaman and Prisoners of War Detained as Prisoners of War: SS *Sangara* (1918), www.findmypast.co.uk.

11 Liverpool Record Office, 387 CRE: Crew Lists, SS *Burutu* (1906), www.ancestry.co.uk; TNA, FO 383 65: Prisoners, Germany (1915): Seamen interned at Ruhleben, www.findmypast.co.uk; 'The Graphic Art', *Lyons' Mail*, October 1950. Leila Kassir, *Lyons Chapbook No. 3: Our Lyons Club, Migration Stories* (London, 2022); Lara Putnam, 'Provincializing Harlem: The "Negro Metropolis" as Northern Frontier of a Connected Caribbean', *Modernism/Modernity*, 20 (3), 2013, 479.

12 This account draws on the 1921 census records, www.findmypast.co.uk.

13 *Births Registered in July, August and September 1898*, Vol. 1c, p.269, www.findmypast.co.uk; 1911 Census, Registration District 28, Deptford East, Piece 2635, www.ancestry.co.uk; LA, LCC EO DIV05 GEY AD 002: Admission and Discharge Register for Infants (8 February 1904), www.ancestry.co.uk; *Baptisms Solemnised in*

the Parish of Christ Church Spitalfields (21 August 1898), www.ancestry.co.uk; 'George Yard Mission and Ragged School', *Survey of London* (September 2019), https://surveyoflondon.org/map/feature/386/detail/.

14 'Air Raid Damage in UK During the First World War', Imperial War Museum Photographic Collection, www.iwm.org.uk/collections/item/object/205193150.

15 'Ministry of Munitions', *The Times*, 21 November 1919.

16 Mrs Robert Henrey, *Julia: Reminiscences of a Year in Madeleine's Life as a London Shopgirl* (London, 1971), 167.

17 Wendy Moore, *Endell Street: The Trailblazing Women Who Ran World War One's Most Remarkable Military Hospital* (London, 2020); Laura Spinney, *Pale Rider: The Spanish Flu of 1918 and How it Changed the World* (London, 2017).

18 'Seven Dials Refreshment House', *The Times*, 25 July 1919.

19 'Bathless Holborn', *Pall Mall Gazette*, 16 February 1920.

20 'Tommy and Jack', *John Bull*, 11 October 1919.

21 'Back to Seven Dials', *HFG*, 11 April 1919.

22 'Private William Cody', *A Street Near You*, https://astreetnearyou.org/person/1629189/Private-William--Cody; 'Rifleman J. McMahon', *A Street Near You*, https://astreetnearyou.org/person/597695/Rifleman---Mcmahon; 'Short Service Attestation of James McMahon' (28 September 1914); *British Army Service Records, 1914–20*, www.findmypast.co.uk.

23 Lieutenant Kenneth George Davies, *A Street Near You*, https://astreetnearyou.org/person/65078/Lieutenant-Kenneth-George--Davies.

24 Mabel Lethbridge, *Against the Tide* (London, 1936).

25 LA, ACC 3445 SIC 01 13: Minutes (3 August 1923); LA, ACC 3445 SIC 01 14: Minutes (4 April 1924).

26 'Advert', *L'Indépendance Belge*, 13 June 1916; TNA, HO 144 22301: 'Closing Orders Made Under Article 10 of Aliens Order 1920' (March 1932).

27 TNA, RG15 01249: 1921 Census, 17 Little Earl Street, www.findmypast.co.uk/.

28 TNA RG15 01250, 1921 Census, 50 Neal Street, www.findmypast.co.uk.

29 'Private Charles Blatchly', *A Street Near You*, https://astreetnearyou.org/person/400848/Private-Charles-Douglas-Carrington--Blatchly; Cathy Sedgwick, 'Private CDC Blatchly', *Sutton Cemetery War Grave* (2021), https://ww1austburialsuk.weebly.com/uploads/4/9/7/8/4978039/blatchly_charles_douglas_carrington.pdf.

30 TNA, RG15 01249, 1921 Census, 38 Great St Andrew Street, www.findmypast.co.uk; 'Vanished in a Taxicab', *Sunday Pictorial*, 28 May 1922; 'Wife's Alleged Attack', *St Pancras Guardian*, 16 June 1922. For Blatchly's extraordinary later life, see Phil Baker, *City of the Beast: The London of Aleister Crowley* (London, 2022); 206–7.
31 Ernest Marke, *In Troubled Waters: Memoirs of my Seventy Years in England* (London, 1986).
32 TNA, RG15 00742, 1921 Census, 22 Liverpool Street, St Pancras, www.findmypast.co.uk.
33 Jacqueline Jenkins, *Black 1919: Riots, Racism, and Resistance in Imperial Britain* (Liverpool, 2008); TNA RG15 17401, 1921 Census, Elder Dempster Hostel, 2 Upper Stanhope Street, Liverpool, www.findmypast.co.uk.
34 Matera, *Black London*, 37; Laura Tabili, *'We Ask for British Justice': Workers and Racial Difference in Late Imperial Britain* (Ithaca, 1994); Lara Putnam, 'Citizenship from the Margins: Vernacular Theories of Rights and the State from the Interwar Caribbean', *Journal of British Studies*, 53 (1), 2014.
35 Carina Ray, *Crossing the Color Line: Race, Sex, and the Contested Politics of Colonialism in Ghana* (Athens, 2015), 11, 164; M. Page Baldwin, 'Subject to Empire: Married Women and the British Nationality and Status of Aliens Act', *Journal of British Studies*, 40, 2001; Lucy Bland, 'White Women and Men of Colour: Miscegenation Fears in Britain after the Great War', *Gender and History*, 17 (1), 2005.
36 Panikos Panayi, *Migrant City: A New History of London* (London, 2020), chapter 4.
37 See *Survey of Seven Dials*.
38 LA, GLC AR HOD 10 007: Plan for Redevelopment: Covent Garden – Seven Dials Area (1957–58).
39 'Holborn Blaze', *Daily Mirror*, 24 August 1929, 3.
40 'Descriptive Map of London Social Conditions', *New Survey of London Life and Labour, Vol VIII* (London, 1933).
41 *Annual Report of the Medical Officer of Public Health for Holborn, 1931* (London, 1932); LA, GLC AR HOD 10 007: Plan for Redevelopment (1957–58).
42 Helen Bosanquet, 'Housing Conditions in London', *Economic Journal*, September 1917; *Annual Report, 1932* (London, 1933).
43 'Protest at High Tenement Rents', *HFG*, 11 June 1926.
44 Bosanquet, 'Housing Conditions'.
45 'Too Many Tenement Houses', *HFG*, 14 August 1925; *Annual Report, 1919* (London, 1920); *Annual Report, 1922* (London, 1923); *Annual Report, 1931* (London, 1932).

46 *Annual Report, 1927* (London, 1928).
47 *Annual Report, 1923* (London, 1924); *Annual Report, 1929* (London, 1930).
48 Lethbridge, *Against the Tide*, 232–4; TNA, RG15 01249, 1921 Census, 5 Lumber Court, www.findmypast.co.uk; 'Disrobed at Dance', *Edinburgh Evening News*, 29 April 1922; LA, LCC MIN 11053: Unlicensed Public Dancing, Brett's Club (27 June 1923); 'Girl Drug Taker's Death', *HFG*, 12 May 1922; 'Girl Drug Taker's Death', *HFG*, 9 June 1922; 'Girl Victim of Drug Habit', *Lancashire Evening Post*, 3 June 1922; 'Black Men's Pyjama Parties', *John Bull*, 4 August 1923. See also Marek Kohn, *Dope Girls: The Birth of the British Drugs Underground* (London, 1994).
49 *Annual Report 1922* (London, 1923).
50 Mrs Robert Henrey, *An Exile in Soho* (London, 1952), 1, 147; Henrey, *Julia*, 135.
51 TNA, J 54 1951 (February 1927); 'Negro Cafe Owner's Libel Suit', *Guardian*, 10 February 1927.
52 'London Editor is Sued', *Ottawa Journal*, 5 March 1927.
53 TNA, HO 144 22301: SDI Frankton to Superintendent (19 February 1927); 'Close up the Black Café', *John Bull*, 19 February 1927; Matera, *Black London*, 22.
54 'The 'Black Man's Cafe' Libel Action', *The Times*, 9 February 1927.
55 Alec Waugh, 'Round About Soho', in St John Adcock (ed.), *Wonderful London, Volume 1* (London, 1924–25).
56 Thomas Burke, *City of Encounters: A London Divertissement* (London, 1932), 26–7; Minkah Makalani, *In the Cause of Freedom: Radical Black Internationalism from Harlem to London, 1917–1939* (Durham, 2011), 166–7; Elizabeth Buettner, '"Going for an Indian": South Asian Restaurants and the Limits of Multiculturalism in Britain', *Journal of Modern History*, 80 (4), 2008.
57 Marke, *In Troubled Waters*, 62–3.
58 Susan Pennybacker, *From Scottsboro to Munich: Race and Political Culture in 1930s Britain* (Princeton, 2009), 88–9.
59 'A Raid in Bloomsbury', *HFG*, 11 April 1919; 'The Coffee Cooler Fined', *HFG*, 18 April 1919. Matera, *Black London*; Laura Tabili, *Global Migrants, Local Culture: Natives and Newcomers in Provincial England, 1841–1939* (Houndmills, 2011); Kennetta Hammond Perry, *London Is the Place for Me: Black Britons, Citizenship, and the Politics of Race* (Oxford, 2015); Susan Okokon, *Black Londoners, 1880–1980* (Stroud, 1998); John Davis, 'Rents and Race in 1960s London: New Light on Rachmanism',

Twentieth Century British History, 12 (1), 2001, 69–92; Harold Carter, 'Building the Divided City: Race, Class, and Social Housing in Southwark, 1945–1995', *London Journal*, 33, 2008, 155–85.

60 'Six Month's Hard for Trafficker in Drugs', *Illustrated Police News*, 16 July 1925; 'Opium Charge against Coloured Men', *Illustrated Police News*, 11 June 1925; LA, PS BOW A 01 098 (3 June 1925); LA, LCC MIN 11066: Presented Papers (14 May 1924).

61 'West End Dance Club Scene', *HFG*, 11 January 1924.

62 'Black Men and White Women', *HFG*, 27 July 1923; 'Undesirable Club Struck Off', *HFG*, 28 September 1923; 'The Worst Place in the West End', *Illustrated Police News*, 4 October 1923; 'Wild Scene at "Black Man's Café"', *HFG*, 15 February 1924; 'Coloured Men in a Club', *HFG*, 9 January 1925; 'Night Club Prison Sentence', *HFG*, 30 January 1925. 'Negroes Chase a Woman', *Thomson's Weekly News*, 21 February 1931; 'Coloured Seamen in West End Club Fracas', *Illustrated Police News*, 5 January 1933.

63 TNA, HO 144 22301: SDI Frankton to Superintendent (19 February 1927).

64 'Scene in Seven Dials', *HFG*, 9 March 1928.

65 Laura Tabili, 'Empire is the Enemy of Love: Edith Noor's Progress and Other Stories', *Gender and History*, 17 (1), 2005; Tabili, 'Outsiders in the Land of Their Birth: Exogamy, Citizenship, and Identity in War and Peace', *Journal of British Studies*, 44 (4), 2005; Lucy Bland, 'British Eugenics and "Race Crossing": A Study of an Interwar Investigation', *New Formations*, 60, 2007; Gemma Romain, *Race, Sexuality, and Identity in Britain and Jamaica: The Biography of Patrick Nelson, 1916–63* (London, 2017).

66 TNA, RG15 00340, 1921 Census, 11 Dimsdale Road; TNA RG15 00234, 1921 Census, 122 Uxbridge Road, both accessed at www.findmypast.co.uk; 'A Coloured Man's Café', *Daily Mail*, 9 February 1927.

67 'London Editor is Sued', *Ottawa Journal*, 5 March 1927.

68 'A Coloured Man's Café', *Daily Mail*, 9 February 1927.

69 'Prince Monolulu', *Gloucestershire Echo*, 24 August 1927; Anita McConnell, 'MacKay, Peter Carl', *Oxford Dictionary of National Biography* (23 September 2004), https://doi-org.bham-ezproxy.idm.oclc.org/10.1093/ref:odnb/76829; Sidney White, *I Gotta Horse: The Autobiography of Ras Prince Monolulu* (London, 1950).

70 'Early Scenes on the Course', *Portsmouth Evening News*, 4 June 1930; Matera, *Black London*, 216–20.

71 'Black Man's Café Scene', *HFG*, 3 February 1928.

72 'Stabbed in the Neck', *Nottingham Journal*, 12 October 1922; 'A Violent Man and a Bad Lot', *Illustrated Police News*, 8 July 1926. 'White Woman's Serious Charge Against Coloured Man', *Illustrated Police News*, 8 November 1928; 'White Women Terrorized by Coloured Scoundrel', *Illustrated Police News*, 14 December 1928.
73 'Opium Charge Against Coloured Men', *Illustrated Police News*, 11 June 1925; 'Coloured King of Dope Traffic', *Sunday News*, 12 July 1925.
74 Arnold Palmer, 'Coloured Nights in Seven Dials', *Sphere*, 1 May 1926; Palmer, *Straphangers* (London, 1927), Chapter XXV.
75 'Black Bullies: Yard to Clean up Plague Spots of London', *People*, 6 June 1926.
76 TNA, RG15 01250, 1921 Census, 82 Neal Street, www.findmypast.co.uk; 'Queen's Park Girl Frightened', *Marylebone Mercury*, 11 August 1923.
77 'Wild Scene at "Black Man's Café"', *HFG*, 15 February 1924; 'Charge of Razor Slashing', *HFG*, 22 May 1925; 'In Blacks' Colony', *Nottingham Journal*, 3 June 1925; 'Knuckle Duster Assault Charge', *HFG*, 26 March 1926; 'A Violent Man and a Bad Lot', *Illustrated Police News*, 8 July 1926; 'The Ups and Downs of Life', *HFG*, 9 May 1924; 'Alleged Hammer Attack in Café', *HFG*, 28 November 1924; 'Scene in Seven Dials', *HFG*, 9 March 1928.
78 'Black Man's Café', *Northern Daily Mail*, 9 January 1925.
79 Barry Pain, 'London Types', *Wonderful London, Vol. 1*, 5.
80 LA, A PMC 98 2: *Public Morality Council Annual Report* (1932); LA, A PMC 98 3: *Public Morality Council Annual Report* (1933).
81 'The Seamy Side', *Daily Mail*, 4 December 1924; Christian Høgsbjerg, 'Rufus E. Fennell: A Literary Pan-Africanist in Britain', *Race and Class*, 56 (1), 2014.
82 'Midnight Incident', *Birmingham Daily Gazette*, 4 August 1920.
83 CLS, B HO M 1 1: Minutes (28 April 1920; 27 October 1926); 'Black Bullies', *People*, 6 June 1926.
84 TNA, HO 144 22301: SDI Frankton to Superintendent (19 February 1927).
85 'Seven Dials Cafe Arrests', *Observer*, 14 October 1923; 'Mystery Powder in Seven Dials', *HFG*, 19 October 1923; 'Unfounded Charge Against Police', *Sunday Post*, 28 October 1923; LA, PS BOW A 01 090 (13, 20, 27 October 1923).
86 'Seven Dials Cafe Arrests', *Observer*, 14 October 1923.
87 LA, PS BOW A04 059 (25 June 1924); LA, PS BOW A04 060 (2 July & 9 July 1924).
88 LA, PS BOW A04 069 (12 January 1927).

89 'Negro runs Amok', *Evening News*, 3 July 1924; 'Violent Scene in Seven Dials' *HFG*, 27 June 1924'; TNA, HO 144 22301: SDI Frankton to Superintendent (19 February 1927). 'Violent Negro Punished', *HFG*, 23 September 1921.
90 TNA, HO 144 22301: SDI Frankton to Superintendent (19 February 1927).
91 'Three Women Victims of Murder', *Reynolds's Newspaper*, 4 October 1931.
92 John Gray, *Gin and Bitters* (London, 1938); Daniel Stephen, *The Empire of Progress: West Africans, Indians, and Britons at the British Empire Exhibition, 1924–25* (Houndmills, 2013),
93 Stephen, *Empire of Progress*, 93.
94 'The Lighter Side', *Nottingham Evening Post*, 1 January 1924. Philip Grant, 'Sierra Leone at the British Empire Exhibition in 1924', *Brent Archives* (February 2014), https://legacy.brent.gov.uk/media/8439336/Sierra%20Leone%20at%20the%20British%20Empire%20Exhibition%20in%201924.pdf.
95 LA, ACC 352 10: Agreement between British Empire Exhibition Incorporated and J. Lyons and Co. Ltd (30 October 1923).
96 LA, ACC 3527 333: *Guide to Lyons' Restaurants and Cafes at the British Empire Exhibition* (London, 1925).
97 Caroline Bressey, 'Black Modernism, Racism, and the Making of Popular British Culture in the Inter-war Years', *Conversation* (12 November 2014), http://theconversation.com/black-modernism-racism-and-the-making-of-popular-british-culture-in-the-inter-war-years-33435); Caroline Bressey and Gemma Romain, 'Staging Race: Florence Mills, Celebrity, Identity, and Performance in 1920s Britain', *Women's History Review*, 28 (3), 2019.

Chapter 2

1 'Beautifying London', *Mercury*, 30 March 1928.
2 Harold Clunn, *The Face of London* (London, 1932), 13. Sally Alexander, 'A New Civilization? London Surveyed, 1928–1940s', *History Workshop Journal*, 64 (1), 2007, 296–320.
3 David Gilbert, '*London of the Future*: The Metropolis Reimagined after the Great War', *Journal of British Studies*, 43 (1), 2004, 82, 94, 95; Helena Beaufoy, 'Order out of Chaos: The London Society and the Planning of London, 1912–1920', *Planning Perspectives*, 12 (2), 1997; Michael Collins, 'The London County Council's Approach to Town Planning, 1909–1945', *London Journal*, 42 (2), 2017, 172–91; Frank Mort, 'Fantasies of Metropolitan London: Planning London in the 1940s', *Journal of British Studies*, 43 (1), 2004;

Erika Rappaport, 'Art, Commerce, or Empire? The Rebuilding of Regent Street, 1880–1927', *History Workshop Journal*, 53 (1), 2002.

4 Professor Adshead, 'Central London', in Sir Aston Webb (ed.), *London of the Future* (London, 1921), 141–2, 143.

5 Gilbert, '*London of the Future*', 115.

6 Gilbert, '*London of the Future*', 102; Erika Rappaport, *Shopping for Pleasure: Women in the Making of London's West End* (Princeton, 2001).

7 Neil Smith, *The New Urban Frontier: Gentrification and the Revanchist City* (London, 1996); David Ley, *The New Middle Class and the Remaking of the Central City* (Oxford, 1996).

8 'HM Office of Land Registry', *Gazette*, 16 July 1920; 'HM Office of Land Registry', *Gazette*, 24 February 1920; 'HM Office of Land Registry', *Gazette*, 10 August 1922.

9 'A Wonderful Opportunity', *The Times*, 23 July 1920.

10 'The Estate Market', *Country Life*, 3 May 1919.

11 'Sales by Auction', *The Times*, 5 April 1919.

12 Ibid.; 'Result of Sale', *The Times*, 10 May 1919.

13 'Results of Auction Sales', *The Times*, 9 May 1919.

14 'Holborn (Shaftesbury Avenue)', *South London Press*, 2 December 1905; 'Shaftesbury Avenue', *Morning Post*, 26 January 1906.

15 'Labour Party Conference', *Labour Leader*, 23 January 1913; 'Visit to the Western Front (March 1918', *Lives of the First World War*, https://livesofthefirstworldwar.iwm.org.uk/story/29465.

16 'Subconscious War Worry', *Hartlepool Northern Daily Mail*, 17 October 1917; Genna Bard, *Resort and Ruin: Dunbar's Hotel Belle-Vue*, https://storymaps.arcgis.com/stories/7d2f721c96da429e9310a1ef6332ff61.

17 *Certificate of Incorporation, No. 158902: Gordon and Smith Limited* (20 August 1919), companieshouse.gov.uk; 'HM Office of Land Registry', *London Gazette*, 9 August 1921; 'Finance', *Kinematograph Weekly*, 15 April 1920; 'Central Flats (London)', *Gazette*, 27 February 1931.

18 'Guests of Holborn's Mayor', *HFG*, 13 July 1923. For Smith, see Grand Lodge of England, Freemason Membership Register: Folio 93, Motherland Lodge (29 November 1921), www.ancestry.co.uk. For Harvey, see Folio 129, Holborn Borough Council Lodge (23 February 1920), www.ancestry.co.uk.

19 'Holborn's Council Candidates', *HFG*, 27 October 1922'; 'Council Election Nominations', *HFG*, 23 October 1925.

20 'HM Office of Land Registry', *Gazette*, 8 December 1922; 'HM Office of Land Registry', *Gazette*, 21 May 1920.

21 'Messrs. SH Davids and Co.', *The Times*, 20 March 1920.

22 'HM Office of Land Registry', *Gazette*, 2 October 1923'; 'Ilford Builders' Affairs', *Eastern Counties Times*, 3 April 1925.

23 Colin Stanley (ed.), *The Surrender of Silence: The Memoirs of Ironfoot Jack, King of the Bohemians* (London, 2018), 116–18; 'Blackmail Charge', *Thanet Advertiser*, 17 April 1931.

24 TNA, MEPO 3 758: Minute 11a, DDI Campion (29 August 1934).

25 CLS, B HO M 1 1: HMBC Minutes (11 January 1928).

26 'Tainted Money, *John Bull*, 12 September 1931.

27 'West End Flat Scandals', *Reynolds News*, 30 August 1931.

28 'Gaol for "Dangerous" Woman', *Illustrated Police News*, 4 June 1931; 'A Ghastly Traffic Revived', *John Bull*, 13 June 1931.

29 LA, GLC AR BR 07 2698: Shaftesbury Hotel, Monmouth Street, Building Act Case File (1916–55).

30 'Close up the Black Café', *John Bull*, 19 February 1927. For this proximity, see Electoral Register, Polling District B, Central St Giles Ward (1922), www.ancestry.co.uk; 'HM Office of Land Registry', *London Gazette*, 9 August 1921.

31 CLS, B HO M 1 1: HMBC Minutes (12 December 1923); 'Holborn Council and Housing', *HFG*, 12 December 1924.

32 CLS, B HO M 1 1: HMBC Minutes (23 July 1924).

33 Paul Calderwood, *Freemasonry and the Press in the Twentieth Century* (London, 2013), 289; 'Holborn Council Freemasons', *HFG*, 27 February 1920.

34 'Important Piccadilly Transaction', *Country Life*, 24 January 1925; '700 Bedrooms', *Weekly Dispatch*, 1 March 1925; 'A Self-Made Man', *Daily Express*, 19 July 1925; 'New Palatial Hotel for London: Gigantic Deal by a Group of Yorkshiremen', *Yorkshire Evening Post*, 6 August 1925; 'Half a Million Deal in London Hotel', *Yorkshire Post*, 7 August 1925.

35 'Architecture Today: A New Hotel', *Westminster Gazette*, 11 March 1926.

36 'New Palatial Hotel for London', *Yorkshire Evening Post*, 6 August 1925; 'Half a Million Deal in London Hotel', *Yorkshire Post*, 7 August 1925; 'Tonic Air for Hotel', *Liverpool Echo*, 27 January 1927.

37 'A Homely Atmosphere and Modern Comfort', *Westminster Gazette*, 28 January 1927.

38 'Romance of London Hotel', *People*, 30 January 1927.

39 Sonia Ashmore, Bronwen Edwards, and David Gilbert, '"Mr Bourne's Dilemma": Consumer Culture, Property Speculation, and Department Store Demise', *Journal of Historical Geography*, 38, 2012, 434–46.

40 'HM Land Registry', *London Gazette*, 4 February 1927; 'Park Lane Hotel', *Financial Times*, 2 July 1943; *Certificate of Change of*

Name: Gordon and Smith Limited (6 January 1927), companie shouse.gov.uk.

41 'HM Land Registry', *Gazette*, 11 March 1927.

42 'Government Refuse Intervention', *Pall Mall Gazette*, 29 January 1919.

43 'Dockyards Condition', *Daily News*, 12 January 1921; 'The Safety Men', *Westminster Gazette*, 25 April 1921; TNA, RG15 01254, 1921 Census: Shaftesbury Hotel, Great St Andrew Street, www.findmypast.co.uk.

44 Hywel Francis, 'Cook, Arthur James (1883–1931)', *ODNB* (3 January 2008), https://doi.org/10.1093/ref:odnb/32539.

45 'Chromatic Film Printers', *Kinematograph Weekly*, 3 February 1921; 'National Conference of Hairdressers Assistants', *Ealing Gazette*, 25 November 1922; 'Touring Contracts', *Westminster Gazette*, 18 September 1924; 'Truce on Stage', *Daily News*, 3 October 1924; 'Big Progress of Socialism in the Country', *Daily Herald*, 2 December 1924; 'The Shaftesbury Hotel', *Stage*, 18 March 1926.

46 'The "Social Socialists"', *Justice*, 8 May 1924; 'Veterans of Labour', *Daily Herald*, 10 October 1924.

47 'Communists as Cross-Examiners', *Daily Herald*, 18 November 1925.

48 'Labour Doubts about Cooperative People', *Daily News*, 14 December 1925.

49 'Frederick Silvester and Co.', *Era*, 4 June 1919. See also 'Artists Cards', *Era*, 2 March 1932.

50 I draw here on a survey of Seven Dials in the 1920s and 1930s [hereafter *Survey of Seven Dials*] The survey uses the 1921 Census (available at www.findmypast.com) and the 1939 Register (available at www.ancestry.co.uk). In addition to these genealogical databases, it also uses the following sources: LSE, GB 97 NSOL 2 19 4: New Survey of London Life and Labour, Holborn survey cards (1930–34); *Kelly's Post Office Directory* (London, 1934); LA, VA GOAD IND: *Insurance Plan of London, Volume VIII* (London, 1938).

51 'Restaurant, Shaftesbury Hotel, Great St Andrew Street' (2 July 1931), postcard in author's collection; 'Applications for Licences', *HFG*, 5 March 1920.

52 'Shaftesbury Hotel, London' (July 1928), postcard in author's collection.

53 *Shaftesbury Hotel: London Weekly Diary of Social Events* (30 May to 5 June 1938), in author's collection.

54 'Financial', *Era*, 4 July 1934. See 'Wanted', *Kinematograph Weekly*, 17 April 1919; 'Cinema Acting', *Daily Mirror*, 11 April 1919;

'Wanted: Pianist who can Speak Lines', *Stage*, 10 April 1919; 'Wanted, Artists for Winter Tour', *Stage*, 30 October 1919.

55 'Husband Who Disappeared', *Acton Gazette*, 11 May 1928; 'Tired of Funerals', *Daily Express*, 12 December 1922; 'Croydon Divorce Suit', *Croydon Times*, 23 December 1922. 'Divorce Case', *Uxbridge and West Drayton Gazette*, 4 January 1929.

56 'Hotel Guest's Money', *Daily News*, 2 July 1935. See 'Committed on Theft Charges', *HFG*, 2 September 1921; 'Love Rivals Shot Dead in Bank', *Daily Mirror*, 6 November 1922; 'Expensive Tastes', *Weekly Dispatch*, 5 November 1922.

57 'The Song Plugging Scandal', *Era*, 6 May 1931.

58 'Secret Talk in Hotel', *Daily News*, 4 July 1932.

59 'Pen Points', *St Pancras Gazette*, 30 March 1928; 'Primrose "Buds" Annual Dinner', *St Pancras Gazette*, 3 April 1931; "Untitled', *Stage*, 21 January 1932; 'Woman Conservatives' Presentation Dinner', *St Pancras Gazette*, 19 May 1933; 'Lodge 21', *Marylebone Mercury*, 12 October 1935; 'Ward 8 Conservatives', *St Pancras Gazette*, 9 December 1938.

60 Victoria Park Toy Dog Association, Annual Supper and Dance Programme (10 December 1931), in author's collection.

61 James Agate, *Ego: The Autobiography of James Agate* (London, 1935).

62 TNA, RG101 0255L 002 4: 1939 Register, Shaftesbury Hotel, Monmouth Street, London, www.findmypast.co.uk.

63 'Green Park Hotel', *Financial Times*, 2 August 1928; '£20,000 Hotel Bought by Ex-Teacher', *Adelaide Advertiser*, 12 September 1928.

64 'Rise to Wealth', *Register News-Pictorial (Adelaide)*, 2 January 1929.

65 'Hotel Pioneer as Parliamentary Candidate', *Western Mail*, 23 May 1932; 'Café Royal', *Scotsman*, 25 September 1930; 'Café Royal', *Financial Times*, 12 April 1935.

66 Diana Bourbon, 'Other Half of the World', *Britannia and Eve*, November 1930.

67 Earl of Meath, 'London as the Heart of Empire', in Webb, *London of the Future*, 252.

68 Meath, 'London as the Heart of Empire', 258. Gilbert, '*London of the Future*', 109–10; Gilbert, '"London in all its Glory – Or How to Enjoy London"' Guidebook Representations of Imperial London', *Journal of Historical Geography*, 25 (3), 1999, 279–97. On decolonising post-independence cities see Siddhartha Sen, *Colonising, Decolonising and Globalising Kolkata: From a Colonial to a Post-Marxist City* (Amsterdam, 2017); Colin Clarke, *Decolonising*

the Colonial City: Urbanisation and Stratification in Kingston, Jamaica (Oxford, 2006).

69 'Free Hold Investments in the Heart of the West End', *The Times*, 27 April 1936; Peter Scott, 'Edgson, (Walter) Stanley (1893–1950)', www.oxforddnb.com/display/10.1093/ref:odnb/9780198614128.001.0001/odnb-9780198614128-e-51906.

70 'Town Houses', *The Times*, 3 April 1929. See also 'Business Premises', *The Times*, 14 September 1926; 'Transfer Books', *The Times*, 1 September 1927; 'Flats and Chambers', *The Times*, 19 June 1931; 'Raglan Property Trust Limited', *The Times*, 28 July 1936; 'Obituary: Alfred Rubens', *Independent*, 28 June 1998.

71 'Men and Women in the Public Eye', *Sphere*, 12 February 1927.

72 'From Teacher to Hotel Owner', *Daily News*, 2 August 1928.

73 '£20,000 Hotel Bought by Ex-Teacher', *Adelaide Advertiser*, 12 September 1928.

74 'Bracewell Smith dies at 81', *Liverpool Daily Post*, 13 January 1966. See also 'Sir Bracewell Smith', *The Times*, 13 January 1966; 'Sir Bracewell Smith Leaves £1,197,000', *Daily Telegraph*, 2 April 1966.

75 Jane Jacobs, *Edge of Empire: Postcolonialism and the City* (London, 1996).

76 Residential Hotels and Caterers Association, *London: What to See and Where to Stay* (London, 1930), 68.

Chapter 3

1 'Holborn Housing Scheme Begun', *HFG*, 29 October 1926; LA, ACC 3445 SIC 10 029: Form of Service for the Opening of St Giles Buildings (1925).

2 LA, ACC 3445 SIC 10 029: Form of Service (1925); LA, ACC 3445 SIC 01 14: Minutes (15, 27 May, 8, 12 & 16 October 1925); LA, ACC 3445 SIC 10 030: *Strike at the Root of Social Unrest* (1926); LA, ACC 3445 SIC 01 025: *Annual Report of the SIC, 1925–26* (London, 1926); 'Houses for the Working Class', *HFG*, 23 October 1925.

3 'Slums in the Dials and the Lane', *HFG*, 23 July 1920.

4 'Abolishing Slums', *Marylebone Mercury*, 20 July 1920.

5 'Disappearing Seven Dials', *Kensington Post*, 17 September 1920.

6 Ibid.

7 Ibid.

8 'Slums in the Dials and the Lane', *HFG*, 16 July 1920.

9 CLS, B HO M 1 1: HMBC Minutes (14 July 1920).

10 'Urgent Problem of Housing', *HFG*, 11 July 1919.

11 'Slums in the Dials and the Lane', *HFG*, 23 July 1920.
12 'Disappearing Seven Dials', *Kensington Post*, 17 September 1920.
13 'Abolishing Slums', *Marylebone Mercury*, 20 July 1920.
14 'Notorious Slum to Go', *Birmingham Gazette*, 19 July 1920.
15 'Abolishing Slums', *Marylebone Mercury*, 20 July 1920.
16 'New Road Subways', *Daily Mail*, 26 September 1921.
17 'Slums in the Dials and the Lane', *HFG*, 23 July 1920.
18 'Abolishing Slums', *Marylebone Mercury*, 20 July 1920.
19 'Disappearing Seven Dials', *Kensington Post*, 17 September 1920.
20 CLS, B HO M 1 1: HMBC Minutes (14 July 1920).
21 'Disappearing Seven Dials', *Kensington Post*, 17 September 1920.
22 'Brilliant Gathering in Holborn', *HFG*, 2 December 1921.
23 Notes and News', *HFG*, 20 August 1920.
24 'Too Many Tenement Houses', *HFG*, 14 August 1925.
25 Stanley Adshead, 'Central London', in Sir Aston Webb (ed.), *London of the Future* (London, 1921), 143.
26 'A Wonderful Opportunity', *The Times*, 23 July 1920.
27 'Disappearing Seven Dials', *Kensington Post*, 17 September 1920.
28 Stephen Heathorn, 'The Battle of the Bridges: Temporal Modernity in the Reimagining of Interwar London's Cityscape', *Journal of British Studies*, 61 (4), 2022.
29 JH Forshaw and Patrick Abercrombie, *County of London Plan* (London, 1943), 56.
30 Webb, *London of the Future*, 146; 'Disappearing Seven Dials', *Kensington Post*, 17 September 1920.
31 CLS, B HO M 1 1: HMBC Minutes (14 July 1926).
32 'New Road Subways', *Daily Mail*, 26 September 1921.
33 'St Paul's Bridge, the Strand, and Seven Dials', *British Builder*, September 1922.
34 'Holborn and Thames Bridges', *HFG*, 25 June 1926; 'Borough Council's Brief Meeting', *HFG*, 16 July 1926; CLS, B HO M 1 1: HMBC Minutes (23 June, 14 July 1926).
35 LA, GLC AR BR 17 040022: TS Hosking, Architect's Department: Model Dwellings Shorts Gardens (6 July 1924).
36 *Annual Reports of the Medical Officer of Health for Holborn, 1933, 1934 & 1935* (London, 1934, 1935 & 1936).
37 'Shorts Gardens Men for Trial', *HFG*, 12 February 1926.
38 LA, GLC AR BR 17 040022: Spurrell to WE Riley, Superintending Architect (26 November 1913); 'Holborn Council', *HFG*, 11 July 1913.
39 'Holborn and the Housing Scheme', *HFG*, 11 April 1919.

40 'Holborn's New Housing Scheme', *HFG*, 25 July 1924.
41 CLS, B HO M 1 1: HMBC Minutes (28 January 1920); 'Holborn's Housing Scheme Vetoed', *HFG*, 16 October 1925.
42 'Housing Bonds in Holborn', *HFG*, 2 July 1920; 'Housing Scheme for Holborn', *HFG*, 10 July 1925.
43 CLS, B HO M 1 1: HMBC Minutes (14 June 1922).
44 LA, ACC 3445 SIC 01 13: Minutes (2 December 1921, 6 January, 24 February, 5 May, 2 June, 3 November & 1 December 1922, 6 April 1923); LA, ACC 3445 SIC 01 14: Minutes (22 February 1924).
45 'Working Class Dwellings Scheme', *HFG*, 23 June 1922. See also CLS, B HO M 1 1: HMBC Minutes (14 June 1922).
46 'Holborn's Biggest Improvement', *HFG*, 26 November 1926; 'Holborn Council Freemasons', *HFG*, 27 February 1920.
47 *Annual Report, 1926*; LA, GLC AR BR 17 040022: Report by Superintending Architect (3 March 1924).
48 CLS, B HO M 1 1: HMBC Minutes (14 January 1925); LA, ACC 3445 SIC 01 14: Minutes (27 June, 1 August 1924). For the origins of these concerns, see e.g. LA, PS BOW A01 115: Registers (12 & 19 March 1928).
49 LA, GLC AR BR 17 040022: R Taylor, LCC Architects Department (22 February 1924); 'Dwellings for Holborn Workmen', *HFG*, 12 October 1923; 'Shorts Gardens Housing Scheme', *HFG*, 30 June 1922.
50 LA, GLC AR BR 17 040022: Superintending Architect to Westcott and Reeves (16 June 1924).
51 LA, ACC 3445 SIC 01 025: *Annual Report of the SIC, 1925–26* (London, 1926); LA, ACC 3445 SIC 01 032: Summary of Estates Records, St Giles Buildings (1925–55).
52 LA, ACC 3445 SIC 08 006: St Giles Buildings, Shorts Gardens, Artists Impressions (1925).
53 'Town Planning a "Try On"', *HFG*, 10 February 1928.
54 'Notes and News', *HFG*, 20 June 1924.
55 'Plain Words to Borough Council', *HFG*, 17 June 1927.
56 Ibid.
57 'Protest at High Tenement Rents', *HFG*, 11 June 1926.
58 LA, ACC 3445 SIC 10 030: *Strike at the Root of Social Unrest* (1926).
59 'Town Planning a "Try On"', *HFG*, 10 February 1928.
60 'Notes and News', *HFG*, 20 August 1920.
61 Rebecca Preston and Andrew Saint, *St Giles-in-the-Fields: The History of a London Parish* (London, 2024), 359.
62 'Untitled', *Daily Herald*, 27 May 1921.

63 'Arresting the Depopulation of Central London', *HFG*, 31 December 1920; 'Lectures', *Daily Herald*, 17 December 1920; 'Comrade Arthur Field', *Communist*, 8 October 1921.
64 'Housing of the Working Classes', *HFG*, 3 December 1920.
65 'Mr Joseph Maloney', *HFG*, 16 October 1925.
66 'Untitled', *Daily Herald*, 27 May 1921; 'Council Election Results', *HFG*, 6 November 1925; 'Holborn's "Red" Candidate', *HFG*, 18 February 1927; 'Criticism of Holborn Council', *HFG*, 28 March 1924.
67 CLS, B HO M 1 1: HMBC Minutes (6 September 1922); Bow Arts, 'Gliksten – the Foremost Name in Timber', *Raw Materials*, https://rawmaterials.bowarts.org/collection/gliksten-timber/.
68 'Letters to the Editor', *Saturday Review*, 30 October 1926.
69 LA, GLC AR BR 17 040022: H Spencer Stowell (13 April 1922); Report by Superintending Architect (1 May 1922); Stowell to Superintending Architect, LCC (8 May 1922). See also CLS, B HO M 1 1: HMBC Minutes (26 January 1921).
70 'Letters to the Editor', *Saturday Review*, 30 October 1926.
71 *Covent Garden Strike* (1924), at www.britishpathe.com/asset/50875/; 'Strike Picket in Court', *HFG*, 29 August 1924.
72 'Councillor and Housing Problems', *HFG*, 27 February 1925.
73 'Moving Covent Garden Market', *HFG*, 26 March 1926.
74 CLS, B HO M 1 1: HMBC Minutes (25 March 1925, 27 January, 28 April 1926; LA, LCC AR TP 02 146: L Walford to LCC (7 February 1936); LA, GLC MA SC 01 210: Clerk of Council to Town Clerk, MBC (5 April 1939).
75 LA, CLS B HO M 1 1: HMBC Minutes (8 July 1925, 25 November 1925).
76 *Annual Reports*, 1920–1940.
77 Ibid., 1937.
78 LA, GLC MA SC 01 210: Medical Officer of Health to Dr JA Struthers (28 August 1939); Medical Officer to Valuer (18 May 1938).
79 Ibid.: MOH, Shelton Street (Monmouth Street) Area (20 March 1939); Seven Dials Areas, Holborn (11 May 1938).
80 Ibid.
81 Ibid.: Seven Dials Areas, Holborn (11 May 1938).
82 Ibid.: MOH, Shelton Street (Monmouth Street) Area (20 March 1939).
83 LSE, GB 97 NSOL 2 19 4: New Survey of London Life and Labour, Holborn survey cards (1930–34); Simon Abernathy, 'Deceptive Data? The Role of the Investigators in the New Survey of London Life and Labour', *Historical Methods*, 50 (1), 2017.

84 LSE, GB 97 NSOL 2 19 4: Holborn survey cards (1930–34).
85 LA, GLC AR HOD 10 007: Plan for Redevelopment: Covent Garden – Seven Dials Area (1957–58).
86 'Town Planning Scheme for Holborn', *HFG*, 30 April 1926; 'Efforts to Save Foundling Estate', *HFG*, 18 June 1926; LA, LCC CL TP 01 005: Town Planning Scheme No. 4 (Holborn and St Pancras) General Papers (1927–35); CLS, B HO M 1 1: HMBC Minutes (11 January, 8 February, 27 June 1928).
87 'Notes and Topics', *Architects' Journal*, 30 December 1937.
88 Ivor Brown, 'Looking Round', *Observer*, 10 October 1937.

Chapter 4

1 S. Theodore Felstead, *Horatio Bottomley: A Biography of an Outstanding Personality* (London, 1936); Julian Symonds, *Horatio Bottomley* (London, 2001).
2 F. A. Mackenzie. 'Foreign London', in St John Adcock, *Wonderful London: The World's Greatest City Described by its Best Writers and Pictured by its Finest Photographers*, volume III (London, 1924–5), 1011.
3 'Dupes Mean Dope', *John Bull*, 6 October 1923, 6; 'Black Snow Man', *John Bull*, 10 November 1923, 8; 'Menace of the Blacks', *John Bull*, 12 July 1924; 'Black and White', *John Bull*, 19 July 1924, 8; 'Audacious Aliens', *John Bull*, 18 July 1925, 11; A Black Betrayal', *John Bull*, 25 July 1925; 'Good News', *John Bull*, 5 September 1925, 8; 'Black-Skinned Blackguards', *John Bull*, 26 September 1925, 16; 'Great P.O. Robbery', *John Bull*, 10 October 1925, 15; 'A Terrible Negro Haunt', *John Bull*, 10 April 1926.
4 'A Black Betrayal', *John Bull*, 25 July 1925.
5 'Menace of the Blacks', *John Bull*, 12 July 1924.
6 'A Terrible Negro Haunt', *John Bull*, 10 April 1926.
7 'Menace of the Blacks', *John Bull*, 12 July 1924.
8 'A Terrible Negro Haunt', *John Bull*, 10 April 1926.
9 Ibid.
10 Charles Pilley, *Law for Journalists* (London, 1924), xv, xvi.
11 Ibid., 7–8.
12 Ibid., 21.
13 W. Valentine Ball, *The Law of Libel and Slander* (London, 1936), 5.
14 Pilley, *Law for Journalists*, vi.
15 TNA, J 54 1951: 'James Kitten versus Odhams Press and E.R. Thompson' (February 1927).
16 Ibid.
17 Ibid.

18 'In the Matter of the Solicitors Act', *London Gazette,* 1 June 1926; 'In the Matter of the Solicitors Acts', *London Gazette*, 23 September 1927.
19 Mervyn Mackinnon and Alan Bell, *Libel for Laymen* (London, 1933), 115–16.
20 Edward Wooll, *A Guide to the Law of Libel and Slander* (London, 1939), 13–14.
21 'The Weather', *The Times*, 10 February 1927.
22 Ernest Marke, *In Troubled Waters: Memoirs of my Seventy Years in England* (London, 1986), 51–2, 55.
23 'Edward Holton Coumbe', *London Wiki*, https://london.fandom.com/wiki/Edward_Holton_Coumbe.
24 'The "Black Man's Cafe" Libel Action', *The Times*, 9 February 1927.
25 'Negro Cafe Owner's Libel Suit', *Guardian*, 10 February 1927.
26 Ibid.
27 'The "Black Man's Cafe" Libel Action', *The Times*, 9 February 1927.
28 Lara Putnam, 'Citizenship from the Margins: Vernacular Theories of Rights and the State from the Interwar Caribbean', *Journal of British Studies*, 53 (1), 2014, 162–91; Carina Ray, *Crossing the Color Line: Race, Sex, and the Contested Politics of Colonialism in Ghana* (Athens, 2015).
29 Laura Tabili, *We Ask for British Justice: Workers and Racial Difference in Late Imperial Britain* (Ithaca, 1994).
30 'Raid on a London Club', *Evening Telegraph*, 16 January 1925.
31 'Black Man's Cafe', *Yorkshire Evening Post*, 9 February 1927; TNA, RG15 012175: *1921 Census*, 8 Martell Road, West Dulwich, www.findmypast.co.uk.
32 'Relief Fund', *Musical Standard*, 5 November 1921; Howard Rye, 'Southern Syncopated Orchestra: The Roster', *Black Music Research Journal*, 30 (1), 2010; Monik Nordine 'Legacy of the Southern Syncopated Orchestra' (9 October 1921), https://moniknordine.ca/2021/10/09/legacy-of-the-southern-syncopated-orchestra/; Matera, *Black London*, 150–1; *SS Rowan Survivors in Dublin* (British Pathé, 1921), www.youtube.com/watch?v=Jxb8y4zlyVM; 'Man Who Didn't Sail on Rowan', *Dundee Evening Telegraph*, 10 October 1921. See Catherine Parsonage, *The Evolution of Jazz in Britain, 1880–1935* (London, 2005).
33 'Reputation of Cafe Kept by Negro', *Yorkshire Post*, 10 February 1927; 'Black Man's Cafe', *Yorkshire Evening Post*, 9 February 1927.
34 Ibid.

35 TNA, RG14 22091: *1911 Census*, 7 Edith Road, Seacombe, Cheshire, www.findmypast.co.uk.
36 'Reputation of Cafe Kept by Negro', *Yorkshire Post*, 10 February 1927; 'The 'Black Man's Cafe' Libel Action', *The Times*, 10 February 1927.
37 'Black Man's Cafe', *Yorkshire Evening Post*, 9 February 1927. See also 'MP and Black Man's Café', *Westminster Gazette*, 10 February 1927.
38 'Life at a Soho Cafe', *Daily Mail*, 10 February 1927.
39 As far as I can tell, Solanke is mentioned only in *The Times*. See e.g. 'The Black Man's Café Libel Action', *The Times*, 9 February 1927.
40 'Called to the Bar', *West Africa*, 1 May 1926; 'Solanke, Oladipo Felix (1893–1958)', *Oxford Dictionary of National Biography* (23 September 2003, https://doi-org.bham-ezproxy.idm.oclc.org/10.1093/ref:odnb/59528).
41 Hakim Adi, *West Africans in Britain, 1900–1960: Nationalism, Pan-Africanism, and Communism* (London, 1998), 24–5.
42 G. O. Olusanya, *The West African Students' Union and the Politics of Decolonisation, 1925–1958* (Ibadan, 1982); Adi, *West Africans in Britain*; Jinny Prais, 'Imperial Travelers: The Formation of West African Urban Culture, Identity, and Citizenship in London and Accra, 1925–1935', PhD dissertation, University of Michigan (2008), 57–59.
43 Marc Matera, *Black London: The Imperial Metropolis and Decolonization in the Twentieth Century* (Berkeley, 2015), 26–36; Olusanya, *West African Students' Union*, 2; Ladipo Solanke, *United West Africa (or Africa) at the Bar of the Family of Nations* (London, 1927), 40, 35; *Wasu*, March / June 1927.
44 Adi, *West Africans in Britain*, 27.
45 Ladipo Solanke, *Yoruba Problems, and How to Solve Them* (Ibadan, 1931).
46 Olusanya, *West African Students' Union*, 5.
47 Solanke, *United West Africa*, 62.
48 Adi, *West Africans in Britain*, 26–7; Matera, *Black London*, 31.
49 Solanke, *United West Africa*, 64.
50 '*Wasu*', *West Africa*, 17 April 1926.
51 Dennis Bardens, *Lord Justice Birkett* (London, 1963), 64, 167; H. Montgomery Hyde, *The Life of Lord Birkett of Ulverston* (London, 1964), 160–2; 'Birkett, Norman, first Baron Birkett (1883–1962), *Oxford Dictionary of National Biography* (23 September 2004, https://doi-org.bham-ezproxy.idm.oclc.org/10.1093/ref:odnb/31899).

52 'Absent Plaintiff', *Westminster Gazette*, 27 January 1927.
53 'The 'Black Man's Cafe' Libel Action', *The Times*, 10 February 1927.
54 H. P. Lansdale-Ruthven, *The Law of Libel for Journalists* (London, 1934), 5.
55 'Reputation of Cafe Kept by Negro', *Yorkshire Post*, 10 February 1927; 'The 'Black Man's Cafe' Libel Action', *The Times*, 10 February 1927.
56 'MP and Black Man's Café', *Westminster Gazette*, 10 February 1927.
57 'Reputation of Cafe Kept by Negro', *Yorkshire Post*, 10 February 1927; 'The 'Black Man's Cafe Libel Action', *The Times*, 11 February 1927.
58 'The 'Black Man's Cafe' Libel Action', *The Times*, 10 February 1927.
59 'Negro Cafe Libel Suit', *Guardian*, 11 February 1927.
60 'Where Women Beat the Men', *People*, 13 February 1927.
61 'Negro Cafe Libel Suit', *Guardian*, 11 February 1927.
62 'The 'Black Man's Cafe Libel Action', *The Times*, 11 February 1927.
63 'Negro Cafe Libel Suit', *Guardian*, 11 February 1927.
64 'The 'Black Man's Cafe' Libel Action', *The Times*, 9 February 1927.
65 'Negro's Cafe', *Yorkshire Post*, 9 February 1927; 'A Coloured Man's Cafe', *Daily Mail*, 9 February 1927; 'Negro Cafe Owner's Libel Suit', *Guardian*, 10 February 1927.
66 'Reputation of Cafe Kept by Negro', *Yorkshire Post*, 10 February 1927.
67 'The 'Black Man's Cafe' Libel Action', *The Times*, 10 February 1927.
68 'Life at a Soho Cafe', *Daily Mail*, 10 February 1927; 'Reputation of Cafe Kept by Negro', *Yorkshire Post*, 10 February 1927.
69 'The Black Man's Café Libel Action', *The Times*, 10 February 1927.
70 'Black Man's Café', *Daily News*, 9 February 1927; 'Prince as Tipster', *Edinburgh Evening News*, 9 February 1927.
71 'The Black Man's Café Libel Action', *The Times*, 10 February 1927.
72 'Black Man's Cafe', *Yorkshire Evening Post*, 9 February 1927.
73 'The Black Man's Café Libel Action', *The Times*, 10 February 1927.
74 Ibid.
75 'Life at a Soho Cafe', *Daily Mail*, 10 February 1927.

76 'Avory, Sir Horace Edmund (1851–1935)', (23 September 2004, https://doi-org.bham-ezproxy.idm.oclc.org/10.1093/ref:odnb/30506
77 'Negro's Cafe', *Yorkshire Post*, 9 February 1927.
78 Lansdale-Ruthven, *Law of Libel*, 146–7.
79 'The 'Black Man's Cafe' Libel Action', *The Times*, 10 February 1927.
80 Solanke, *United West Africa*, 62.
81 'Black Man's Cafe', *Scotsman*, 11 February 1927; 'Criminals Haunt', *Westminster Gazette*, 11 February 1927.
82 Wooll, *Guide to the Law of Libel*, 3.
83 'Negro Cafe Owner's Libel Suit', *Guardian*, 10 February 1927.
84 'Disorderly Premises', *Hansard*, Volume 202 (27 February 1927), www.hansard.parliament.uk/; TNA, HO 144 22301: Section 432194 / 20, Sandon to Secretary of State (15 February 1927).
85 TNA, HO 144 22301: Section 432194 / 20 (February 1927).
86 'Disorderly Premises', *Hansard*, Volume 202 (27 February 1927), www.hansard.parliament.uk/.
87 87 Paul Mulvey, *The Political Life of Josiah C. Wedgwood* (London, 2010), 113; Josiah Wedgwood, *Memoirs of a Fighting Life* (London, 1940). 116–17.
88 'Dominions and Colonial Affairs Appropriation Bill', *West Africa*, 7 August 1926; 'Letter to the Editor', *West Africa*, 24 April 1926.
89 'Colonial Policy in Relation to Coloured Peoples', *Hansard* (11 December 1929), www.hansard.parliament.uk/.
90 'The Sierra Leone Dinner Club's London Gathering', *West Africa*, 10 July 1926. H. E. Conway, 'Labour Protest Activity in Sierra Leone during the Early Part of the Twentieth Century', *Labour History*, 15 (1968), 49–63; Akintola Wyse, 'The 1926 Railway Strike and Anglo-Krio Relations: An Interpretation', *International Journal of African Historical Studies*, 14 (1), 1981, 93–123; Wyse, *H.C. Bankole-Bright and Politics in Colonial Sierra Leone, 1919–1958* (Cambridge, 1990).
91 Wedgewood, *The Future of the Indo-British Commonwealth* (London, 1921).
92 'Close up the Black Café'. *John Bull*, 19 February 1927; 'Kitten Gets Scratched', *John Bull*, 7 April 1928.
93 'Costs of Libel Action', *The Times*, 24 March 1928; 'Kitten, James', *London Gazette*, 27 May 1927, 3504; 'Kitten, James', *London Gazette*, 3 June 1927, 3689; 'Kitten, James', *London Gazette*, 28 February 1928, 1471. 'Stepney Man Charged at Bow Street', *East End News*, 23 August 1929.
94 LA, PS BOW A01 116: Registers (11 June 1928).

95 Ibid.: Registers (30 April 1928); 'Prison for Desertion', *East London Observer*, 11 August 1928; TNA, BT 350: Merchant Seaman Identity Certificate 302151, Isaac Jackson (1918), www.findmypast.co.uk. For other cases see LA, PS BOW A01 116: Registers (12 April 1928; 25 June 1928).

96 LA, PW BOW A01 114: Registers (2 February 1928); LA, PS BOW A01 115: Registers (2 March 1928); 'Scene in Seven Dials', *HFG*, 9 March 1928. See also 'Black Man's Café Scene', *HFG*, 3 February 1928; 'All Blacks Fight', *Daily Herald*, 27 December 1928.

97 'The Hammond Spencer Estate', *The Times*, 26 March 1928; 'The Hammond Spencer Estate', *Daily Chronicle*, 14 April 1928; 'The Estate Market', *The Times*, 20 March 1928. For the sale see 'Little Earl Street', *The Times*, 28 July 1928.

98 'Costs of Libel Action', *The Times*, 24 March 1928.

99 Minkah Makalani, *In the Cause of Freedom: Radical Black Internationalism from Harlem to London, 1917–1939* (Chapel Hill, 20214), 19.

Chapter 5

1 'Prince's Treasure Hunt', *Edinburgh Evening News*, 26 June 1924.

2 This discussion draws on *Survey of Seven Dials*.

3 'A Treasure Hunt', *Free Press and Mail*, 6 August 1924.

4 'Prince's Treasure Hunt', *Edinburgh Evening News*, 26 June 1924; D. J. Taylor, *Bright Young People: The Rise and Fall of a Generation, 1918–1940* (London, 2008).

5 'Rebuke for the Prince', *Daily Herald*, 28 July 1924.

6 Seth Koven, *Slumming: Social and Sexual Politics in Victorian London* (Princeton, 2006).

7 George Goodchild, *Jack O'Lantern* (London, 1929), 128–9.

8 Virginia Woolf, 'Street Haunting: A London Adventure' (1930), in *The Death of the Moth, and Other Essays* (London, 1942); Woolf, *Between the Acts* (London, 1941).

9 *The Missions and Charities Handbook* (London, 1949), 118.

10 'National Refuges Working Boys and Training Homes, London', *Children's Homes*, www.childrenshomes.org.uk/LondonWBSH/.

11 'The Straits of Central London', *Quiver*, vol. 37 (1902), 930–7, 115; 'Seven Dials Mission House', *Builder*, 22 April 1905.

12 'New Vicar of Ashburnham', *Sussex Agricultural Express*, 23 April 1926.

13 'Mission Hall Bones', *Daily Mirror*, 7 January 1925; 'Bones in Mission Hall', *Daily News*, 7 January 1925.

14 CLS, B HO M 1 1: Holborn MBC Minutes (14 July 1920).
15 LA, ACC 3445 SIC 01 14: Minutes (1922–1930) 'Miss E Dibdin', *Norwood News*, 18 March 1938; 'Bequest in Will of Norwood Lady', *Norwood News*, 13 May 1938; 'Borough Council Elections', *The Times*, 4 November 1919; TNA, RG14 1172: *1911 Census*, 62 Torrington Square, Bloomsbury, www.findmypast.co.uk. For Norah March see March, *Towards Racial Health: A Handbook on the Training of Boys and Girls* (London, 1915); March, *Sex Knowledge, Economics of Maternity and Child Welfare Work* (London, 1922).
16 Charles Marson, *God's Cooperative Strategy* (London, 1914), 108.
17 'Duchess of Seven Dials', *Bioscope*, 22 January 1920; British Film Institute, 54485: *The Duchess of Seven Dials*, https://collections-search.bfi.org.uk/web/Details/ChoiceFilmWorks/150050941.
18 'Duchess of Seven Dials', *Kinematograph Weekly*, 22 January 1920.
19 'Highgate Empire', *Holloway Press*, 5 February 1921.
20 'Ripley Empire', *Ripley and Heanor News*, 1 April 1921.
21 'Duchess of Seven Dials', *Kinematograph Weekly*, 22 January 1920.
22 Ibid.; 'Duchess of Seven Dials', *Bioscope*, 22 January 1920.
23 Ibid.
24 'London on the Screen', *Picturegoer*, 1 January 1922.
25 'Shaftesbury Pavilion', *Movie-Land*, 10 January 1921.
26 'Shadowland', *Picturegoer*, April 1921; 'Shadowland', *Picturegoer*, November 1921; 'In Full Cry (1921)', *Internet Movie Database*, www.imdb.com/title/tt0185376/mediaviewer/rm2235877377/?ref_=tt_md_1.
27 'Police Stop Filmmakers', *Guardian*, 10 December 1926.
28 'A Specialist in Shorts', *Kinematograph Weekly*, 7 January 1926; 'London After Dark', *Bioscope*, 29 April 1926; 'HB Parkinson', *Bioscope*, 12 December 1928.
29 'London After Dark', *Hull Daily Mail*, 11 December 1926.
30 'Police Stop Film', *Manchester Evening News*, 9 December 1926.
31 'MGM Buy British Films for Australia', *Bioscope*, 22 September 1927; 'The Story of Budock Vean's Pioneer Movie Maker Owner', www.budockvean.co.uk/news/the-story-of-budock-veans-pioneer-movie-maker-owner/. Only the film on Elephant and Castle survives, so it is unclear if the controversial scene is cut. See *London After Dark* (1926), https://player.bfi.org.uk/free/film/watch-london-after-dark-1926–online.
32 Goodchild, *Jack O'Lantern*, 128–9.

33 Norah James, *Hail! All Hail!* (London, 1929). See Lucy Bland, *Modern Women on Trial: Sexual Transgression in the Age of the Flapper* (Manchester, 2013).
34 Arnold Palmer, 'Books', *Britannia and Eve*, 1 July 1933.
35 Joseph Broadhurst, *From Vine Street to Jerusalem* (London, 1936), 38; Edgar Wallace, *The Hand of Power* (London, 1927), 116.
36 Graham Greene, *Brighton Rock* (London, 1938).
37 Victoria and Albert Museum, *Diaghilev and the Golden Age of the Ballets Russes, 1909–1929* (London, 2010).
38 'Fairies in Seven Dials', *Weekly Dispatch*, 27 July 1919. James Beechey and Richard Shone, 'Picasso in London, 1919', *Burlington Magazine*, October 2006.
39 'A Club in Seven Dials', *The Times*, 9 December 1924; *Post Office London Directory* (London, 1925), 2239. See TNA, BT350: Merchant Seaman Identity Certificate 848093, Felice Tapporo (1918), www.findmypast.co.uk; TNA, HO 396, World War Two Internees (Alien) Index Cards, 795727, Felice Tapporo (1940), www.ancestry.co.uk.
40 'Raided Club', *Daily News*, 16 June 1925; 'The Imported Rogue', *John Bull*, 11 July 1925. A year later Francesco Russo is fined £30 for selling alcohol without a licence from his shop opposite the Shaftesbury. See 'A Soho Licensing Offence', *The Times*, 16 October 1926.
41 *Arnold Bennett's Letters to his Nephew* (London, 1936), 202.
42 'Round of the Day', *Westminster Gazette*, 29 September 1927. Bennett and Cohen are seen again a week later: 'Gaiety in Seven Dials', *Era*, 5 October 1927.
43 Philip Kelleway, *Highly Desirable: The Zinkeisen Sisters* (Leiston, 2016), 30; Elizabeth Darling, 'The Cave of Harmony', in *Queer Spaces* (London, 2022), 74–5.
44 'Mariegold', *Sketch*, 5 October 1927.
45 Rohan McWilliam, 'Elsa Lanchester and Bohemian London in the Early Twentieth Century', *Women's History Review*, 23 (2), 2014, 172; Virginia Nicholson, *Among the Bohemians: Experiments in Living, 1900–1939* (London, 2002); Elsa Lanchester, *Elsa Lanchester, Myself* (New York, 1984); Lanchester, *Charles Laughton and I* (San Diego, 1938).
46 Kathleen Hale, *A Slender Reputation: An Autobiography* (London, 1994), 185.
47 *The Journals of Arnold Bennett* (London, 1932), 51.
48 'Mariegold', *Sketch*, 5 October 1927.
49 Hale, *Slender Reputation*, 132.
50 'Cave of Harmony', *Stage*, 15 March 1928.

51 'The Round of the Day', *Westminster Gazette*, 29 September 1927.
52 Hale, *Slender Reputation*, 132; 'Modernities', *Graphic*, 15 October 1927; 'Matisse and Armstrong', *Daily Chronicle*, 14 January 1928.
53 'New "Little Theatre"', *Dundee Evening Telegraph*, 29 November 1927; 'Plays and Pictures', *Nation and Athenaeum*, 11 February 1928.
54 'Gaiety in Seven Dials', *Era*, 5 October 1927.
55 'Seven Dials Club for Noted Men', *Daily Chronicle*, 30 September 1927.
56 'Club Premises in Seven Dials',' *The Times*, 30 September 1927.
57 *Journals of Arnold Bennett*, 271.
58 'Seven Dials Club for Noted Men', *Daily Chronicle*, 30 September 1927.
59 'Club Premises in Seven Dials', *The Times*, 30 September 1927.
60 'Mainly for Women', *Sunday Pictorial*, 2 October 1927.
61 Hale, *Slender Reputation*, 185; 'Mariegold', *Sketch*, 5 October 1927.
62 'Modernities', *Graphic*, 15 October 1927.
63 'A Cave of Harmony', *Stage*, 15 December 1927; 'Dramatis Personae', *Observer*, 29 January 1928; 'New "Little Theatre"', *Dundee Evening Telegraph*, 29 November 1927.
64 'The Perfect Plot', *Daily Mirror*, 12 March 1928.
65 'Gossip of London', *Daily Chronicle*, 13 March 1928.
66 Tom Laughton, *Pavilions by the Sea: The Memoirs of an Hotel Keeper* (London, 1977), 95–6.
67 CEM Joad, 'The Twenties: The Age of Release', *Saturday Book* (London, 1952), 282; Elsa Lanchester, *Elsa Lanchester, Herself* (London, 1983), 54; *The Player's Theatre, Covent Garden* (1938), www.britishpathe.com/asset/207920/.
68 'Gossip of London', *Daily Chronicle*, 13 March 1928; Hale, *Slender Reputation*, 131.
69 'The Presiding Genius', *Sketch*, 5 October 1927.
70 John Collier and Iain Laing, *Just the Other Day: An Informal History of Great Britain since the War* (London, 1932), 136–7.
71 Stella Gibbons, *Cold Comfort Farm* (London, 1932), 186–7.
72 'Round of the Day', *Westminster Gazette*, 29 September 1927; Lanchester, *Elsa Lanchester*, 59; Jane Marcus, *Virginia Woolf and the Languages of Patriarchy* (Bloomington, 1987), 168; Elizabeth Darling, 'Class, Sexuality, and Home in Interwar London', in Brent Pilkey, Rachel Scicluna, Ben Campkin, and Barbara Penner (eds), *Sexuality and Gender at Home* (London, 2017).
73 Radclyffe Hall, *The Well of Loneliness* (London, 1928), 258.

74 'Today's Gossip', *Daily Mirror*, 29 September 1927; Terry Castle, *Noel Coward and Radclyffe Hall: Kindred Spirits* (New York, 1996).
75 British Library, EC Z3 605: Harold Scott to Edith Craig (10 January 1928); Katherine Cockin, *Edith Craig and the Theatres of Art* (London, 2017), 216.
76 Sylvia Townsend Warner, *Collected Poems* (New York, 1980), 90.
77 'New "Little Theatre"', *Dundee Evening Telegraph*, 29 November 1927.
78 E. P. Leigh-Bennett, 'Night Lights: No. IX', *Bystander*, 25 January 1928.
79 Hale, *Slender Reputation*, 185.
80 'Surprise for Smart Set', *Edinburgh Evening News*, 23 June 1928.
81 TNA, BT 31 29734 219185: Cave of Harmony Ltd. (1927–32).
82 *Late Joys at the Players' Theatre* (London, 1943), 14–15.
83 TNA, CRIM 1 735: Jack Neave and Others (1934); TNA, MEPO 3 758: Caravan Club, 81 Endell Street, Disorderly House (1934); TNA, DPP 2 224: Jack Neave and Others, Disorderly House (1934); Mark Benney, *What Rough Beast? The Story of 'Ironfoot Jack'* (London, 1939), chapter 10; Colin Stanley (ed.), *The Surrender of Silence: The Memoirs of Ironfoot Jack* (London, 2018), chapter 5.
84 Constance Collier, *Harlequinade: The Story of My Life* (London, 1929), 142–4.
85 Elisa Rolle, 'Frank Vosper', *Queer Places*, http://www.elisarolle.com/queerplaces/fghij/Frank%20Vosper.html.
86 John Gielgud, *Early Stages* (London, Macmillan, 1939), 123–4.
87 Ibid. Sheridan Morley, *John G: The Authorised Biography of John Gielgud* (London, 2001). Charles Laughton lodges on nearby Long Acre: Laughton, *Pavilions by the Sea*, 50.
88 *London Electoral Register, Central St Giles Ward* (London, 1932), 40, www.ancestry.co.uk.
89 'Dollars to Donat', *Photoplay*, August 1939.
90 Avril Blake, *Misha Black* (London, 1984), chapter 1; Harriet Atkinson, 'Lines of Becoming: Misha Black and Entanglements through Exhibition Design', *Journal of Design History*, 34 (1), 2021, 37–53; V&A Archive of Art and Design, GB 73 AAD 1980 3 157: Letter head by Studio Z (1929).
91 Lynda Morris and Robert Radford, *The Story of the Artists International Association, 1933–1953* (Oxford, 1983).
92 V&A, GB 73 AAD 1980 3 130: National Registration Identity Card, Mischa Black.
93 'Duchess of Seven Dials', *Kinematograph Weekly*, 22 January 1920.

94 Mabel Lethbridge, *Fortune Grass* (London, 1934); Lethbridge, *Against the Tide* (London, 1936).
95 Lethbridge, *Fortune Grass*, 225.
96 Lethbridge, *Against the Tide*, 231.
97 Lethbridge, *Fortune Grass*, 177, 204.
98 Ibid., 219.

Chapter 6

1 *Bertie Alexander Meyer*, https://en.wikipedia.org/wiki/Bertie_Alexander_Meyer; Alan Powers, *Serge Chermayeff: Designer, Architect, Teacher* (London, 2001).
2 Avery Drawings and Archives Collections, Columbia University [Avery]: Serge Chermayeff architectural records and papers: Series III, Box 12 Folder 6, Cambridge Theatre, interior design (1932) and Series III, Subseries 4 Request Box 15, Folder 1, Souvenir of Cambridge Theatre (1930).
3 Noel Coward, *Present Indicative* (London, 1937), 200.
4 'London Stage's Reply to "Talkies"', *Daily Mail*, 25 June 1929.
5 'New Theatres', *Sheffield Daily Telegraph*, 25 August 1928; 'Cambridge Theatre Seven Dials', *Architects' Journal*, 8 October 1930.
6 'London Stage's Reply to "Talkies"', *Daily Mail*, 25 June 1929.
7 'New Theatres', *Sheffield Daily Telegraph*, 25 August 1928, 8.
8 'London Stage's Reply to "Talkies"', *Daily Mail*, 25 June 1929.
9 'New Companies', *The Stage*, 4 June 1931; 'New Companies', *Financial Times*, 28 May 1931.
10 Charles Graves, 'Theatre Money', *Nash's Pall Mall Magazine*, June 1934. This summary draws on LA, GLC DG EL 03 E001: Public Control Department (Entertainments): Cambridge Theatre, Earlham Street (1932–55); Claire Cochrane, *Twentieth Century British Theatre: Industry, Art, and Empire* (Cambridge, 2011); Tracy Davis, *The Economics of the British Stage, 1800–1914* (Cambridge, 2000); Rohan McWilliam, *London's West End: Creating the Pleasure District, 1800–1914* (Oxford, 2020).
11 'Sales by Auction', *The Times*, 5 April 1919; 'Result of Sale', *The Times*, 10 May 1919; 'A Wonderful Opportunity', *The Times*, 23 July 1920; 'John D. Wood and Co.', *The Times*, 11 December 1928.
12 See *Survey of Seven Dials*. On Bennett, see Register of Soldiers' Effects, Francis William Bennett (25 January 1919), www.ancestry.co.uk.

13 'London's New Theatres', *The Stage*, 25 July 1929. For the theatre's construction, see LA, GLC AR BR 19 4158: Theatre Cases, Cambridge Theatre, Seven Dials (1929–50).
14 'The New Seven Dials Theatre', *The Stage*, 4 September 1930.
15 *Cambridge Theatre Souvenir Programme* (October 1930).
16 Barbara Tilson, 'The Modern Art Department, Waring and Gillow, 1928–1931', *Journal of the Decorative Arts Society*, 8, 1984, 40–9.
17 This description draws on Avery, Series III, Box 12 Folder 6, Cambridge Theatre, interior design (1932) and Series III, Subseries 4 Request Box 15, Folder 1, Souvenir of Cambridge Theatre (1930); *The Cambridge Theatre, Earlham Street, London*, http://www.arthurlloyd.co.uk/CambridgeTheatre.htm; *Cambridge Theatre*, https://westendguides.com/cambridge-theatre/. See also *Anthony Gibbons Grinling*, http://www.antonygibbonsgrinling.co.uk.
18 'Who Said a Theatre Slump?' *Daily Mail*, 9 September 1930.
19 Cadbury Research Library, University of Birmingham [CRL], MS38 1369: 'Reply to the Talkies', *People*, 7 September 1930; 'London's Latest Theatre', *Architects' Journal*, 3 September 1930.
20 Avery, Series III, Box 12 Folder 6, Cambridge Theatre, interior design (1932).
21 'The New Seven Dials Theatre', *The Stage*, 4 September 1930.
22 *Souvenir of Cambridge Theatre, Seven Dials* (NP, 1930), in author's possession.
23 Richard Hornsey, 'Listening to the Tube Map: Rhythm and the Historiography of Urban Map Use', *Environment and Planning D: Society and Space*, 30 (4), 2012, 675–93.
24 CRL, MS38 1369: *Charlot's Masquerade*, by Ronald Jeans (1930), theatrical programme.
25 CRL, MS38 1369: 'The Cambridge', *The Stage*, 11 September 1930; James Ross Moore, *Andre Charlot: The Genius of Intimate Musical Revue* (London, McFarland, 2005), 121–2.
26 CRL, MS38 1369: 'Charlot's Masquerade at the Cambridge Theatre', unattributed cutting, 17 September 1930.
27 'At the Play', *Bystander*, 17 September 1930.
28 'The Cambridge', *The Stage*, 4 September 1930.
29 CRL, MS38 1369: 'Breathless!' *Sunday Dispatch*, 7 December 1930.
30 'Cambridge Theatre Seven Dials', *Architects' Journal*, 8 October 1930.
31 Professor C. H. Reilly, 'Landmarks of the Year', *Architects' Journal*, 14 January 1931.
32 'Modernity in Seven Dials', *Observer*, 31 October 1930.

33 'The Cambridge', *The Stage*, 4 September 1930.
34 'London's Latest Theatre', *Sphere*, 6 September 1930.
35 *Cambridge Theatre Souvenir Programme* (October 1930).
36 CRL, MS38 1369: 'Reply to the Talkies', *People*, 7 September 1930.
37 Ibid.: 'Charlot's Masquerade', *Sunday Times*, 7 September 1930.
38 'Colour Talkies', *Daily Mail*, 26 May 1930.
39 CRL, MS38 1369: 'Breathless!' *Sunday Dispatch*, 7 December 1930.
40 'Court and Society', *Daily Mail*, 6 December 1930 'Duchess and Charity', *Daily Mail*, 20 December 1930.
41 'We Take Off Our Hat To', *Sketch*, 1 April 1931.
42 'Who Said a Theatre Slump?' *Daily Mail*, 9 September 1930.
43 'A 31 Hours Wait', *Daily Mail*, 4 September 1930; CRL, MS38 1369: 'Charlot's Masquerade at the Cambridge Theatre', unattributed cutting, 17 September 1930.
44 'The Cambridge Theatre: Modernity in Seven Dials', *Observer*, 31 October 1930.
45 'George William Leech, RI (British, 1894–1966)', http://www.cambridgeprints.com/artists/l/LEECH.HTML.
46 CRL, MS38 1369: 'The Cambridge', *Stage*, 11 September 1930. See also *Souvenir of Cambridge Theatre, Seven Dials* (NP, 1930), 9.
47 'London's Latest Theatre', *Sphere*, 6 September 1930.
48 Ibid; 'Untitled', *Architects' Journal*, 2 December 1931.
49 CRL, MS38 1369: 'The Passing Shows', *Tatler*, 24 September 1930.
50 'Who Said a Theatre Slump?', *Daily Mail*, 9 September 1930.
51 See e.g., *White Cargo, Souvenir Programme* (1935) – copy in author's collection.
52 This discussion draws on *Survey of Seven Dials*.
53 CRL, MS38 1369: 'The Passing Shows', *Tatler*, 24 September 1930.
54 See e.g. 'Seven Dials: 1930', in *Souvenir of Cambridge Theatre, Seven Dials* (1930).
55 CRL, MS38 1369: 'Beatrice Lillie's Return', *Morning Post*, 6 September 1930. See the short film *Charlot's Masquerade*, British Pathé (1930), www.britishpathe.com/asset/57044/.
56 James Moore, 'Jeans, Ronald (1887–1973)', *Oxford Dictionary of National Biography*, 2008, https://doi.org/10.1093/ref:odnb/73132.
57 CRL, MS38 1369: 'Charlot's Masquerade', *Sunday Graphic*, 7 September 1930.
58 Ibid.: 'The Passing Shows', *Tatler*, 24 September 1930; 'Charlot's Masquerade', *Sunday Graphic*, 7 September 1930.
59 Ibid.: 'Beatrice Lillie's Return', *Morning Post*, 6 September 1930.

60 Ibid.: 'The Cambridge', *Stage*, 11 September 1930.
61 Ibid.: 'Charlot's Masquerade', *Observer*, 7 September 1930.
62 Ibid.: Untitled cutting, *Daily Mirror*, 6 September 1930.
63 CRL, MS38 4525: *White Cargo* (1923–53). 'White Cargo Revived', *Stage*, 21 November 1935.
64 'African Melodrama', *Arbroath Herald*, 29 November 1935.
65 'Olga Lindo', *Daily News*, 7 November 1935; 'Flashes from the Footlights'. *Daily Mirror*, 18 November 1935.
66 'White Cargo Revived', *Stage*, 21 November 193.
67 TNA, RG15 01990: *1921 Census*, 7 Belvedere Crescent, York Road, Lambeth, www.findmypast.co.uk; TNA, RG101 0854H 002 6, *1939 Register*, 2 Lancaster Road, Haringey, www.findmypast.co.uk.
68 'White Cargo Revived', *Stage*, 21 November 1935.
69 'In Seven Dials', *Era*, 6 May 1931; CRL, MS38 5056: 'The Sign of Seven Dials', *The Stage*, 4 June 1931.
70 CRL, MS38 5056: 'The Sign of Seven Dials', *Stage*, 4 June 1931.
71 Harry Ransom Center, Box 158.4: B. J. Simmons and Co., Costume Design Records, Job 740, *Sign of the Seven Dials*, Cambridge Theatre (1931).
72 CRL, MS38 5056: 'The Sign of the Seven Dials', *Punch*, 10 June 1931.
73 Ibid.
74 Ibid.: 'The Sign of Seven Dials', *Stage*, 4 June 1931.
75 Ibid.: 'The Sign of the Seven Dials', *Punch*, 10 June 1931
76 Ibid.: 'Seymour Hicks in a New Show', *Evening News*, 3 June 1931.
77 Ibid.: 'The Sign of the Seven Dials', *Sunday Times*, 7 June 1931; James Agate, *Ego: The Autobiography of James Agate* (London, 1935), 379.
78 CRL, MS38 5056: 'Seymour Hicks', *Sunday Express*, 7 June 1931.
79 'For Sale', *Stage*, 2 July 1931.
80 *Souvenir of Cambridge Theatre* (October 1930).
81 For a partial list of the productions staged in the 1930s, see *Theatricalia*, https://theatricalia.com/place/8k/cambridge-theatre-london/past?page=2/.
82 'Cambridge Theatre', *Kinematograph Weekly*, 28 February 1935.
83 Later the theatre hosted exhibitions by the Society for Cultural Relations between Peoples of the British Commonwealth and the USSR (1942) and the Jewish Fund for Soviet Russia's screening of *The Proud Village* (1944): LA, GLC DG EL 03 E001 (1932–55); 'The Cambridge Theatre, Seven Dials', *Music Hall and Theatre History*

Site, http://www.arthurlloyd.co.uk/CambridgeTheatre.htm. On the International Brigade Dependents' and Wounded Aid Committee, see Marx Memorial Library, SC ORG DWAC (1936–39).

84 G. B. Shaw, 'Subsidizing the Theatre', *The Times*, 13 September 1937.

85 See the film of this performance *Katherine Dunham* (1952), www.britishpathe.com/asset/79063/.

Chapter 7

1 W. R. Titterton, 'Among the Squares and Circuses', in St John Adcock (ed.), *Wonderful London: The World's Greatest City Described by its Best Writers and Pictured by its Finest Photographers*, vol. II (London, 1924–25), 664; Rebecca Preston and Andrew Saint, *St Giles-in-the-Fields: The History of a London Parish* (London, 2024), 407.

2 'Where is St Giles Circus?', *HFG*, 24 December 1920. For the wider interest in these questions, see 'Names of Famous Old Streets', *HFG*, 18 July 1919.

3 'Arthur Field', https://en.wikipedia.org/wiki/Arthur_Field_(trade_unionist).

4 'St Giles or Bloomsbury Circus', *HFG*, 31 December 1920.

5 'St Giles or Bloomsbury Circus', *HFG*, 21 January 1921. For a later reprisal of the argument see CLS, B HO M 1 1: HMBC Minutes (25 March 1925).

6 CLS, B HO M 1 1: Holborn Metropolitan Borough Council Minutes (13 May 1936). See also LA, LCC CL TP 01 060: Street Naming Subcommittee, Conference with Holborn MBC on General Question: Clerk of Council to Town Clerk, Holborn (10 September 1935); LA, GLC AR BR SN 01 045: Circulated information of naming, renaming, numbering, and renumbering of streets and buildings, correspondence (1925–84).

7 LA, LCC MIN 12261: Street Naming Subcommittee, Presented Papers (22 October 1935); LA, LCC MIN 12258: Street Naming Subcommittee, Minutes (22 October 1935).

8 LA, LCC MIN 12259: Street Naming Subcommittee, Minutes (10 March 1936; 31 March 1936).

9 LA, LCC CL TP 01 060: Clerk of Council to Town Clerk, Holborn (10 September 1935); CLS, B HO M 1 1: HMBC Minutes (13 May 1936); LA, LCC MIN 12261: Street Naming Subcommittee, Presented Papers (14 July 1936).

10 LA, LCC MIN 12261: Street Naming Subcommittee, Presented Papers (3 November 1936; 24 November 1936).

11 LA, LCC MIN 12262: Street Naming Subcommittee, Presented Papers (29 June 1937).
12 LA, LCC CL TP 01 060: Holborn Street Names which are Repeated Outside the Borough (1936); LA, LCC MIN 12259: Street Naming Subcommittee, Minutes (14 July 1936); CLS, B HO M 1 1: HMBC Minutes (13 January 1937); CLS, B HO M 1 1: HMBC Minutes (10 February 1937).
13 LA, LCC MIN 12261: Report by the Superintending Architect (8 December 1936).
14 'Seven Dials Protest', *Daily Mail*, 19 September 1936.
15 'Not Copyright', *Sheffield Daily Telegraph*, 4 June 1930.
16 'At Random', *Observer*, 7 August 1938.
17 This account draws on LA, LCC MIN 12261: Report by the Superintending Architect (8 December 1936); LA, LCC CL TP 01 060: Report of the Street Naming Subcommittee (8 December 1936).
18 LA, LCC MIN 12259: Street Naming Subcommittee, Minutes (8 December 1936). See also CLS, B HO M 1 1: HMBC Minutes (10 February 1937).
19 'London Day by Day', *Edinburgh Evening News*, 21 September 1936.
20 LA, LCC MIN 12261: Street Naming Subcommittee, Presented Papers (8 December 1936). See also LA, LCC CL TP 01 060: Report of the Street Naming Subcommittee (8 December 1936).
21 LA, GLC MA SC 01 210: LCC Public Health Department, Housing (1936 Act) Borough of Holborn, Seven Dials areas (1938–39).
22 Ibid.: Holborn Medical Officer of Health, Shelton Street (Monmouth Street) Area (20 March 1939).
23 Ibid.: Public Health Department, special report (15 March 1939).
24 LSE, GB 97 NSOL 2 19 4: New Survey of London Life and Labour, Holborn (1930–34).
25 'Decree for Dorothy Dix', *Kensington News*, 10 November 1933.
26 This discussion draws on *Survey of Seven Dials*.
27 LA, GLC MA SC 01 210: Medical Officer of Health, Shelton Street (Monmouth Street) Area, Holborn (20 March 1939).
28 'Girl Drug Takers Death', *HFG*, 12 May 1922; 'Girl Drug Takers Death', *HFG*, 9 June 1922; 'Drug Victim's Tragic Death', *HFG*, 16 June 1922; 'Black Men's Pyjama Parties', *John Bull*, 4 August 1923.
29 LA, LCC MIN 12263: Petition as to changing the name of Lumber Court (1 March 1938). See also LA, LCC MIN 12260: Street Naming Subcommittee, Minutes (1 March 1938).
30 LA, LCC MIN 12263: Street Naming Subcommittee, Presented Papers LCC MIN 12263 (1 March 1938).

31 'The Ambassadors Theatre', *Music Hall and Theatre History Site*, http://www.arthurlloyd.co.uk/AmbassadorsTheatre.htm.
32 LA, LCC MIN 12263: Petition as to changing the name of Lumber Court (1 March 1938). See also LA, LCC MIN 12260: Street Naming Subcommittee, Minutes (1 March 1938). The wider discussion draws on *Survey of Seven Dials.*
33 LA, LCC MIN 12260: Street Naming Subcommittee, Minutes (1 March 1938); LA, LCC MIN 12263: Street Naming Subcommittee, Presented Papers (1 March 1938).
34 LA, LCC MIN 12263: Petition as to changing the name of Lumber Court (1 March 1938); LA, LCC MIN 12260: Street Naming Subcommittee, Minutes (1 March 1938).
35 *Pictorial London: Views of the Streets, Public Buildings, Parks, and Scenery of the Metropolis* (London, 1906), 162, xxi. For first-hand accounts of the markets, see Mrs Robert Henrey, *An Exile in Soho* (London, 1952), 105; Henrey, *Julia: Reminiscences of a Year in Madeleine's Life as a London Shopgirl* (London, 1971), 165.
36 'Sunday Street Trading', *Somerset Guardian*, 22 June 1928.
37 'Ban on Sunday Street Trading', *HFG*, 28 October 1927.
38 'Law Everyone Breaks', *Daily Mail*, 12 March 1929; 'Banned by Law of 1677', *Daily Mail*, 26 March 1929.
39 'Pushed off the Kerb', *John Bull*, 12 January 1929. See also 'Mr Chartres Biron', *John Bull*, 6 April 1929.
40 'Council and Sunday Trading', *HFG*, 11 November, 1927.
41 'Sunday Trading Ban', *HFG*, 27 April 1928; CLS, B HO M 1 1: HMBC Minutes (23 October 1929). For Mrs Day, see 'Veteran Costers', *Western Mail*, 15 May 1929.
42 'Sunday Street Trading', *Somerset Guardian*, 22 June 1928.
43 'Lords Day Observance Act', *Western Daily Press*, 26 March 1929; 'Street Trading on Sunday', *Eastern Post*, 30 March 1929.
44 'Veteran Costers', *Western Mail*, 15 May 1929.
45 For an example of this concern in a different context see LA, LCC CL TP 01 060: R. L. Graves, Marylebone Town Clerk, to Clerk of Council (17 October 1936).
46 CLS, B HO M 1 1: HMBC Minutes (10 February 1937; 13 May 1936).
47 Ibid.: HMBC Minutes (23 June 1937); LA, LCC CL TP 01 060: Report of the Street Naming Sub-Committee (8 December 1936).
48 'London Street Names', *Observer*, 8 May 1938; CLS, B HO M 1 1: HMBC Minutes (13 May 1936; 23 June 1937). LA, LCC MIN 12262: Street Naming Subcommittee, Presented Papers (13 July

1937); LA, LCC MIN 12259: Street Naming Subcommittee, Minutes (13 July 1937).

49 LA, LCC MIN 12263 Street Naming Subcommittee, Presented Papers (15 February 1938); LA, LCC MIN 12260: Street Naming Subcommittee, Minutes (15 February 1938).

50 LA, LCC MIN 12260: Street Naming Subcommittee, Minutes (22 November 1938).

51 Ibid.: Street Naming Subcommittee, Minutes (11 July 1939).

52 'London Street Names', *Observer*, 8 May 1938. See also 'New Street Names', *Yorkshire Post*, 9 May 1938.

53 LA, LCC MIN 12259: Street Naming Subcommittee, Minutes (18 February 1936); LA, LCC MIN 12261: Street Naming Subcommittee, Presented Papers (18 February 1936).

54 Ibid.: Street Naming Subcommittee, Presented Papers (22 October 1935).

55 On the London Society, see www.londonsociety.org.uk/page/about. St John Adcock, *Wonderful London*, Vols I–III (London, 1924–5). *Wonderful London*, dir. Harry Parkinson and Frank Miller (1924).

56 'London after Dark', *Bioscope*, 29 April 1926; 'London after Dark', *Westminster Gazette*, 10 December 1926.

57 'At Random', *Observer*, 7 August 1938.

58 'From the Post-bag', *Observer*, 3 April 1938.

59 'St Giles or Bloomsbury Circus', *HFG*, 31 December 1920.

60 Ibid.

61 CLS, B HO M 1 1: HMBC Minutes (13 May 1936).

62 LA, LCC MIN 12261: Street Naming Subcommittee, Presented Papers (3 November 1936; 24 November 1936).

63 CLS, B HO M 1 1: HMBC Minutes (13 January 1937). See also LA, LCC MIN 12261: Street Naming Subcommittee, Presented Papers (3 and 24 November 1936); LA, LCC MIN 12259: Street Naming Subcommittee, Minutes (24 November 1936; 2 February 1937; 29 June 1937).

Denouement

1 TNA, RG101 0254F 015 1: *1939 Register*, 37 Mercer Street, www.findmypast.co.uk; LA, GLC MA SC 01 210: Medical Adviser's Department, Slum Clearance, Seven Dials Areas (1938–39).

2 Certificate of Death, Jim Kitten: No. 115 Abbots Langley, Watford (18 October 1940); Certificate of Marriage, Emily Kitten and James Tucker: No. 207, Holborn Register Office (9 June 1943);

Register of Civil Deaths and Burials, Vol. 5D, 381 (20 January 1962); *Probate Death Index, London* (28 June 1962), www.findmypast.co.uk; TNA, BT 364: Merchant Seaman, Identity certificate: 374210, James Tucker (1919).

3 J. M. Lee, 'Commonwealth Students in the United Kingdom, 1940–1960', *Minerva*, 44 (1), 2006, 1–24; Thomas Molony, *Nyerere: The Early Years* (London, 2014), 181.

4 J. H. Forshaw and Patrick Abercrombie, *County of London Plan* (London, 1943), 23–4.

5 LA, GLC AR HOD 10 007: Plan for Redevelopment: Covent Garden – Seven Dials Area (1957–8).

6 David Bieda, *Seven Dials: Reinventing a Lost Neighbourhood* (2009), www.sevendials.com/web/viewer.html?file=/resources/Reinventing_a_Lost_Neighbourhood.pdf.

7 Nicholas Albery and Christine Mills, *The Neal's Yard Story* (London, 1987).

8 Jonathan Nunn, 'Hippy, Capitalist, Guru, Grocer: The Forgotten Genius Who Changed British Food', *Guardian*, 23 January 2024.

9 *Covent Garden's Moving: Covent Garden Area Draft Plan* (London, 1968); *Covent Garden: The Next Step* (London, 1971); *The Greater London Council (Covent Garden) GLC Action Area Plan* (London, 1978).

10 London County Council, *Survey of London, Volume V* (London, 1914), 114.

11 Bieda, *Seven Dials*.

12 'From Demolition to Conservation', *Seven Dials Trust*, www.sevendials.com/history/from-demolition-to-conservation.

13 The company's portfolio of *c.*640 buildings is valued at £4.8 billion: see Shaftesbury Capital, www.shaftesburycapital.com/en/about-us.html; www.novaloca.com/retail-premises/to-let/london/211195.

14 *Seven Dials Trust*, www.sevendials.com.

15 Searching for 'Seven Dials' at www.londonpicturearchive.org.uk is the easiest way to do this.

16 *Shaftesbury Capital*, www.shaftesburycapital.com/en/about-us.html; www.novaloca.com/retail-premises/to-let/london/211195.

17 Historic England: *Cambridge Theatre: List No. 1342096* (11 January 1999), https://historicengland.org.uk/listing/the-list/list-entry/1342096. On the campaign to list the Cambridge: LA, GLC DG PRB 35 020 365: GLC Public Information Branch Press Office, 'List These Theatres, Says GLC' (1 August 1973).

18 *The Seven Dials Trust People's Plaques and Street History Plaques Project*, www.sevendials.com/resources/brochure_archive/

People-s_and_Street_History_Plaques_Project_Brochure_2015-11-23.pdf. See also 'Seven Dials Conservation Area', *Bloomsbury Conservation Areas Advisory Committee*, https://bloomsburyconservation.org.uk/conservation-areas/seven-dials-conservation-area/.

19 I draw here on Anna Minton, *Big Capital: Who is London For?* (London, 2017).

Note on sources

This book reconstructs a lost urban world and the lives of those who lived, worked, and played there. At its heart is a survey of Seven Dials in the 1920s and 1930s, which interweaves genealogical sources, including the records of the 1921 Census and 1939 Register, published street directories and electoral registers, social surveys like *The New Survey of London Life and Labour* (1930–35) (Archives and Special Collections, London School of Economics) and the fire insurance plans produced by Charles E. Goad Ltd (London Archives). It is a painstaking task, but putting the neighbourhood's people, businesses, and institutions back in their place allows us to understand what was at stake in Seven Dials' remaking and unmaking after the Great War.

The tensions and conflicts animated by this process often played out through the institutions of law and police. The book draws on the records of the Bow Street Magistrates Court (London Archives) and the Metropolitan Police, Home Office, and High Court of Justice (National Archives). Concerns about urban change, gentrification and decline, and the area's changing character and culture were shaped – and often amplified – by the sensational reporting of newspapers, periodicals, and magazines. The book thus also surveys Seven Dials' place in the local and national press.

The 'problem' of Seven Dials was always political, and its history braced by the efforts of politicians, planners, and developers to remake London in their own image. To understand how this happened, the book draws on newspapers and periodicals, trade publications, and the records of the London County Council (London Archives), Holborn Metropolitan Borough Council (Camden Local Studies and Archives), and Land Registry. If the tensions that coalesced around Seven Dials were local and personal, they had national and imperial resonance. To explore why this was the case, the book draws on the records of the Home, Foreign, and Colonial Offices (National Archives), and Parliamentary Debates (Hansard).

Finally, the book tries to evoke how London looked and felt in the 1920s and 1930s. To do this – to understood how people thought and talked about Seven Dials – it draws on guidebooks, travelogues, novels, and autobiographies (British Library; Bishopsgate Institute). It makes particular use of visual and material sources, including films, newsreels, and photographs (BFI National Archive, British Film Institute; British Pathé online archive; London Picture Archive); paintings, illustrations, and architectural plans and drawings; theatrical ephemera, programmes, costumes, and props (Avery Drawings and Archives, Avery Architectural and Fine Arts Library, Columbia University; Cadbury Research Library, University of Birmingham; Harry Ransom Centre, University of Texas; Victoria and Albert Museum, National Art Library and Archives); and contemporary maps and plans (London Archives).

Further reading

This list is not exhaustive, but if you are interested in reading more – about histories of London or the 1920s and 1930s – here are some recommendations:

Hakim Adi, *West Africans in Britain, 1900–1960* (1998).

Hakim Adi, *African and Caribbean People in Britain: A History* (2023).

Kate Atkinson, *Shrines of Gaiety* (2022).

Rob Baker, *Beautiful Idiots and Brilliant Lunatics: A Sideways Look at Twentieth Century London* (2017).

Lucy Bland, *Modern Women on Trial: Sexual Transgression in the Age of the Flapper* (2013).

Stephen Brooke, *London 1984: Conflict and Change in the Radical City* (2024).

Kieran Connell, *Multicultural Britain: A People's History* (2024).

Elizabeth Darling, *Re-forming Britain: Narratives of Modernity Before Reconstruction* (2007).

John Davis, *Waterloo Sunset: London from the Sixties to Thatcher* (2022).

Laura Doan, *Fashioning Sapphism: The Origins of a Modern English Lesbian Culture* (2001).

Juliet Gardiner, *The Thirties: An Intimate History* (2011).

David Hendy, *The BBC: A People's History* (2022).

Christopher Hilliard, *The Littlehampton Libels: A Miscarriage of Justice and a Mystery About Words in 1920s England* (2017).

Matt Houlbrook, *Queer London: Perils and Pleasures in the Sexual Metropolis, 1918–57* (2005).

Stephen Inwood, *City of Cities: The Birth of Modern London* (2011).

Jacqueline Jenkins, *Black 1919: Riots, Racism, and Resistance in Imperial Britain* (2008).
Marek Kohn, *Dope Girls: The Birth of the British Drug Underground* (2024).
Julia Laite, *The Disappearance of Lydia Harvey: A True Story of Sex, Crime, and the Meaning of Justice* (2022).
Claire Langhamer and Hester Barron, *Class of '37* (2022).
Michael John Law, *1938: Modern Britain: Social Change and Visions of the Future* (2017).
Alison Light, *Mrs Woolf and the Servants: The Hidden Heart of Domestic Service* (2007).
Minkah Makalani, *In the Cause of Freedom: Radical Black Internationalism from Harlem to London, 1917–1939* (2011).
Marc Matera, *Black London: The Imperial Metropolis and Decolonization in the Twentieth Century* (2015).
Rohan McWilliam, *London's West End: Creating the Pleasure District, 1800–1914* (2020).
Anna Minton, *Big Capital: Who is London For?* (2017).
Frank Mort, *Capital Affairs: London and the Making of the Permissive Society* (2010).
Mo Moulton, *Mutual Admiration Society: How Dorothy L Sayers and her Circle Remade the World for Women* (2019).
Virginia Nicholson, *Among the Bohemians: Experiments in Living, 1900–1939* (2002).
Panikos Panayi, *Migrant City: A New History of London* (2020).
Kennetta Hammond Perry, *London is the Place for Me: Black Britons, Citizenship, and the Politics of Race* (2016).
Rebecca Preston and Andrew Saint, *St Giles-in-the-Fields: The History of a London Parish* (2024).
Carina Ray, *Crossing the Colour Line: Race, Sex, and the Contested Politics of Colonialism in Ghana* (2015).
Gemma Romain, *Race, Sexuality, and Identity in Britain and Jamaica: The Biography of Patrick Nelson, 1916–1963* (2017).
Cathy Ross, *Twenties London: A City in the Jazz Age* (2003).
The Seven Dials Trust, website at https://www.sevendials.com.
Neal Shashore, *Designs on Democracy: Architecture and the Public in Interwar London* (2022).
Jane Shaw, *Octavia, Daughter of God: The Story of a Female Messiah and her Followers* (2011).
Laura Spinney, *Pale Rider: The Spanish Flu of 1918 and How it Changed the World* (2017).
Gavin Stamp, *Interwar: British Architecture, 1919–39* (2024).

Daniel Stephen, *The Empire of Progress: West Africans, Indians, and Britons at the British Empire Exhibition, 1924–25* (2013).
D. J. Taylor, *Bright Young People: The Rise and Fall of a Generation, 1918–1940* (2008).
Dan Todman, *The Great War: Myth and Memory* (2005).
Jenny Uglow, *Sybil and Cyril: Cutting Through Time* (2021).
Francesca Wade, *Square Haunting: Five Women, Freedom, and London Between the Wars* (2020).
Judith Walkowitz, *Nights Out: Life in Cosmopolitan London* (2012).
Sarah Waters, *The Paying Guests* (2014).
Jerry White, *London in the Twentieth Century: A City and its People* (2008).

Illustrations

0.1 Seven Dials, 1938. From London Archives, GLC MA SC 01 210 (1938–39). Courtesy of London Archives. *page* 14

1.1 Shops in Great White Lion Street, 1913. From LA, SC PHL 01 157 75 3784. Published courtesy of The London Archives (City of London Corporation). Courtesy of London Archives. 32

1.2 'A sketch of the Kitten's Cafe, from a recent photograph'. From 'Close up the Black Cafe', *John Bull*, 19 February 1927. Courtesy of the British Library Board. All rights reserved. With thanks to The British Newspaper Archive (www.britishnewspaperarchive.co.uk). 37

2.1 Postcard of Shaftesbury Hotel, London, undated. Copy in author's collection. 57

2.2 Corner of Earlham Street and Monmouth Street, 1938(?). Published courtesy of the Seven Dials Trust. 71

3.1 'A sketch of St Giles Buildings, Seven Dials', included in a Society for the Improvement of the Condition of the Labouring Classes fundraising appeal, from 'Help us Abolish the Slums', *The Times*, 7 December 1926. © News Licensing. 80

3.2 St Giles Buildings, Shorts Gardens, Artist's Impressions, 1925. Courtesy of London Archives, ACC 3445 SIC 08 006. Published courtesy of the Peabody Trust, London. 93

4.1 Statement of Claim, 1926. From National Archive, J 54 1951: James Kitten versus Odhams Press and E. R. Thompson (February 1927). Courtesy of the National Archives of the United Kingdom. 110

4.2 'An Ideal Block for Future Development', 1928. From 'The Hammond Spencer Estate', *The Times*, 26 March 1928. © News Licensing. 137

5.1 'Scene from "The Duchess of Seven Dials"', 1920. From 'Duchess of Seven Dials', *Bioscope*, 22 January 1920. Courtesy of the British Library Board. All rights reserved. With thanks to The British Newspaper Archive (www.britishnewspaperarchive.co.uk). 146

5.2 Harold Scott and Elsa Lanchester in the vaults of the Cave of Harmony, 1928. Copy in author's collection. 155

5.3 Nightclub in Seven Dials, London, 1927–28. Anonymous photographer for the General Photographic Agency. Published courtesy of Getty Images. 162

6.1 'Architect's drawing of the new Cambridge Theatre'. From 'Who Said a Theatre Slump?', *Daily Mail Atlantic Edition*, 9 September 1930. Published courtesy of DMG Media Licensing. 175

6.2 Foyer of the Cambridge Theatre, 1930. From Avery Architectural and Fine Arts Library, University of Columbia, Papers of Serge Chermayeff, Series III, Box 12 Folder 6, Cambridge Theatre, interior design (1932). 181
6.3 Scene from *At The Sign of the Seven Dials*, 1931. From Cadbury Research Library: Special Collections, University of Birmingham: CRL, MS38 5056: unattributed newspaper clipping. 198
7.1 Great White Lion Mercer Street, 1938. Courtesy of London Archives, LCC AR BA 05 352: Street naming and numbering plan, 8059 (1938). 206
7.2 Proposed clearance area: Monmouth Street and Shelton Street, 1939. Courtesy of London Archives, GLC MA SC 01 210 (1938–39). 212
8.1 Shops in Mercer Street, 1956. Courtesy of London Archives, SC PHL 01 163 56 3257. 232
8.2 Vacant Site in Earlham Street, 1975. Courtesy of London Archives, SC PHL 01 152 75 5008. 235

Endpapers Seven Dials, 1938. From Charles Goad's *Insurance Plan of London*, Volume VIII (London, 1938). Courtesy of London Archives, LCC VA GOAD VIII 1938.

Acknowledgements

It has taken me more than twenty years to work out how best to tell this story – to see how a brief Home Office file, a libel trial, and the history of Seven Dials and its people might allow us to understand how London was made modern in the 1920s and 1930s. In being able to make these connections, I am indebted to the remarkable scholars who have transformed our understanding of the imperial metropolis over the past two decades, particularly those who have shown how histories of race and ethnicity, gender and sexuality, and class are central in shaping modern urban life. It is a pleasure to acknowledge the foundational importance of their work here, and in the endnotes which underpin this book. Of course, there are different ways to tell this story, just as there are countless different stories to tell about those people whose lives passed in and out of Seven Dials in the 1920s and 1930s. I would be delighted to share my research notes with anyone who wants to follow these threads.

Writing a book like this would have been impossible – even unthinkable – twenty years ago, before the digitisation of archival sources on an industrial scale and the keyword searchable genealogical and newspaper databases that allow us to trace ordinary people through their fleeting encounters with the institutions of state, law, and media. A century after it was completed, the online publication of the 1921 Census was a breathtaking and transformative moment. I have still relied on the historian's old ways, though – the craft through which we navigate physical archives and libraries. And so, I have also relied on the wisdom and guidance of those archivists and librarians who know their collections better than anyone. I owe a debt of gratitude to those who have generously enabled my research at the Avery Architectural and Fine Arts Library, Columbia University; the British Film Institute National Archive; the Bishopsgate Institute; the British Library; the Cadbury Research Library, University of Birmingham; Camden Local Studies and Archives; the Harry Ransom Centre, University of Texas; the London Archives; Archives and Special Collections, London School of Economics; the National Archives of the United Kingdom; and the Victoria and Albert Museum, National Art Library and Archives.

I am struck now by the conversations I hear echoing through this book. History making is a collective endeavour, and I owe so much to those colleagues and friends who have shared ideas or sources, inspired me with their scholarship, and otherwise shaped my thinking about London and the 1920s and 1930s. Thank you to Harriet Atkinson, Rob Baker, David Bieda and the Seven Dials Trust, Jonathan Boff, Stephen Brooke, Nathan Cardon, Michell Chresfield, Elizabeth Darling, Laura Doan, David Hendy, Chris Hilliard, Matthew Hilton, Katie Hindmarch-Watson, Victoria Iglikowski-Broad, Michelle Johansen, Leila Kassir, Seth Koven, Julia Laite, Claire Langhamer, Chris Moores, Eloise Moss, Mo Moulton, Lawrence Napper, Insa Nolte, Will Pooley, Carina Ray, Mary Scoltock,

Jane Shaw, Kate Skinner, Alison Twells, Christine Wagg and the Peabody Trust, Judith Walkowitz, Chris Waters, Emma West, and Sarah Wise. For all these things, and for their generous and critical friendship in reading drafts I thank Max Jones, Simeon Koole, and Mark Williams. Jacob Fredrickson's craft and graft built the survey of Seven Dials that underpins this book, just as his own imaginative scholarship helped me think differently about the 1920s and 1930s.

Working with Manchester University Press has been a privilege. My first conversation with Kim Walker was about another project entirely, but her instinctive grasp of what *this* book might become has been inspiring. In completing the manuscript, I have benefited immensely from Alun Richards' good sense and intuitive commentaries on my writing. Together Kim and Alun have pushed, encouraged, and supported me to write something I did not think possible. I thank the three anonymous readers who engaged constructively with my prospectus and manuscript.

As always, my greatest debts are to my family. It never feels enough, but for being and doing everything, I offer my gratitude and love to Adam, Christine, and Zoe; to Mum and Dad; and to Sarah – the centre of my world, guide, exemplar and inspiration. This book is for Frankie and Kitt, who know better than most the power of stories to shape how we might know and change the world.

Index

Abercrombie, Patrick 233–4
activism
  housing 95, 226, 236–7, 243
  political 2, 38–9, 41, 65, 120, 129, 133, 138, 168, 225
actors 2, 66, 142, 164–7, 172, 174, 194, 197, 214
Adelphi theatre 7, 178
Adshead, Stanley 53, 85–6
Agate, James 68, 200
Aldwych 52, 83, 105
Alexandra Hotel 69, 75
Ambassadors theatre 170, 172, 176, 218
Andrews, Sybil 140, 200
architects 2, 78, 91, 97, 176, 180, 186, 236
architecture, modernist 174, 179, 186–7, 201
artisans 9, 215, 220, 228
artists 7, 140–2, 163–4, 167–9, 172
Artists' International Association (AIA) 167–8, 172, 202
At the Sign of the Seven Dials (1931) 198, 201–2, 221
avant-garde 2, 9, 13, 153, 156, 159
Avory, Sir Horace 116, 128–30
Baird, John Logie 188–9, 240
Bankhead, Tallulah 139, 153, 172
Bartlett, G. E. 103–4
Belgium, migrants from 21, 26–7, 30, 103, 214
belonging 3, 9, 49–50, 117, 171, 228, 231
Bennett, Arnold 152–4, 156
Binder, Pearl 168, 172
Birkett, Norman 1, 122–30
Biron, Sir Chartres 46–7, 156
Black
  business owners 36, 46, 76, 108–9, 122, 138, 156
  'colony' 3, 10, 42–5, 50, 69, 78, 108, 111–13, 127, 129–30, 141, 150, 195, 197, 202, 230–1
  community 3, 36, 38–45, 116, 118–19, 135–6
  culture 108, 160, 196, 230
  migrants 28–31, 37–8
Black, Misha 167–9, 236

Bloomsbury 10, 39, 43, 99, 105, 112, 144, 154, 168, 204, 234, 237
bohemians 2, 9, 59, 143, 151–4, 157, 160–1, 163, 172, 189, 208
Booth, Charles 4, 33, 88
Bovill, William Forster 24, 81, 95
Brighter London Society 54, 85
Bright Young People (BYP) 2, 139–40, 161, 208
Britannia and Eve 70, 150
British Empire Exhibition 48–50, 120–1, 131, 134
British Legion 26, 89

Cadby Hall 20–1, 41, 49
Cafe and Restaurant, The
  Bracewell Smith's complaints 60–3, 123–4
  closure 135, 137, 173, 229, 233
  customers 36–45, 164, 197
  John Bull articles 107–8, 112–14
  libel trial 118–19, 124–7, 130–4
  opening 17–18
  police harassment 46–8, 135–6, 190
  see also Kitten, Emily; Kitten, Jim
Café Royal 58, 69, 75
Cambridge Circus 36, 79, 177, 192
Cambridge Theatre 13, 72, 96, 167, 173–202, 208–9, 229, 233, 240
capital 8–9, 11–12, 15, 40, 63, 226, 241
  power of 54, 73, 84–6, 94, 96, 102, 105, 124, 137, 168, 180, 192, 202, 231, 242
Caravan Club 59, 162–4
Caribbean, migrants from 2, 19, 43
Castle Street 7, 27, 56, 59–60, 86, 178, 180, 194, 208
Cave of Harmony 13, 152–63, 169, 208, 240
change, urban 11, 13, 138, 239
Charing Cross Road 3, 35, 136, 177
Charlot, André 185, 196
Charlot's Masquerade 185, 196, 202
Charlotte Street 40, 43, 112, 168
Chermayeff, Serge 173–4, 182–4, 187, 191
Christie, Agatha 6, 142
cinemas 10, 53–4, 178, 218
citizenship 9, 27, 42, 108, 111, 112, 117, 133
class 2, 9, 11, 46, 86, 128, 188, 268, 242
  differences 11, 52, 109, 129
  hierarchies 19, 171
  inequalities 31, 76, 130
  privileges 8, 156
clubs 35, 60, 152, 155
  queer 159–60, 163–4
  see also nightclubs
Cody, Mary Ellen 24–6
Cohen, Harriet 152, 156
Cold Comfort Farm (1932) 158–9
colonialism 120–1, 134
'colour bar' 10, 29–30, 36, 39, 42, 50, 109, 113, 117, 119–20, 122, 127–8, 132–3, 138, 231, 242
Coloured Alien Seamen Order (CASO) (1925) 29, 117, 132
commercialisation 81, 92, 94–6, 102
community 39, 78, 94, 116–17, 170–1, 211, 226, 231, 238

Comyn Ching 58, 166, 214, 227, 237, 242
conflict
  class 11, 28, 94
  industrial 28, 64, 140
consumerism 40, 54, 86, 241
  mass 9, 35, 150, 218
  upmarket 12, 238
cosmopolitanism 36, 150, 187, 219, 240
  dangers of 45, 142
  limits of 124, 134
Coumbe, Edward Holton 116–19, 122, 127, 130
councillors 60, 80–1, 88–91, 95, 98–100, 104, 144, 223–5
Covent Garden Community Association 237, 243
Covent Garden market 3, 7, 11, 23, 26, 31, 55, 97–100, 102, 106, 140, 214–15, 220, 233–6
crime 42, 88
  associated with Black culture 108, 112, 127
  associated with Seven Dials 3–4, 46, 48, 113, 125, 130, 142, 147, 149–50, 209
Cruikshank, George 4, 154
culture 11–12, 107, 109, 153, 156, 167, 201
  Black 108, 120, 141, 230
  mass 53, 169, 187–9, 196, 219
  metropolitan 9, 197

dance halls 39, 118, 154, 178, 187
Davies, Reverend Wilfred 25–6, 33, 81, 98, 144
Davis, Lillian 35–6, 217
de Bear, Archibald 198–200, 202, 221
decline, urban 3, 9, 12, 15, 45, 55, 105–6, 169, 174, 199, 210, 217, 235, 241
decolonisation 70, 137, 232
department stores 10, 52, 54, 243
depopulation 11, 15, 33, 59, 86, 95, 169, 226
deportation 29, 42, 112, 152
dereliction 15, 31, 33, 238
designers 167–8, 187, 236
development
  case for 78, 81, 97, 136
  commercial 53–5, 73–4, 98, 210, 233–4
  planned 3, 87, 105
  residential 13, 56, 73, 89, 231
  speculative 53, 84, 105, 233
  urban 60, 70, 76, 179, 187, 211, 217, 223, 226, 242–3
  see also redevelopment
Dibdin, Emily 81, 144–5
Dibdin, Robert 24, 77, 81, 89–90, 94–5, 144
Dickens, Charles 4, 154
disorder 127, 132, 209, 221
Donat, Robert 166–7, 172
Drake, William 1, 114
dressmakers 9, 28, 31, 35, 214, 217, 220
drugs 35, 42, 45, 47, 112, 125, 217
Drury Lane 7, 35, 52, 57, 100, 143
Du Cann, C. G. L. 93–4
Duchess of Seven Dials, The (1920) 145–7, 149

Earlham Street 208, 235
East End 5–7, 18, 43, 143, 209, 221, 231
Edward, Prince of Wales 2, 139, 141, 151, 161
Elvey, Maurice 188–9

empire 9, 19, 27–8, 36, 49–50, 121–2, 133, 231
Endell Street 15, 22, 59, 77, 97, 100, 163, 164
Erskine, Uriah 40, 44, 117
estate agents 59–60, 136, 179

Farmer, Tommy 88, 139
Field, Arthur 95–6, 204, 225–7
film industry 2, 188–9, 198, 201
films about Seven Dials 6, 44, 142, 145–9, 189, 196, 198, 205, 224
Fitzrovia 154, 230
Forshaw, J. H. 233–4
Foundling Hospital 99, 105, 237
France, migrants from 2, 27, 36–8, 124, 214
French, Laurie 40, 42
Frith Street 57, 189

Gal, Madeleine (Mrs Robert Henrey) 15, 23, 36
gambling 45, 47, 88, 107, 112, 132
Garrick Club 156, 161
Garvey, Amy Ashwood 38, 138
General Strike 29, 65, 94
gentrification 3, 9, 12, 76, 141, 165, 169, 192, 214, 226, 237, 242
Gibbons, Stella 158–9
Gielgud, John 165–6, 169, 240
Gilbert and Sullivan 5, 128, 145
Globe House 73, 235
Goodchild, George 142, 149
Gordon, Thomas 56–7
Grape Vine Club 152, 155
Grapes Inn 56, 152, 154, 167, 240
Great Earl Street 13, 33, 45, 55–6, 86, 95, 139–72, 178, 188, 195, 208
Great Queen Street 90–1
Great St Andrew Street 13, 26, 33, 51–76, 79, 100, 124, 143, 192, 208, 210–11, 213–15, 217, 222–3
Great War, aftermath 8, 11, 22–9, 52, 54, 58, 72, 78
Great White Lion Street 13, 17–50, 52, 56, 61–2, 67, 70, 108, 124–5, 132, 135–6, 138–9, 143, 160, 172–3, 227–9, 231, 240–1
Greater London Council 12, 236
Greece, migrants from 30, 46, 216
Green Park Hotel 69, 75
Grey, John 20, 29

Hale, Kathleen 153–4, 157, 161
Hall, Radclyffe 153, 156, 159–60, 172
harassment, official 47, 119, 135–6, 231
Harvey, George 58, 69, 84–5, 90–1
Holborn Council 10, 13, 57–8, 60–2, 77, 79, 81, 84, 87, 89–90, 95–6, 100, 105, 123, 134, 164, 177, 205, 210–11, 221–3, 227
homelessness 81, 84, 141
housing
- activists 226, 236–7
- affordable 26, 78, 92
- crisis 82, 84, 89, 92, 104–5, 213
- insanitary 33, 82, 104, 241
- modern 91–2, 94–6, 99–100, 237
- municipal 53, 89, 95, 104–5
- 'slum' 14, 202, 238
- social 10, 239

immigration 47, 111–12, 116, 128, 133
'improvement'
challenges of 88, 104, 200
contradictions of 70, 84, 93–4, 104–5, 201, 226, 229
and decolonisation 70, 232
ideas of 6, 9, 11, 95–6, 103, 129, 216, 222
politics of 77–106
process of 79, 82, 87, 179, 232
urban 78–9, 81–2, 243
inequalities 11–12, 31, 33, 53, 70, 76, 130, 243
Ireland, migrants from 3, 34, 36
Italy, migrants from 2, 30, 36–8, 46, 73, 76, 124, 169, 214, 216

Jeans, Ronald 196–7
Jewish
entrepreneurs 30, 46, 76, 150, 156, 221
migrants 124, 214
John Bull 1, 24, 60, 108–9, 111–14, 116–18, 120–1, 122–3, 126, 128–9, 133, 135, 197, 221, 227
Johnson, Joseph 20, 41
journalists 2, 41, 43, 45, 77, 84, 108, 113, 122, 127, 131, 142, 172, 174, 178, 180, 189–90, 195
muckraking 108, 111–14, 116, 127, 231
Joynson-Hicks, Sir William 62, 133–4

Kennedy, Frank Obadiah 41, 118–19, 122, 135–6, 160, 197
Kingsway 5, 52, 87, 100
Kitten, Emily (née Bridger) 1, 8, 16–18, 21–2, 27, 36, 41–2, 44, 48, 58, 61, 69, 126, 171, 193, 202, 227, 229–30
Kitten, Jim 1, 8, 16–20, 22, 26–30, 37–8, 41, 44, 47–8, 58, 61, 69, 130, 171, 190, 195, 202, 227, 229–30
see also Cafe and Restaurant, The; libel trial; Ruhleben internment camp
Knightsbridge 69, 231

labourers 9, 28, 38, 180, 220
labour market 9, 31, 36, 98, 194, 213
Lanchester, Elsa 153–9, 161–2, 172, 199, 236, 240
Lansbury, George 68, 85
Leech, George William 191–2, 200
Leibovitch, Paul 192–4
leisure 10, 31, 54, 67, 75, 82, 99, 174, 184, 219, 226
Lethbridge, Mabel 26, 170–1
libel
actions 111, 113, 115, 122, 129, 133
law 109, 114, 122, 131, 138
trial 1–2, 8–11, 13, 16, 107–38, 227, 232–3, 242–3
Lieber, Kalman 18, 73
Lieber, Woolf 73–4, 235
Litchfield Street 170, 201
Little Earl Street 13, 26, 33, 72–3, 79, 100, 124, 136, 207–8, 217–21, 225
Little St Andrew Street 13, 23, 33, 72–3, 79, 100, 166–7, 205, 207–8, 210–11, 213–15, 217, 222–3, 227
Little White Lion Street 13, 56, 64, 80, 86, 173–202, 227

London County Council (LCC) 5, 14, 31, 34, 52, 58, 61, 79, 81, 84, 87, 91, 100–1, 105, 123, 134, 205, 207–8, 210–11, 215, 217–18, 221, 223, 227, 237
London Film Studios 145, 147
London Society 53, 78, 224, 237
Long Acre 7, 15, 22, 31, 55, 95–7, 108, 142, 227
Louise Caroline Alberta, Princess (Duchess of Argyll) 77–8, 100
Lumber Court 4, 34, 166, 170, 217–20
Lyons' teashops 20–1, 45, 49

Manning, Edgar 36, 217
marginalisation 9, 176, 222, 228, 234
Marke, Ernest 28, 39, 116
Marylebone 82, 85, 204
Maternity and Child Welfare Committee 81, 91, 144–5
Mayfair 69, 72, 106, 147–8, 161, 196
McMahon, Elizabeth 24–6
Mercer Street 30, 108, 227–30, 235
merchant seamen 2, 19–20, 28, 37, 43, 46, 135, 152, 230
Metro-Goldwyn-Mayer 189, 194, 218, 220
Meyer, Bertie 173, 176, 185, 198
Meyrick, Kate 35, 125
migrants 3, 13, 31, 168–9, 228, 231
Miller, Frank 44, 224
Miners' Federation of Great Britain 28, 65
Ministry of Health 79, 89
missionaries, Christian 5, 141, 143, 145, 197
modernity 35, 49, 52, 73, 106, 163, 174, 180, 185, 187, 191, 195
Monmouth Street 74, 100, 102, 219, 223
Monolulu, Prince Ras (Peter Charles McKay) 19, 41
Monro, George 97–8
Moore, John 47, 126
morality 45, 127, 153, 159
municipal authories 5, 14, 45–7, 76, 78, 87, 100, 105, 156, 220–1, 227, 237, 239
Municipal Reform Party 81, 85, 94, 96, 99, 218
musicians 2, 38–9, 47, 118–19, 160, 197

National Unemployed Workers' Movement 66, 168
Neale, Thomas 3, 239
Neal Street 24–6, 30, 33, 43, 55, 60, 67, 88, 92, 97, 101, 139, 169, 194, 216, 236
Neal's Yard 32, 80, 236, 242
Neave, Jack 59, 162–4
New Compton Street 40, 118
New Oxford Street 5, 79
New Survey of London Life and Labour (1933) 32, 103
Nigeria, migrants from 2, 119, 197
nightclubs 10, 54, 57, 112, 141–2, 151–64, 208
  see also clubs
Norgate, Matthew 154, 161
Nottingham Court 91–2, 101, 139
novels about Seven Dials 142, 149–50

Odhams Press 1, 9, 22, 31, 108, 111, 114, 116, 122–3, 129–30, 134, 136, 227
overcrowding 4, 18, 21, 33–4, 81–2, 104, 241
Oxford Street 54, 178, 184, 204, 214

Padmore, George 39, 138
Palmer, Arnold 42, 150
Park Lane Hotel 62–4, 74, 123
Parker, Sir George 79–81, 84, 87, 90, 92, 94, 97
Parkinson, Harry 44, 148, 150, 224
philanthropists 2, 5, 21, 39, 78, 92, 94, 99, 141, 143, 145, 169, 190
Piccadilly 63, 69, 75, 177, 183–4
planners 2, 9, 11–12, 32–3, 78, 80, 84, 102, 105, 183, 191, 203, 205, 231, 233–4, 238
planning
  blight 11, 74, 105, 169, 233
  failings of 84, 106, 234
  postwar 87, 106, 234
  rational 15, 53, 86
  urban 81, 87, 105
pleasure-seekers 13, 35, 54, 141–3, 151, 153, 163, 169, 176, 183, 203, 209
Poland, migrants from 36, 215
police 2, 4, 21, 45, 47, 50, 76, 88, 131–2, 148, 150, 190
  raids 39–40, 46–7, 107, 135–6, 152, 164, 231
politicians 1, 12, 24, 32–3, 42, 45, 59, 78, 81–4, 89, 98, 105, 205, 231
  Conservative 2, 52, 58, 62, 65, 103–4, 132, 225–6
  Labour 24, 56, 68, 81, 85, 95–6, 105, 132, 204, 225, 227, 231
  local 55, 99, 204
  visions of 9, 11, 102, 183, 203, 223, 238, 242
politics 93, 109, 153, 167, 231, 243
  and capital 8–9, 11–12, 39, 192, 228
  cultural 153, 187
  of 'improvement' 77–106
  local 13, 65, 78, 217, 222–3, 225, 227
  racial 30, 40–1, 109, 116–17, 121–2, 134, 138, 168
  radical 4, 65, 121, 201–2
porters 9, 21, 26, 28, 38, 54, 77, 98, 151, 214
poverty 21, 34, 140
  realities of 81, 104, 169, 202
  of Seven Dials 3, 12, 33, 142, 147, 149, 170–1, 238, 241
  urban 4, 159, 174, 228
power 12, 75, 91, 134, 178
  financial 54, 58, 84, 96, 104, 202, 233
  political 43, 49–50, 62, 85, 104, 124, 127, 137, 138, 226
precarity 21, 28, 34, 40, 56, 98, 104, 118, 148, 163, 193, 213, 241
preservationists 12, 53, 105, 224, 226, 236–7
property
  developers 3, 9–10, 12–13, 53, 55, 59, 69, 72–3, 75–6, 86, 89, 102, 136, 177, 179, 183, 191, 203, 211, 227, 231, 233–4, 238
  market 9, 13, 31, 36, 52, 54, 59, 75–6, 105, 169, 194, 213, 231
  values 54, 84, 98, 222
prostitution 4, 23, 47, 60, 107, 127, 132, 164

public health 2, 24, 34, 59, 100–1, 199, 211
public order 29, 45, 107, 132, 135

race 2, 11, 47, 109, 122, 130–1, 231
racial
  difference 11, 45, 49, 52, 108, 111, 124, 129, 196, 202
  fault lines 10, 20, 29, 112, 118, 133, 196, 242
  hierarchies 19, 30, 43, 124, 129, 160, 171
  inequality 9, 31, 76, 115, 130, 134
  politics 30, 40–1, 109, 116–17, 121–2, 134, 138, 168
  prejudice 36, 39, 114, 117, 120–1, 128
  pride 20, 41
  privilege 8, 86, 128
  violence 11, 29, 70, 111
racism 1, 47, 50, 109, 120, 122, 131, 133, 196, 242
Raffle, Dr Andrew 101–2
redevelopment 2, 70, 86, 102, 176, 178, 236–7
  commercial 75, 243
  pace of 9, 15, 53, 69, 224
  urban 54, 76, 200
  see also development
refugees 26, 103, 143
regeneration 237–9
Regent Street 52, 54, 58, 184
relationships
  interracial 30, 41, 118, 126–7, 129, 131
  same-sex 159–60, 165–6
rents
  cheap 59, 141, 151, 154, 165, 169, 213
  rising 33, 92, 242
respectability 5–6, 46, 67, 103, 109, 117, 124, 129–30, 171, 190, 220
restaurants 31, 34, 36, 38, 53–4, 57, 107, 150, 171, 203, 237
Reynolds, Billy 59, 162–4
Rich, James 40, 42, 44, 112, 164
Rigiani, Nellie (Jarni) 34–5, 170–1, 219
Robeson, Paul 21, 45, 50
Royal Army Service Corps 22, 24
Ruhleben internment camp 18–20, 22, 29, 41, 117, 230
Russia, migrants from 2, 36, 38, 97, 151–2, 168–9
Russo, Francesco 18, 62
Ryder, Dudley (Viscount Sandon) 62, 132, 134

Saunders, Nicholas 236, 242
Savoy Hotel 21, 28, 30, 38, 67, 107
Scott, Harold 153–8, 160–2, 200, 236
Seven Dials and Drury Lane Improvement Scheme 81–7, 92–4, 105, 144, 177, 191, 204, 226, 233, 236
Seven Dials Mission 24, 143–4
sexuality 11, 35, 150, 153, 160
Shaftesbury Avenue 3, 5, 15, 17, 27, 36, 42, 56, 61, 79, 87, 97, 118, 136, 142–3, 147–8, 164, 168, 179–80, 209, 223, 227
Shaftesbury Capital 238–9, 242
Shaftesbury Hotel 13, 17, 52, 55–8, 60, 62, 64–9, 70, 72–3, 75–6, 123, 136, 151, 167, 200, 214, 229, 231, 233, 241
  see also Smith, Bracewell
Shaftesbury Social Club 152, 155

Shelton Street 91, 102, 169, 189, 208
shopkeepers 2, 9, 124, 211, 215–16, 219–20, 243
Shorts Gardens 4, 13, 22, 24, 26, 33, 55, 59, 64, 77–106, 140, 143, 163
Sierra Leone, migrants from 1, 18–21, 28, 41, 107, 116, 118, 160, 197, 216, 230
Sketches by Boz (1836) 4, 154
'slum'
  as description of Seven Dials 3, 5–6, 12, 31, 45, 75, 78, 82, 88, 141–2, 146, 149, 180, 191, 231
  clearance 5, 81–2, 87–8, 96, 101–2, 179, 211–13
  housing 14, 101, 202, 238
slumming 2, 21, 141–71, 189, 198, 208–10
Smith, Bracewell 2, 8, 11, 13, 16, 51–2, 54, 55–8, 60–6, 68–9, 72, 74–6, 84–5, 123–4, 127, 132, 134, 152, 177–8, 214–15, 218
Smith, Sir Hubert Llewellyn 32, 103
Society for Improving the Conditions of the Labouring Classes 13, 77, 90, 94, 97, 144
Society for the Protection of Ancient Buildings 105, 224
Soho 7, 10, 27, 38, 43, 57, 59, 141–2, 230, 234
Solanke, Ladipo 2, 119–22, 129–31, 133, 138
Spurrell, E. F. 81–4, 87
St Giles 3, 5, 22–3, 205, 239
St Giles Buildings 13, 77–8, 92–3, 98, 100–1, 103–5
St Giles Circus 204, 225
St Martin's Lane 15, 55, 57, 79, 97, 150, 169, 176, 178, 188, 199, 209, 213, 223
St Martin's theatre 170, 176
Stapleton, Alan 7–8
Strand 21, 104, 107, 142
street markets 3, 163, 166, 220–2, 225, 242–3
Street Naming Subcommittee 205, 210, 223
street renaming 13, 203–28, 240, 243

Taffurelli, Pietro 73–4, 216, 235
tailors 2, 28, 31, 164
Thackeray, Charles 18, 124
theatregoers 50, 170, 174, 182–3, 185–6, 188, 192–5, 199, 209
theatreland 67, 82, 173–202, 218
Thompson, Edward Roffe 1, 114
Times Laundry Company 137, 229
Titterton, William 203–5
Tottenham Court Road 40, 43, 118, 177, 204
Tower Street 33, 189, 194, 217–18, 221
tradespeople 33, 124, 134, 214–15, 219, 221–2, 243
Troubridge, Una 160, 172
Tucker, James 20, 230
Two Brewers 166, 216

unemployment 28–30, 83, 88
United States, migrants from 30, 36, 103, 118, 160
urban life 8, 106, 138, 234, 241–3
utopian plans 10, 15, 78, 87, 92, 105, 145, 174, 184, 191, 202–3, 226, 233, 238, 243

vice 4, 42, 46, 48, 113, 130
violence
  associated with Seven Dials 46, 112, 127, 199, 202
  racist 29, 49, 70, 111

waiters 2, 9, 19, 21, 28, 30, 38, 151–2, 159, 166, 220
Wallace, Edgar 150, 189
Waterloo Bridge 86–7
Wedgwood, Josiah 132–4
Well of Loneliness, The (1928) 156, 159–60
West African Students' Union (WASU) 39, 120, 122, 230
West End 3, 5, 10, 21, 31, 35, 54, 57, 60, 66, 72, 140, 151, 184–8, 190, 194, 197, 200–1, 218, 223, 229
West Street 24, 143–4, 88–9, 218
Westminster 82, 85, 87, 204, 227
Wheeler, Edwin 207–10
women
  freedom of 23–4, 35, 150
  older 34, 104
  queer 156, 159–60
  single 34–5
Wonderful London (1924–26) 148, 224
Wooll, Edward 115, 131
working-class
  housing 31, 89, 98, 174
  neighbourhoods 3, 10, 12, 226, 238
  people 1–3, 11, 31, 34, 38, 76, 78, 167, 213, 233
  voters 226–7

Yorke, Arthur 20, 28

EU authorised representative for GPSR:
Easy Access System Europe, Mustamäe tee 50,
10621 Tallinn, Estonia
gpsr.requests@easproject.com

www.ingramcontent.com/pod-product-compliance
Lightning Source LLC
Chambersburg PA
CBHW010909150426
42813CB00072BB/3445/J

* 9 7 8 1 5 2 6 1 8 1 9 5 4 *